ACCLAIM FOR

Jean Carper's Complete Healthy Cookbook

"Jean Carper has the most amazing ability to translate nutrition science into easy, practical messages for healthy eating. Her advice is up-to-date, sensible and, best of all, delicious."

—JENNIE BRAND-MILLER, PhD,
professor of Human Nutrition, University of Sydney, immediate past
president of the Nutrition Society
of Australia, and coauthor of the *New York Times*–
best-selling *New Glucose Revolution* series

■

"This is the nutrition cookbook you've been waiting for—packed with the latest exciting scientific facts, lively writing and dynamite recipes. As a nutrition researcher, I always find Jean Carper's advice and her understanding of the science behind it, the best! I give this book five big stars. So will you."

—GENE SPILLER, PhD,
director and founder of the Health Research
and Studies Center in Los Altos, California

■

"Jean Carper does it again, combining nutritional mastery with culinary delights. This new book, full of advice and recipes, is one you should read and heed."

—NORMAN E. ROSENTHAL, MD,
medical director, Capital Clinical Research Associates,
and author of *The Emotional Revolution*

Jean Carper is one of America's most respected authorities on nutrition and health. An acclaimed *New York Times* best-selling author, she writes the popular column "EatSmart" for *USA Weekend* magazine, which is circulated in 600 newspapers and read by 50 million people weekly. Her best-selling books, sold throughout the world and translated into fifteen languages, include *Food-Your Miracle Medicine*, *Stop Aging Now!*, *Miracle Cures*, and *Your Miracle Brain*. Her nutrition reports can be heard on XM radio's *Take Five*. Carper sits on the boards of the American Aging Association and the American Botanical Council. A former award-winning senior medical correspondent for CNN, she lives in Florida and Washington, D.C.

Jean Carper's Complete Healthy

A Comprehensive,
Science-Based
Nutrition Guide with
More than **200**
Delicious Recipes

Jean Carper

Cookbook

MARLOWE & COMPANY
NEW YORK

Published by
Marlowe & Company
An Imprint of Avalon Publishing Group, Incorporated
245 West 17th Street • 11th Floor
New York, NY 10011-5300

AVALON
publishing group inc unpublished

An earlier edition of this book was published in 2004 in different form as *EatSmart:
The Nutrition Information You Can't Live Without.* This edition has been updated and expanded, with
more than 50 additional recipes (most of which have been previously published in *USA Weekend*
magazine) and other additional material.

Library of Congress Cataloging-in-Publication Data
Carper, Jean.
    Jean Carper's complete healthy cookbook: a comprehensive, science-based nutrition
guide with more than 200 delicious recipes / Jean Carper.
        p.cm.
    Rev. ed. of EatSmart. 2004.
    Includes index.
    ISBN-13: 978-1-56924-326-8 (trade paper)
    ISBN-10: 1-56924-326-3 (trade paper)
    1. Nutrition. 2. Cookery. I. Carper, Jean. EatSmart. II. Title.
    RA784.C2845 2007
    641.5'63—dc22

9 8 7 6 5 4 3 2 1

Designed by Pauline Neuwirth, Neuwirth & Associates, Inc.

Printed in the United States of America

Contents

PART 3: The Recipes

Why This Book?

I HAVE BEEN writing "EatSmart" for *USA Weekend* magazine since 1994. One of the high points is being in touch with millions of Americans who read the column. At this writing, the weekly circulation of *USA Weekend* magazine, published by Gannett Co. and distributed in 600 newspapers, is 19 million copies with nearly 50 million readers.

Many readers write me e-mails and letters, requesting reprints of the columns and recipes that they have clipped, stashed away and have now lost. Often, they suggest that I put it all together in a book. So, I did.

I could not include all of my columns, but I have selected and updated the most popular and important ones, reporting the latest research on how to eat to keep your health, avoid or reverse chronic diseases, slow aging, and perhaps prolong your life. I've also included information on the value of specific supplements.

I have also chosen more than 200 of my favorite recipes, nearly all of them previously published in *USA Weekend*. Thus, the recipes have been tested by not only myself, my family, and my friends, but also by millions of readers.

I am by no means a chef, but I do like to create recipes that require relatively few common ingredients, are easy and quick to make, taste good and, most important, are good for you. They are typically low calorie, high in good fat, low in bad fat, low in blood-sugar-spiking activity, moderately low in sodium and full of antioxidants from fruits and vegetables,

herbs and spices. Since I do not eat red meat myself, the recipes do not contain red meat—beef, lamb, pork, veal—with one exception. If you are a beef eater, you'll find a recipe on page 262 that shows you how to reduce the carcinogens in cooked hamburgers.

Many of the recipes are either vegetarian or contain fish. Some also contain poultry, which researchers say may be more healthful than red meat.

You can contact me at jeancarper.com.

Enjoy!

HOW TO EAT SMART

Ten Rules for Smart Eating

HERE ARE THE ten most important things you can do to improve your diet, boost your health, fend off disease, and live longer.

1 EAT FATTY FISH

It's not just fish, but fatty fish—fresh and canned salmon, tuna, sardines, herring, mackerel—that keep arteries clear, hearts in rhythm, and the brain and joints functioning well. In research, eating fatty fish only once a week slashed fatal heart attack risk by 44 percent.

2 EAT WHOLE GRAINS

To reduce your odds of heart disease, cancer, diabetes, obesity, and premature death, eat whole grains. Examples include: oatmeal, shredded wheat, whole-grain bread, popcorn, brown rice, wild rice, quinoa, and bulgur wheat. Whole grains, unlike refined grains, deliver loads of fiber, antioxidants, anticancer agents, cholesterol reducers, clot-blockers, plus essential minerals, such as zinc, selenium, and magnesium.

3 USE OLIVE OIL

People who eat lots of olive oil have better blood cholesterol and blood pressure, less heart disease, less cancer (notably of the colon, breast, prostate, and pancreas), less arthritis, and live the longest! Research even finds that diets rich in olive oil help prevent wrinkles. Olive oil is packed with antioxidants and good monounsaturated fats. The best type is extra virgin because it contains more antioxidants from the pressing of the olives.

4 EAT NUTS

A daily ounce of tree nuts (walnuts, almonds, pecans) or peanuts can cut your risk of heart disease up to 50 percent. A University of Toronto study shows that a very high-fiber vegetable-grain diet, including 2.3 ounces of nuts daily, lowered bad LDL cholesterol 30 percent in a week! The diet worked as well as cholesterol-reducing "statins," such as Lipitor and Mevacor, say researchers. Eating nuts also increases longevity, according to other research.

5 DRINK TEA

Real brewed tea (from bags or loose tea) has amazing powers to help detoxify the body and discourage strokes, heart attacks, cancer, and neurological damage. According to studies, black and green tea are both beneficial, but green teas have about double the antioxidant activity. Green tea also possesses EGCG, a unique anticancer agent and possible brain cell protector against Alzheimer's and Parkinson's. To extract the most antioxidants, brew tea for five minutes. Instant, bottled, and herbal teas don't work; they lack antioxidants.

6 EAT FRUITS AND VEGETABLES

Plant foods are the best antidote to virtually all chronic ailments, including high blood pressure, heart disease, diabetes, arthritis, cancer, stroke, wrinkles, obesity, and age-related mental decline. Fruits and vegetables are rich cocktails of vitamins, minerals, antioxidants, and fiber. Your best bets are deeply colored greens, brightly colored berries, and citrus fruits. Eat at least five, and preferably seven to nine servings a day.

7 EAT GOOD CARBOHYDRATES

"Bad" carbs spike blood sugar and insulin; "good" carbs ("low glycemic index" foods) do not. Keeping insulin low is a secret to longevity, research shows. Eating good carbs, such as dried beans, lentils, peanuts, oatmeal, yogurt, cherries, and prunes, can help prevent colon cancer, heart disease, diabetes, obesity, and poor memory.

8 RESTRICT MEAT, ANIMAL FAT AND TRANS FATS

These foods are hazardous to your health. Red meat, especially grilled or fried (as in bacon), is linked to several cancers, primarily colon cancer. Saturated fats in whole milk, butter, cheese, sausage, steak, and poultry encourage inflammation, leading to heart disease, cancer, and degenerative brain diseases. Trans-fatty acids found in many margarines, processed snack foods, and baked goods, such as donuts, are even worse for your heart than animal fats. Check labels for amounts of trans fats in processed foods.

9 EAT LESS

"Cutting portion sizes in half would do more to improve Americans' health than anything," says one expert. Compelling research shows that obesity is a major cause of disease and premature death. Eating excessive calories accelerates aging, leads to obesity, and contributes to cancer, heart disease, diabetes, and Alzheimer's disease. Drastically trimming calories by 30 percent is the only reliable way known to increase life span in animals.

10 TAKE A MULTIVITAMIN/MINERAL PILL

The supplement is insurance against nutritional inadequacies that can promote chronic diseases. A lack of micronutrients—such as folic acid, vitamins B_{12} and B_6, niacin, vitamins C and E, and zinc—actually damages genetic DNA the same way radiation and chemical carcinogens do, setting the stage for cancer, according to landmark studies by researchers at the University of California–Berkeley. Correcting even minor deficiencies can boost immunity, curb chronic diseases, and perhaps prolong life.

Fats: The Good, the Bad, and the Ugly

A GUIDE TO DIETARY FATS

Contrary to popular belief, not all fat is bad. Your body needs good fats to survive and thrive. Indeed, the type of fat you eat is far more important than the amount of fat you eat. For example, the lifesaving Mediterranean diet is high in fat (as much as 40 percent of calories), but most of it is good fat from olive oil and fish. In one large study, eaters of a Mediterranean diet had 70 percent lower death rates from all causes than eaters of a low-fat American-type heart diet (about 30 percent calories from fat)

Indeed, long-term Harvard studies have never found any link between a high percentage of calories from fat and any important disease, including heart disease, cancer, and weight gain, but they have found that the type of fat you eat can dramatically affect your health.

BAD FATS

- **Animal fats (including butter, cheese, lard, and the fat contained in meat, poultry, and milk).** Most experts agree that the saturated fat in animal products is a prime enemy in raising bad cholesterol, promoting inflammation, and clogging arteries, leading to cardiovascular disease. It may harm immune functioning and increase risk of cancer, diabetes, and cognitive decline, including Alzheimer's, as you grow older.

- **Corn oil:** In a six-month study by Harvard researcher George L. Blackburn, daily doses of corn oil doubled the odds of recurrence and spread of colon cancer. Corn oil is high in omega-6 fatty acids and also rapidly oxidizes (saturates with oxygen), releasing floods of disease-causing free radicals inside the body. Experts say nearly everyone should cut back on corn oil, as well as regular safflower and sunflower seed oils (all laden with omega-6 fatty acids).

- **Trans fats (also called partially hydrogenated vegetable oils):** These are the worst of the bad fats for clogging your arteries and promoting diabetes and obesity. Trans fats increase the risk of infertility in women by as much as 70 percent. They also make you fatter than do other fats. Researchers at Wake Forest University in North Carolina found that monkeys fed the same number of calories either from trans fats or olive oil gained four times more weight when eating the trans fats. Worse, the extra fat deposits settled in the abdominal area, which boosts risk for diabetes. I have only one message about trans fats: don't eat them. In fact, these fats are so bad for you, I've devoted an entire section to them, starting on page 9.

SO-SO FATS

- **Soybean oil:** Soybean oil contains desirable monounsaturated fatty acids, but is also high in hazardous omega-6 fatty acids that can over-run cells, promoting cancer, inflammatory reactions, and immune function. Although safer than corn oil, soybean oil is not nearly as healthful as olive oil and canola oil. Unfortunately, much soybean oil is hydrogenated—i.e., hardened—making it particularly harmful. It's okay to eat tofu (soybean curd), soy milk, and whole soybeans that have little oil and high antioxidants.

- **Peanut oil:** Peanut oil is very similar in fatty acid composition to soybean oil. Use only occasionally.

- **Tropical fats such as palm and coconut oils:** Other vegetable fats have little saturated fat, but these tropical fats are 50 to 85 percent saturated fat. Nevertheless, they do not appear to destroy arteries. Research shows they raise good HDL blood cholesterol. They also are high in lauric acid, found to be anti-inflammatory, antiviral, and antibacterial. They're okay to eat occasionally.

GOOD FATS

- **Olive oil:** Its fat is mainly monounsaturated, which promotes health. Studies show that people whose main source of fat is olive oil live longer and have less heart disease, cancer, and arthritis. Olive oil also contains antioxidants, similar to those in tea and red wine, which combat disease processes. Choose extra-virgin olive oil because it is richer in antioxidants than are other olive oils.

- **Fish oil (omega-3 fat):** Overwhelming research shows omega-3 oils in fatty fish can help save you from cardiovascular disease (especially sudden cardiac death), cancer, respiratory problems, inflammatory conditions (such as arthritis), neurological disorders (including depression), and Alzheimer's disease. Best sources of omega-3's include salmon, herring, sardines, and tuna, both canned and fresh. Eat fish at least twice a week. Even one weekly serving conveys great benefits.
- **Canola oil:** Canola oil is very low in saturated fat, high in monounsaturated fat, and rich in beneficial omega-3 fatty acids. Use it in salad dressings, for sautéing or frying, or in any recipe that calls for cooking oil.
- **Macadamia nut oil:** This is the highest of all salad oils in monounsaturated fats.
- **High oleic-acid safflower oil:** It ranks high as a monounsaturated fat, along with olive oil. Previously, safflower oil consisted mainly of less desirable omega-6-type fatty acids. Now, most safflower oil is about 75 percent good oleic-acid of the type in olive oil. Be sure the label on safflower oil indicates "high oleic-acid."

- **Grapeseed oil:** In studies, it has raised good HDL cholesterol. It's also high in antioxidants.
- **Avocado oil:** Like avocados, it's rich in beneficial monounsaturated fat.
- **Walnut oil:** High in beneficial plant omega-3's.

TRANS FATS: The Worst Fat of All

Of all fats, the ugliest—more vicious even than animal fat—are trans fats. Such fats are created when liquid oils are solidified by a process called *partial hydrogenation* that stretches processed foods' shelf life and changes "safe" unsaturated fats into dangerous ones. Trans fats are concentrated in solid vegetable shortenings, stick margarines, donuts, crackers, cookies, chips, some cereals, cakes, pies, some breads, and foods that have been fried in hydrogenated fats, such as chicken, fish, and potatoes.

Harvard nutritionist Walter Willett blames trans fats for at least 30,000 premature deaths a year, calling their introduction into the diet the "biggest food-processing disaster in U.S. history." Mary G. Enig, PhD, a pioneering trans-fats researcher, formerly at the University of Maryland, says, "Several decades of research show that consumption of trans fats promotes heart disease, cancer, diabetes, immune dysfunction, obesity, and reproductive problems."

What's bad about trans fats?

Everything about them is bad, especially when it comes to blood fats that affect the heart, says Willett. Mainly, trans fats increase bad LDL cholesterol, triglycerides, and insulin levels, reduce beneficial HDL cholesterol, and promote

what about cholesterol?

CHOLESTEROL-RICH FOODS, such as eggs and shrimp, pose little or no threat to most people. A comprehensive analysis of 224 scientific studies conducted over twenty-five years by Wanda Howell, PhD, University of Arizona, concludes that eating cholesterol only slightly affects blood cholesterol. The primary villain is saturated animal fat, she says. A British study showed that cutting 50 milligrams of dietary cholesterol a day reduces blood cholesterol less than one point.

In a large Harvard study, men and women who ate an egg a day did not have more heart attacks than those who ate an egg only once a week. So an egg a day (rich in choline, needed for brain development and B vitamins that may discourage heart disease) is generally okay, say most experts.

inflammation that helps bring on heart attacks. Harvard research found a one-and-a-half-times-higher heart attack risk in women who ate the most trans-fats, primarily in margarine, compared with women eating the least. In men, the risk was more than double.

Margarine, a special villain

Margarine accounts for about 20 to 25 percent of all trans fats consumed, says Dr. Enig. Eating an extra teaspoon of trans-fat-rich margarine a day boosted men's chances of heart attack 10 percent, according to the famed Framingham Heart Study. Generally, the harder the margarine, the more the trans fat. Tufts research shows that eating stick margarine sent triglycerides 18 percent higher than did semiliquid squeeze-bottle margarine.

In fact, trans-fat-rich margarines are worse for cholesterol than butter. Butter's saturated fat raises bad LDL, but margarine's trans fats both boost LDL and depress good HDL cholesterol, doubling the damage. Dutch research found that trans fats depressed good HDL cholesterol 21 percent more than saturated fats did. Thus, eating trans fats is extra harmful if you already have low HDLs, warn experts. Further, trans fats raise Lp(a), another artery-destroying blood fat.

> **When trans fatty acids are absorbed into human cell membranes, they create abnormal body chemistry, which can cause fat deposits in the arteries, liver and other organs, potentially leading to heart attack, stroke or circulatory occlusion.**
>
> **—National Nutritional Foods Association**

How much trans fat is okay for the heart? Virtually none, according to an analysis of fifty-nine heart-diet studies by Dutch researcher Peter L. Zock at the Wageningen Centre for Food Sciences. He finds the best diet strategy is not to lower total fat, but to severely restrict saturated fats and to get trans-fats intake to near zero.

Trans fats promote these additional health hazards:

Cancer: Dutch researchers found elevated trans fats in the breast tissue of women with breast cancer. A University of North Carolina study reported that a high consumption of sweetened baked goods and oils and condiments high in trans fats doubled the odds of colon polyps that may lead to cancer.

Reproductive Problems: Pregnant and lactating women should minimize intake of trans fats. Research shows that pregnant women with the highest levels of a common trans fat had seven times the risk of the complication preeclampsia, characterized by high blood pressure and edema. High trans fats may also harm fetal and infant development. Nursing mothers who eat trans fats pass them on to infants during breast feeding. Infants feasting on trans fats may have diminished visual acuity and brain development.

Diabetes: Trans fats appear to reduce the body's ability to handle blood sugar by lowering responses to the hormone insulin, which is particularly dangerous to diabetics.

how to avoid trans fats

* Use olive oil and canola oil for virtually all cooking.
* Use trans-fat-free soft tub or liquid margarines instead of stick margarines. Generally, the softer the margarine the better, and liquid is the best. A tablespoon of stick margarine has about 1.9 grams of trans fat; a tablespoon of regular tub margarine, .8 grams. Check the label for trans-free brands. By government standards, "trans-fat-free" means less than 0.5 grams per serving.
* Make sure all of the packaged foods you purchase list the number "0" next to "trans fats" on the nutrition facts label. Foods that list "0" next to trans fats on the label are allowed by the government to contain very small amounts of this fat, so follow up by making sure the words "partially hydrogenated" are not listed in the ingredients list. These are just another way of saying "trans fats."
* Avoid deep-fried foods, apt to be oozing trans fats. A batter-dipped deep-fried whole onion—an appetizer popular at steak houses—has 18 grams of trans fats, according to the Center for Science in the Public Interest. Other trans-fat horrors: cheese fries, onion rings, and fried clams, fish, scallops and shrimp, and chicken. Additional special hazards include baked goods. Half a cookie's fat may be trans fats. A donut contains from 4 to 9 grams of trans fats.

Why Fish Can Save Your Life

EAT FISH! YOU'VE heard it before, but now the case for fish oil is so compelling that you absolutely must pay attention or face overwhelming health risks. Fish's secret is its unique oil, called omega-3 fatty acids, essential for proper cell functioning. Most Americans get only 15 percent of what they need.

HERE'S HOW EATING FISH PROTECTS YOU

- **Stops fatal heart attacks:** More than 250,000 Americans die suddenly of heart attacks every year; half have no warning signs. Yet, eating fatty fish could stop an astonishing 80 percent of such unexpected deaths in men, says Harvard research involving 22,000 male physicians. It's the first time fish oil has been found lifesaving in people with no history of heart disease. The higher the men's blood omega-3 fats, the lower their risk of death from heart attack. A probable reason: fish oil helps suppress arrhythmias (irregular heartbeats) that can trigger cardiac arrest.
- **Prevents heart disease:** The more often women eat fish, the less likely they are to have a heart attack or die of a "cardiac event," says other Harvard research, tracking 85,000 female nurses. Eating fish only once a week cut heart attack risk 29 percent; the figure jumped to 34 percent in women who ate fish five times a week. Researchers credit the omega-3 fats in fish.

- **Cuts strokes:** Fish was even more dramatic in preventing strokes in the nurses. Women who ate fish more than five times a week suffered only half as many strokes as occasional fish eaters, primarily strokes due to blood clots.
- **Blocks cancer:** Research in France found that women with the highest amounts of omega-3's in breast fatty tissue were nearly 70 percent less apt to have breast cancer than were women with the least omega-3's. In a Swedish study, women who ate fatty fish (salmon and herring) twice a week cut their risk of endometrial cancer by 40 percent, compared with women who ate fatty fish less than once a month. Eating lean fish, such as cod and flounder, did not reduce cancer risk. The same Swedish investigators found that prostate cancer rates were two or three times higher in non-fish eaters than in men who ate moderate or high amounts of fish.
- **Soothes brains, saves memory:** Fish eaters around the world are less apt to be depressed, violent, and suicidal. One probable reason: omega-3's boost serotonin, one of the brain's feel-good chemicals. Low blood omega-3's also predict a greater risk of memory loss and Alzheimer's disease as you age. In fact, in a study of 815 older men and women in China, those who ate fish at least once a week reduced their risk of developing Alzheimer's disease by an amazing 60 percent, compared with those who rarely or never ate fish. In Israeli research, short-term memory improved in 74 percent and long-term memory in 58 percent of Alzheimer's patients given fish oil. Fish oil is essential for fetal and infant brains. In Danish research, pregnant women who ate fish once a week cut their risk of premature delivery by a third.

THE FISH WITH THE MOST OMEGA-3'S

The fattiest fish have the highest concentrations of omega-3s. They include mackerel, anchovies, herring, sardines, salmon, tuna, halibut, turbot, blue-fish, trout, and sablefish. Fish with moderate to low omega-3's include catfish, cod, dolphin fish, flounder, grouper, haddock, perch, pike, and red snapper. Shellfish generally have low levels of omega-3 fats.

Contrary to popular belief, farmed salmon contains as much omega-3 healthy oils as does wild salmon, says the United States. Department of Agriculture. But there are other concerns. Farmed salmon is fed artificial color, may pollute the ocean, and may contain more environmental toxins called PCBs. Unfortunately, fresh wild salmon is costly and not always available. Tip: buy canned. Almost all canned salmon is wild. Still, most experts agree that the health benefits of all salmon—wild, farmed, or canned—far outweigh potential hazards.

HOW TO GET THE MOST FROM FISH

- **Best cooking methods:** Bake, poach, steam, microwave, stir-fry, sauté in a little canola or olive oil, or simmer as in fish stew. Deep-frying can destroy fish benefits.
- **Cut Back on Bad Fats:** So-called proinflammatory omega-6 fats, found in corn oil, regular safflower and sunflower seed oils, margarines, shortenings, and to a lesser extent in soybean oil, can overwhelm and neutralize the omega-3's in your cells. So if you eat a salad dressing made with corn oil or soybean oil along with salmon, the omega-3 benefits are diminished.

Critically important is the ratio of good omega-3 to bad omega-6 fats. You should not eat more than four times as much omega-6 fat as omega-3 fat. Unfortunately, Americans eat ten to twenty times more "bad" omega-6's than good omega-3's.

On a regular basis this can be disastrous. Many experts blame our excess of omega-6's and deficiency of omega-3's for much of our epidemic of chronic diseases, including cardiovascular disease, inflammatory diseases, such as arthritis and asthma, and mood and memory disturbances, including Alzheimer's.

Good Carbs, Bad Carbs
How to Tell the Difference

THE BIGGEST MYTH about carbohydrates is that they are all equal in the way they affect the body. "It's become quite clear that not all carbohydrates are the same," says Harvard nutritionist Walter Willett. "It's not only the amount of carbohydrate you eat, it's the type that matters." Pioneering researchers Jennie Brand-Miller, PhD at University of Sydney in Australia, and Thomas M. S. Wolever, MD, PhD, at the University of Toronto, Canada, agree, as they explain in their excellent book *The New Glucose Revolution* (Marlowe & Company, third edition, 2007).

What really matters is how much and how fast a carbohydrate spikes your blood sugar. When you eat a carbohydrate—any sugary or starchy food—your blood sugar goes up. If your blood sugar rises slowly, it's good. If it soars quickly, it can be a serious health threat. There's a vast difference between the way your body processes carbohydrates from white bread and from peanuts, for example. Eating white bread quickly sends blood sugar levels sky high. Peanuts induce blood sugar to rise gradually and only moderately. Chronic blood sugar spikes are linked to weight gain, heart disease, diabetes, some cancers, premature aging, and poor intellectual functioning and memory loss in older people.

Thus, diets high in the wrong carbohydrates may do you in, but the right carbs can dramatically improve your health. The key is knowing the difference.

To determine a carb's blood-sugar raising capacity, Dr. Brand-Miller and colleagues have fed specific foods to carefully chosen groups of individuals and measured how high and how rapidly blood sugar rises. A food gets a high *glycemic index* (GI) number if it causes blood sugar to spike, and a low glycemic index number if it induces gradual rises in blood sugar. A food with a GI of under 55 is considered low-glycemic. For example, lentils have a low GI of 29. Since how much you eat of a carb also matters, researchers now calculate the blood sugar raising power in a common serving of various foods; this is called its *glycemic load*, or GL.

the glycemic load of 25 common foods

THE LOWER THE figure, the less apt the food is to spike blood sugar.

Food	Value	Food	Value
Peanuts	1	Wonderbread	11
Carrots, peeled, boiled	2	Apple juice	12
Kellogg's All-Bran	4	Banana	13
Lentils	5	Coca-Cola	14
Grainy breads	6	Donut, cake	17
Apple	6	Spaghetti, white, boiled 5 minutes	18
M&M's, peanut	6	Sushi, average	19
Baked beans	7	Jelly beans	22
Chick peas	8	Corn Flakes	24
Microwave popcorn	8	Bagel, white	25
Ice cream, average	8	Potato, baked	26
Oatmeal, regular, cooked	9	Mars bar	27
		Raisins	28

For the glycemic ratings of hundreds of other foods, search online at www.glycemicindex.com or consult *The New Glucose Revolution* and other books by authority Jennie Brand-Miller.

HOW "BAD" CARBS CAN HARM YOU

High-glycemic foods that trigger a jump in blood sugar increase your odds of chronic diseases.

- **Heart Disease:** Blood-sugar-boosting carbs double women's risk of heart disease, according to a major Harvard study. The higher the load of high glycemic foods, the greater the odds of fatal and nonfatal heart attacks.
- **Diabetes:** Bad carbs double or triple your risk of developing type 2 diabetes, according to many studies.
- **Weight:** High glycemic carbs frustrate your attempts to lose weight. A

low-glycemic-index diet is an excellent way to control overeating and weight gain. In studies of obese teenage boys, those eating high-glycemic foods consumed 80 percent more calories over a certain period than those on a low-glycemic-index diet, reported researchers at Children's Hospital in Boston.

- **Cholesterol:** The wrong carbs depress good HDL cholesterol, discovered British researchers. The best dietary way to raise HDLs, they found, was a low-glycemic diet. Also, substituting low-glycemic-index foods for high-glycemic index foods in a low-fat diet lowers blood triglycerides by 15 to 25 percent, says research at the State University of New York–Buffalo.

- **Insulin resistance:** Blood sugar jumps lead to *insulin resistance* that promotes high blood pressure, clogged arteries, heart attacks, and strokes. Eating a low-glycemic index diet for a month has reversed insulin resistance.

- **Inflammation:** High-glycemic carbs incite inflammation in blood vessels, which research identifies as a culprit in heart disease, strokes, and Alzheimer's disease. Harvard research found nine times more inflammation in the blood of women who ate the highest-glycemic-index foods, compared with those who ate the lowest-glycemic foods.

- **Cancer:** Bad carbs encourage certain cancers. Italian women eating the highest as opposed to the lowest-glycemic-index diet were 40 percent more apt to develop breast cancer. Harvard research suggests that women who are overweight and inactive more than double their risk of pancreatic cancer by eating a very high-GL diet compared with a very low one. Both colon and breast cancers have also been tied to consuming high-GL diets.

- **Aging:** The wrong carbs can damage cells, causing accelerated aging of all tissues and organs, according to University of California–Berkeley, researchers. Plain sugar (sucrose) especially produces signs of accelerated aging in cells.

bottom line

EATING A low-glycemic diet is one of the best ways to improve overall health, control weight, ward off disease and prolong life.

SIX WAYS TO CONTROL BAD CARBS

1 EAT LOTS OF LEGUMES. They are digested slowly, causing gradual rises in blood sugar, and thus have low ratings. These include baked beans, butter beans, lentils, chickpeas, kidney beans, navy beans, soybeans, and peanuts (which technically are legumes, not nuts).

2 KNOW YOUR STARCHES. White potatoes and white rice can raise blood sugar faster and higher than eating candy. Sushi rice (made with vinegar), basmati rice, brown rice, and especially Uncle Ben's converted rice have a lower glycemic index. Dr. Brand-Miller also says it's a myth that pasta makes you fat. All pastas, says Dr. Brand-Miller, are fairly low-glycemic, helping dampen blood sugar, appetite, and weight gain. You can lower pasta's glycemic index by undercooking it—to the al dente stage.

3 ADD VINEGAR OR LEMON JUICE TO FOODS. Studies show eating 4 teaspoons of vinegar in a salad dressing with an average meal lowers blood sugar as much as 30 percent. Dr. Brand-Miller found that adding vinegar to high-index white potatoes reduced expected blood sugar surges by 25 percent. The reason: acid slows stomach emptying and digestion. She advises eating a salad with a vinegar or lemon-juice dressing with high-glycemic meals. Drinking orange and grapefruit juice also may help. Acidity explains why yogurt and sourdough bread have low GI ratings.

4 COMBINE HIGH- AND LOW-GLYCEMIC-INDEX FOODS. If you eat high-glycemic foods, combining them, such as dried beans and rice, for example, produces an intermediate glycemic index rating. When you eat snacks alone, choose snacks with a low rating, such as apples, peanuts, or popcorn. A high-glycemic food, such as jelly beans, eaten alone is sure to spike your blood sugar.

5 EAT LOTS OF VEGETABLES. You can think of salad vegetables as "free" foods, with no significant impact on blood sugar. Their glycemic rating is effectively zero, says Brand-Miller. Meat does not raise blood sugar, but its fat promotes insulin resistance. It's important to restrict high-fat foods as well as high-glycemic-index foods, she cautions.

6 **RESTRICT PROCESSED FOODS.** Bread, cereals, cookies, and crackers made with finely ground flour have a high rating because the fine particles of starch zip right through your digestive tract. Many cereals and breads have a rating of 70 or more, higher than table sugar's 60–65. Some cold cereals with a low rating include the following: All-Bran with extra fiber, Bran Buds with psyllium, Special K, and muesli.

a quick guide to the best carbs

* Choose whole-grain foods over highly processed ones.

* Eat more legumes (dried beans, lentils, and peanuts).

* Restrict "white" foods, such as sugar, white bread, and white potatoes.

* Eat more high-fiber fruits and vegetables.

* Restrict sugary soft drinks and other high-sugar beverages.

* Eat spaghetti undercooked (al dente); avoid canned spaghetti.

* Add vinegar or lemon juice to carbs; the acid lowers the glycemic index.

* Choose sourdough bread over other breads.

* Choose oatmeal and All-Bran over highly processed cereals.

* Choose basmati or Uncle Ben's converted rice; they are lower glycemic index than brown or white rice. Instant rice is high.

Eat Fiber, Live Longer

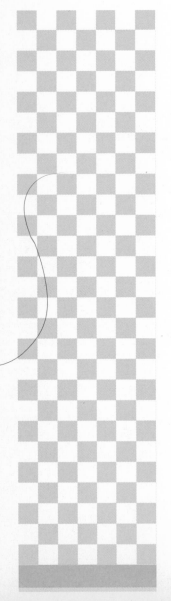

FIBER IS THE stuff that in food that doesn't get fully digested. Two types exist: water soluble (found in oats, legumes, fruits, whole grains, and some vegetables) and insoluble (wheat bran).

HOW EATING HIGH FIBER FOODS HELPS YOU

Stay alive: A British report shows that men and women who ate the most fiber cut their odds of death from all causes by one-third during the eleven-year study, compared with the skimpiest fiber eaters. Surprisingly, fiber was more powerful than antioxidant intake in staving off death. High fiber intakes cut the risk of heart disease in women by nearly half.

Stay slim: In a study of 2,900 young adults by Boston's Children's Hospital, those who ate the most fiber gained 5 percent less weight than those who ate the least. In fact, fiber was more important in preventing weight gain than fat was in promoting it. Why? Fiber suppresses the hormone insulin, which is tied to hunger.

Improve your heart: The Boston study, like many others, found that high-fiber foods lower bad LDL cholesterol, blood pressure, and triglycerides, which are all risk factors for heart disease. A major Harvard study has found that women who ate 23 grams of fiber a day, mostly from cereal, were 23 percent less likely to suffer a heart attack than were those who ate 11 grams a day. In men, a high-fiber diet slashed the odds of heart attack by 36 percent.

Fight cancer: Two studies show that a high-fiber diet dramatically slashes colon cancer risk. In the largest diet-cancer study ever done, researchers studied the diets of 519,978 people in ten European countries for four and a half years. Those who ate the most dietary fiber (35 grams a day) had a 40 percent lower risk of colon cancer than did those who ate the least fiber (15 grams a day or less). Another American study found that eating more than 30 grams of fiber daily reduced the risk of polyps that can lead to colon cancer by 20 percent, compared with those who ate less than 15 grams per day. High fiber may also help prevent cancers of the breast, stomach, thyroid, and mouth.

Protect your gut: A diet high in fiber, especially wheat bran, helps prevent diverticulosis, pockets in the intestinal wall that afflict half of Americans over age sixty. Diverticulosis is due to years and years of lack of fiber, say gastroenterologists. Plus: A high-fiber diet can halve the risk of ulcers and cut the risk of gallstones by a third.

super sources of fiber

FOOD	FIBER GRAMS
⅓ cup All-Bran Bran Buds	13.0
½ cup All-Bran Extra Fiber	13.0
½ cup Fiber One	13.0
½ cup lentils	9.0
½ cup kidney beans	8.0
½ cup barley	7.0
½ cup oat bran	6.0
½ cup corn or green peas	4.5
¼ cup almonds	4.0
1 large pear or apple, with skin	4.0
1 orange	3.6
4 prunes	3.0

EASY WAYS TO EAT MORE FIBER

If your current diet is low in fiber, add high-fiber foods gradually and drink plenty of water.

- Eat high-fiber cereals. Check labels; some cereals have zero fiber; others have as much as 13 grams per serving. An acceptable cereal should have at least 3 grams of fiber per serving, preferably more.
- Top cereals with fresh berries, apples, pears, or dried fruit.
- Eat whole-wheat or whole-grain bread with at least two grams of fiber per slice.
- Use less-processed grains, such as brown rice and whole-grain pasta.
- Add dried beans to stews, casseroles, and soups.

how much fiber do you need?

Adults: Experts advise 21 to 38 grams grams a day. That range breaks down to 38 g for men and 25 g for women younger than fifty; 28 g for pregnant women and and 29 g for lactating women; 30 g for men and 21 g for women older than fifty. Most Americans eat half what they need.

Children: Add five to their age to get the recommended amount of fiber. That means 13 grams daily for an eight year-old. Only one-third of American children between ages seven and ten eat the recommended amount of fiber.

Grains
The Whole Truth

EAT TWO TO THREE WHOLE GRAIN FOODS A DAY.

That simple act may do more to keep you healthy than any other dietary change, says convincing evidence. If you're like 80 percent of Americans, you eat less than one serving of whole grains per day, and you're probably not even sure what a whole grain food actually is.

WHAT "WHOLE GRAIN" MEANS

Whole-grain foods are made with intact kernels, rather than with "refined" or crushed, processed kernels. Whole grains are high in fiber (whole wheat has five times the fiber of refined wheat, for example). Whole grains are also rich in an array of disease-fighting chemicals—antioxidants, tumor suppressors, cholesterol reducers, insulin regulators, antithrombotic agents, phytoestrogens, and nutrients vitamin E, folic acid, zinc, selenium, and magnesium.

Whole grains are what our ancestors ate before modern food processing began pulverizing kernels into superfine powder, reducing their health value and robbing our bodies of protection against chronic diseases.

When whole wheat flour is refined, it is stripped of 95 percent of its vitamin E, 87 percent of its vitamin B_6, 85 percent of its magnesium, 52 percent of its selenium, and 40 percent of its folic acid and vitamin B_{12}. Research shows how essential it is to return to a diet of whole grains. In fact, findings even suggest that you will live longer if you eat whole grains.

HOW WHOLE GRAINS PROTECT YOU

Slash heart disease: In a large Harvard study, women who ate 2.5 servings of whole grains a day were one-third to one-half less apt to get or die of heart disease than were women eating less than half a serving daily. Strongest heart-savers: whole-grain breakfast cereals, brown rice, popcorn, and bran. In fact, eating a daily bowl of cold breakfast cereal (with about 5 grams of fiber) cuts your chances of heart disease by about one-third, researchers said.

Block cancer: Eating lots of whole grains lowers your cancer risk—as much as 50 percent for stomach and colon cancer, 40 percent for ovarian, 20 percent for prostate and pancreatic cancer, and 10 percent for breast cancer, Italian research finds.

Ward off diabetes: Three daily servings of whole grains cut the risk of type 2 diabetes by 21 percent, in a University of Minnesota study of 36,000 women. In the Harvard study, women who ate the equivalent of a bowl of oatmeal and two pieces of whole wheat bread were only one-third as apt to develop type 2 diabetes as women who ate the least whole-grain foods. Researchers credit multiple factors in whole grains that keep blood sugar and insulin under control.

Promote GI health: Unquestionably, whole-grain, high-fiber foods are the best medicine for keeping stools soft and bulky. This not only combats constipation, but helps prevent diverticular disease, a potentially serious irritation and inflammation of tiny pouches inside the colon.

Suppress appetite: When you eat whole grains, you're less hungry, less likely to overeat, and less likely to gain weight, because whole grains are high in fiber and tend to keep blood sugar levels more stable, says Tufts University's Susan Roberts, PhD.

LOOK FOR WHOLE-GRAIN CEREALS

Many cereal boxes now state whether the cereal is whole grain. You can't go wrong with these six cereals that boast more than 90 percent whole grains: Cheerios, regular (not instant) oatmeal, shredded wheat, Wheaties, Nutrigrain Golden Wheat, and Toasty-O's. For others, check labels for "whole grain" or "rich in whole grain."

An exception: All-Bran cereal is not technically whole grain, but University of Minnesota researcher Joanne Slavin, PhD, says it's so "loaded with bran" and fiber it has the value of whole grain. So it's kind of an honorary whole grain.

CHECK THE LABELS

The only way to be sure bread, pasta, crackers, and so on are whole grain is to read the labels very carefully. It can be tricky. Some breads, for example, say "seven grain," or "bran" or "made with wheat flour," giving the impression they're whole grain when they're not. In order to be a whole-grain food, the first ingredient on the label list must have the word "whole" in it, such as whole wheat (another name is graham flour), whole oats, whole rye flour, and whole barley. Look for whole wheat crackers such as Triscuits, whole wheat tortillas, and whole-grain bagels, couscous, and pasta.

DON'T LOOK FOR SHORT CUTS

Important: There's no way to find a substitute for whole grains. Researchers aren't even sure which of whole grains' many components account for their remarkable disease-fighting powers. It's probably not any individual chemical, such as fiber or folic acid. That's why you have to eat the grain's "entire package," to get its benefits, say experts.

Whole Grains:

Wild rice, brown rice (including instant), popcorn, bulgur wheat, whole wheat kernels, wheat berries, oats and oatmeal, barley (including pearled barley), buckwheat, kasha (buckwheat groats), cracked wheat, quinoa (pronounced "keenwa"), amaranth.

Not Whole Grains:

White rice, cornmeal, and whole-kernel corn (it's a vegetable).

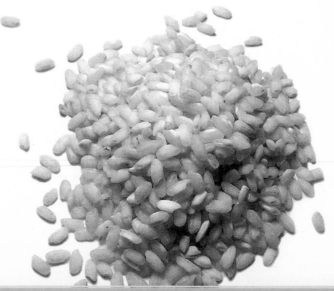

Strong Medicines in Fruits and Vegetables

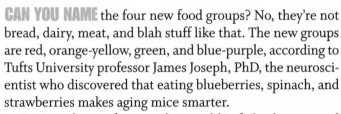

CAN YOU NAME the four new food groups? No, they're not bread, dairy, meat, and blah stuff like that. The new groups are red, orange-yellow, green, and blue-purple, according to Tufts University professor James Joseph, PhD, the neuroscientist who discovered that eating blueberries, spinach, and strawberries makes aging mice smarter.

Dr. Joseph says fruits and vegetables fight disease, and especially those that are deeply and brightly colored—red, orange-yellow, green, and blue-purple. The more brilliant and intense a food's pigment, the greater the food's disease-fighting properties.

Extensive research shows that eating fruits and vegetables helps protect against cancer, heart disease, stroke, high blood pressure, asthma, diabetes, cataracts, inflammatory diseases, and pulmonary troubles. The main reason: Pigments in fruits and vegetables contain phytochemicals or antioxidants that act as cancer inhibitors, cholesterol regulators, anti-inflammatories, and brain cell protectors.

Each fruit and vegetable is a unique package, so you need to eat a variety to get the broadest spectrum of protection. For example, eat purple grapes and blueberries to get *anthocyanins*, and tomatoes and corn to get red and yellow *carotenoids*. Different antioxidants protect different organs.

antioxidant facts and advice

* Frozen fruits and vegetables are as potent as fresh.

* Cooking tomatoes and carrots activates antioxidants.

* When possible, eat the colorful skins, which hold the most antioxidants.

* Always choose the brightest, deepest colors. For example, pick broccoli that is deep blue-green, not yellowish.

* Ripe fruits and vegetables contain the most antioxidants.

* Juices count. Citrus juice in particular is linked to lower disease risk.

* Dried fruits, notably prunes (dried plums) and raisins, have extremely high concentrations of antioxidants.

* Be sure to eat deep green vegetables such as collard or mustard greens; they're the most neglected of all, and are packed with antioxidants.

get your quota

SERVINGS OF fruits and vegetables recommended by the National Cancer Institute:

Children: at least five daily servings
Women: at least seven daily servings
Men: at least nine daily servings

What is a serving?
One medium piece of fruit, such as an apple, pear, or banana
1 cup leafy greens, such as spinach and lettuce
½ cup chopped vegetables, raw or cooked
½ cup chopped fruit, raw or cooked
6 ounces fruit juice or vegetable juice

EIGHT GREAT REASONS TO EAT FRUITS AND VEGETABLES

1 Heart disease risk plunged 72 percent in men and women who ate more than five fruits and vegetables a day, compared with those who ate less than one a day, finds a large Greek study.

2 Women who ate the most dark yellow, orange, and green vegetables had 20 to 35 percent lower odds of breast cancer, in Vanderbilt University research.

3 Eating fruit and vegetables every day reduced deaths from liver, stomach, and lung cancer by 20 to 35 percent, according to Japanese research.

4 Eating lots of fruit as a child cuts risk of cancer as an adult by almost 40 percent, finds a British study.

5 Men and women who ate the most fruits and vegetables were 20 percent less likely to have heart disease, according to Harvard research. Adding just one fruit or vegetable a day cuts heart disease risk by 4 percent.

6 In a Dutch study of male smokers, those who ate the most fruit were only half as likely to die of lung cancer as were those who ate the least.

7 Eating more fruits and vegetables is more effective at combating excess weight than eating less high-fat/high-sugar food, according to research at the State University of New York–Buffalo.

8 Women who eat at least five daily servings of fruits and vegetables reduce their risk of diabetes by 40 percent, compared with women who don't eat them daily, according to a study by the federal Centers for Disease Control and Prevention.

HERE'S HOW common fruits and vegetables stack up in *total antioxidant capacity* (TAC), according to the United States Department of Agriculture. The higher the TAC, the greater their antioxidant activity.

FRUIT		TOTAL ANTIOXIDANT CAPACITY (TAC)
Apple		
Fuji	1	3,578
Gala	1	3,903
Golden Delicious	1	3,685
Granny Smith	1	5,381
Red Delicious	1	5,900
Apricot	1	469
Avocado, Haas	1	3,344
Banana	1	1,037
Blackberries	1 cup	7,701
Blueberries		
Cultivated	1 cup	9,019
Lowbrush	1 cup	13,427
Cantaloupe	1 cup cubed	499
Cherries	1 cup	4,873
Cranberries	1 cup	8,983
Dates	½ cup	3,467
Figs, dried	½ cup	2,537
Grapes		
Green	1 cup	1,789
Red	1 cup	2,016
Grapefruit	½	1,904
Honeydew	1 cup diced	410
Kiwifruit	1	698
Mango	1 cup sliced	1,653
Nectarine	1	1,019
Orange	1	2,540
Peach	1	1,826
Pear		
Green	1	3,172
Red	1	2,943

Pineapple	1 cup diced	1,229
Plums	1	4,118
Prunes	½ cup	7,291
Raisins	½ cup	2,490
Raspberries	1 cup	6,058
Strawberries	1 cup	5,938
Tangerines	1	1,361
Watermelon	1 cup diced	216

VEGETABLE		TOTAL ANTIOXIDANT CAPACITY (TAC)
Vegetables are raw unless otherwise noted		
Artichoke hearts	½ cup cooked	3,952
Asparagus	½ cup	2,021
Beans, green	½ cup	147
Beans, dried, cooked		
Black	½ cup	4,181
Navy	½ cup	2,573
Pinto	½ cup	11,864
Red	½ cup	13,727
Beets	½ cup	1,886
Broccoli	½ cup	700
Cabbage		
Green	½ cup	476
Red	½ cup	788
Carrot	1 medium	741
Cauliflower	½ cup	324
Celery	½ cup	344
Corn	½ cup frozen	428
Cucumber	½ cup	74
Eggplant	½ cup	1,039
Lettuce		
Butterhead	3 oz	1,209
Green leaf	3 oz	1,320
Iceberg	3 oz	383
Red leaf	3 oz	1,519
Onion		
Yellow	½ cup	823
Red	½ cup	917

VEGETABLE		TOTAL ANTIOXIDANT CAPACITY (TAC)
Peas, green	½ cup frozen	480
Pepper, sweet		
Green	1	664
Red	1	1,072
Orange	1	1,830
Yellow	1	1,905
Potatoes		
Red	8 oz	2,494
Russett	8 oz	2,996
White	8 oz	2,383
Radishes	½ cup sliced	1,107
Spinach	3 oz	2,249
Sweet Potato	5 oz	1,173
Tomato	1 raw	415
	½ cup cooked	552

AN APPLE A DAY . . .

Exciting research shows that apples contain potent disease-fighting antioxidants, similar to those in tea, chocolate, and red wine.

HERE'S HOW APPLES IMPROVE YOUR HEALTH

Help you breathe better: A large British study of 2,500 middle-aged men showed that those who ate five or more apples a week had nearly four times better breathing capacity and lung function than non-apple eaters—even among current and former smokers. Suspected reason: antioxidants in apples protected the lungs from atmospheric pollutants and irritants, including cigarette smoke.

Ward off cancer: High apple consumption cut the risk of lung cancer by 40 percent, in a University of Hawaii study, and by 60 percent, in a Finnish study of 10,000 women and men. Further, Finns who ate the most *flavonoids*—a type of antioxidant concentrated in apples—were 20 percent less likely to develop any type of cancer. Investigators suggest that such antioxidants inhibit enzymes that activate carcinogens. Cornell University test tube studies even show that fresh apple extract suppresses growth of colon and liver cancer cells.

Prevent strokes: Those who ate the most apples were the least likely to suffer a blood clot-type stroke over a twenty-eight-year period, finds research by Finland's National Public Health Institute. Eating half an apple a day or more cut their risk of thrombotic stroke by about 40 percent, according to lead researcher Paul Knekt, PhD.

Fight heart attacks: In previous research, Knekt found that the women who ate the most apples were 43 percent less apt to diet of heart disease than were those who ate the least. Apple fiber, notably pectin, tends to lower bad LDL cholesterol. Research says apple antioxidants benefit vascular function and have anticoagulant activity similar to that of aspirin. A analysis finds that some apples are super sources of one particularly promising flavonoid called *procyanidins*, also abundant in red wine and chocolate. In fact, University of California researchers–Davis, found that Red Delicious apples averaged 208 milligrams of procyanidins each, compared with 165 milligrams in a 1.3-ounce chocolate bar and 22 milligrams in 3½ ounces of red wine.

LEAFY GREENS FOR LUTEIN

Why are spinach, kale, and other greens so good for you? One reason: they are packed with an antioxidant called *lutein*. It's a yellow pigment (covered by chlorophyll in green leaves) with newly discovered powers to fight disease. So far the evidence is impressive.

HERE'S HOW LUTEIN BOOSTS HEALTH

Saves aging eyes: Lutein is most hailed as a possible way to protect eyes from macular degeneration, a leading cause of blindness in older people. A landmark Dutch study in men showed that taking 10 milligrams of lutein ester (a specific form of lutein) daily for three months increased pigment thickness in an area of the retina known as the macula by 22 percent, presumably reducing its vulnerability to damage and loss of vision. Further, Harvard researchers found that eating 6 milligrams lutein per day in food (roughly ¼ cup cooked spinach) lowered the odds of macular degeneration by 43 percent. Remarkably, eating sautéed spinach four to seven times a week for three months even reversed some early signs of macular degeneration, discovered Stuart Richer, PhD, at the North Chicago VA Medical Center. Loading up on lutein also seems to reduce the odds of cataracts (opacity of the lens) by 20 to 50 percent, according to research.

how much do you need?

THE AVERAGE American consumes about 1 milligram of lutein each day. Experts recommend at least 4 to 6 milligrams daily.

Discourages cancer: A study by Tufts University and Korean investigators revealed a dramatic 88 percent drop in breast cancer risk in women with the highest blood concentrations of lutein. University of Utah Medical School researchers found that the highest consumers of lutein (a mere 2.4 mg daily) were 17 percent less apt to develop colon cancer than were those who ate the least (300 mcg). Generally, the more lutein consumed, the lower the risk.

High lutein has also been linked to less prostate, lung, and ovarian cancers. In animals, lutein even slowed the growth of breast tumors, and, in test tubes, caused the death of cancer cells. Researchers speculate lutein switches off carcinogenic activity and boosts immune functioning.

Prevents clogged arteries: At the University of Southern California, professor James H. Dwyer measured the thickness of the carotid (neck)

get your lutein here

BEST FOOD SOURCES	PER ½ CUP
Kale, cooked	10.0 mg
Collard greens, cooked	7.7 mg
Spinach, raw	3.3 mg
Spinach, cooked	6.3 mg
Broccoli, raw	1.0 mg
Broccoli, cooked	1.7 mg
Brussels sprouts, cooked	1.7 mg
Yellow corn, cooked	1.2 mg

Egg yolks also have small amounts of lutein (about 200 mcg per yolk) because chickens eat corn. However, egg lutein is particularly well absorbed by the body. Tufts University research showed that blood levels of lutein shot up 200 to 300 percent higher after eating egg yolks than after eating spinach!

Supplements: Lutein is also available as pills. Experts say from 4 to 10 mg daily may be needed to convey benefits shown in eye studies—the amount in ¼ to ½ cup cooked spinach.

arteries of 480 middle-aged men and women. He repeated it a year and a half later. He discovered that those with the lowest blood lutein had the greatest progression of thickening—a sign of blood-vessel clogging throughout the body. In fact, the carotid thickening was four times greater in those with the lowest blood lutein than in those with the highest blood lutein. The conclusion: lutein helped prevent artery clogging.

A probable reason: lutein-bathed cells were less apt to promote bad LDL cholesterol's ability to stick to artery walls.

Delays lung aging: People who eat the most lutein have younger lungs, finds research at the State University of New York of Buffalo. In fact, high lutein intake shaved one to two years off lung aging as indicated by standard lung function tests in 1,616 men and women, aged 35 to 79. (High vitamin E intake also boosted breathing capacity.) The new discovery could be lifesaving, because impaired lung function boosts the risk of death, said researchers. Lutein appears especially important for smokers, they added.

SPINACH: A HEALTH POWERHOUSE

In addition to lutein found in all greens, spinach is packed with a powerful array of other health-enhancing vitamins, minerals, and antioxidants.

Scientists constantly discover new reasons to eat spinach:

- Eating cooked spinach more than twice a week cuts the need for cataract eye surgery in men by half, according to Harvard University research. Including at least two servings a week in your diet cuts the odds of macular degeneration (a leading cause of blindness) in half, says the National Eye Institute.
- Feeding spinach to laboratory animals helped prevent and reverse memory loss, report Tufts University investigators.
- People who eat at least one serving of greens, including spinach, each week are 20 percent less likely to develop colon cancer, according to Italian research.
- In a large-scale Harvard study, leafy greens, including spinach, were singled out as most protective against stroke.
- Because it's high in vitamin K, spinach also helps build stronger bones, lowering the risk of hip fracture from osteoporosis as much as 30 percent, suggests a joint Harvard-Tufts study.

> Eat spinach raw. Eat it cooked. Eat it any way you can find to eat it. I call it the king of vegetables.
>
> —Steven Pratt, ophthalmologist, Scripps Clinic in La Jolla, California.

Spinach's secret weapons: Spinach is rich in antioxidants beta and alpha carotene, lutein, and zeaxanthin as well as potassium, magnesium, vitamin K, and particularly all-important folic acid. Spinach is the richest plant source of folic acid, which helps prevent serious birth defects and suppresses homocysteine, a blood factor tied to higher rates of heart disease, strokes, depression, and Alzheimer's. One-half cup of cooked spinach provides two-thirds of the daily value for folic acid.

One downside: Spinach is rich in oxalic acid, which may contribute to kidney stones in some susceptible people.

THE DISEASE-FIGHTING antioxidants in spinach are better absorbed from cooked spinach with a little added fat, such as olive or canola oil.

tip

Red Hot Health Food

Until the 1800s, Americans considered the tomato a poisonous fruit, and either rarely ate it or boiled it for hours to destroy its "toxins." All of that has radically changed in the last few years. Now that scientists have discovered spectacular disease-fighting antioxidants, including the red pigment lycopene and an anticlotting agent known as *P3 tomato factor*, the tomato has become a hot health food to help prevent and even reverse disease.

Experts urge you to eat more tomatoes in any form—fresh or canned, raw or cooked, or processed in soups or as sauce, paste, juice, or ketchup.

HOW TOMATOES BOOST HEALTH

Fight cancer: Researchers have long known tomatoes might help prevent certain cancers. In a Harvard study, eating lycopene-rich tomato sauce two to four times weekly cut prostate cancer risk by 35 percent. The news is that lycopene may even *shrink* existing prostate tumors. Before surgery, one group of prostate cancer patients at the Barbara Ann Karmanos Cancer Institute in Detroit was given lycopene extract for three weeks; another group got a placebo. Tumors in the lycopene group were smaller and less likely to spread.

Protect lungs: Eating tomatoes helps shield lungs from bad air and cigarette smoke. In a University of North Carolina test, people were exposed to high levels of ozone, an air pollutant. Those who drank a 12-ounce can of tomato-rich V-8 juice daily in the three-week test showed 20 percent less DNA damage in lung cells than those not getting V-8. Other research suggests lycopene helps ward off lung cancer.

Combat heart disease: Tomatoes can make you less prone to clogged arteries and heart disease. Dramatic evidence from Finland shows that middle-aged men with low lycopene are three times more apt to suffer heart attacks or strokes and 18 percent more apt to have narrowed carotid (neck) arteries. Probable reasons: Tomatoes help detoxify bad LDL cholesterol, hindering plaque buildup. In one test, eating 60 milligrams of lycopene daily (the amount in 1½ cups of tomato sauce or 2.2 pounds of fresh tomatoes) for three months reduced LDL cholesterol by 14 percent.

Also, an aspirin-like substance in the yellow jelly around tomato seeds helps thwart blood clots, according to Scottish research. The amount in only four tomatoes reduced clot-provoking blood stickiness by a surprising 72 percent.

Save vision: Tomatoes may protect the eyes by deterring macular degeneration, a cause of vision loss in older people, suggests University of Maryland research that found high levels of lycopene in eye tissue.

Protect skin: German research shows that eating 1.3 ounces of tomato paste daily reduced sun-induced skin damage by 40 percent.

Slow aging: Tomatoes are anti-aging nourishment for the brain. In a classic study at the University of Kentucky, elderly women with the highest lycopene blood levels remained the most mentally and physically active.

How to Get the Most Benefits

- **Eat at least five weekly servings of tomato-based foods.**
- **Eat tomatoes cooked, processed and prepared with a little olive oil.** Heating helps release lycopene, and you get the most lycopene in concentrated, processed products such as tomato paste and sauce, canned tomatoes, juice, soup, and ketchup. In tests at Ohio State University, over a two-week period, blood lycopene rose 192 percent from a daily serving of tomato sauce, 122 percent from tomato soup, and 92 percent from V-8 juice. Other research shows that adding olive oil to tomatoes increases lycopene absorption.
- **Eat a variety.** Lycopene isn't the sole tomato power. For example, tomato soup has more antioxidant activity than can be attributed to lycopene alone, meaning it contains other antioxidants. Raw tomatoes are lower in lycopene, but still may be good at combating blood clots. Rather than sticking only with tomato products known to be high in lycopene, consume a variety of tomato products—sauce, soup, whole tomatoes, juice, and so on—for optimal protection.

BRAIN-BOOSTING BERRIES

Imagine! Eating blueberries (also strawberries and spinach) may help save and rejuvenate your aging brain, says James Joseph, PhD, Tufts University. That's what he found when he fed aged laboratory animals modest amounts of berries and spinach. "They became smarter and younger," he says.

They ate the human equivalent of a pint of strawberries or a large spinach salad or a cup of blueberries every day. The results were startling.

In one test, Dr. Joseph took old rats—between 65 and 70 years old in human terms—with diminished memory, motor coordination, and balance. All the rats fed blueberries, spinach, or strawberries regained short-term memory. In other words, their memory had returned to being "young" or "middle-aged" again. Blueberries proved most potent in rejuvenating brain functions.

Blueberries, but not strawberries and spinach, also reversed the age-related loss of motor coordination and balance in the old animals, which Dr. Joseph called amazing. "I know of no drug that could do the same thing," he says. Examinations revealed that the blueberries apparently had partially repaired the age-induced damage to brain cells, accounting for the rejuvenation.

A slew of evidence confirms the powers of blueberries. Elderly rats fed blueberry extract beat younger rats on memory tests at the University of Houston. In Canadian studies, feeding lab animals blueberries reduced stroke damage.

In a test of senior citizens, those who ate a cup of blueberries a day for a month had faster reaction times and made fewer errors on a computer test, according to a study reported at the 2003 annual conference of the American Aging Association. The improvement was enough to prevent the expected decline in reaction speed due to a year or two of aging, concluded researchers.

Spice Up Your Health!

SPICES, HERBS, AND peppers are more than seasonings to please your palate. Although we eat them in small doses, they can have a major impact on our health.

Herbs and spices act as antioxidants, antibiotics, anti-inflammatory agents, blood thinners, stomach-soothers, bloodsugar, regulators, brain-cell protectors, even cancer fighters and calorie burners.

The strongest antioxidants, beginning with the most potent: oregano, thyme, sage, cumin, rosemary, saffron, turmeric, nutmeg, ginger, cardamom, coriander (cilantro), basil and tarragon. A test at the University of California–Davis declares thyme equal to vitamin E in antioxidant power.

The strongest antibiotics (beginning with the most effective): onion, garlic, allspice, oregano, thyme, tarragon, cumin, cloves, bay leaf, capsicum pepper (cayenne), rosemary, marjoram, mustard, mint, sage, coriander, dill, basil, parsley, black and white pepper, ginger. They are the most ferocious killers of thirty different bacterial species, according to Cornell University tests.

BEST HEALTH BOOSTERS

Oregano: "No wonder oregano has been used since antiquity to fight infections," says Harry Preuss, MD, George Washington University. He found oregano oil as effective as the common antibiotic drug vancomycin, in treating staph infections in mice. The oregano also wiped out an infectious fungus, reduced blood pressure, and improved blood sugar and insulin sensitivity in diabetic rats.

Turmeric: The yellow spice turmeric, a constituent of curry powder, is rich in curcumin, a potent antioxidant that may help stifle cancer. In test tubes, 80 percent of malignant prostate cells exposed to curcumin died. Feeding mice curcumin slowed the growth of implanted human prostate cancer cells, and may do the same to breast and colon cancer cells.

Moreover, curcumin's anti-inflammatory activity reduces the swelling of arthritis and progressive brain damage in animals. Eating food laced with low doses of curcumin slashed Alzheimer's-like plaque in the brains of mice by 50 percent, says UCLA research. Researchers suspect curcumin in curry powder may be one reason the population of India has low rates of Alzheimer's disease.

Ginger: As a natural anti-inflammatory, ginger may help relieve inflammation in arthritis, heart disease, stroke, Alzheimer's, and possibly cancer. Ginger compounds (gingerols) reduce pain in animals and act as Cox-2 inhibitors, similar to the antiarthritis drug Celebrex, according to Australian scientists at Sydney University. Further, gingerols thin the blood "just like aspirin," the Aussies noted, confirming that ginger is a mild anticoagulant. When given ginger for six weeks, arthritis patients at the University of Miami had less knee pain than did those not getting ginger. Ginger is also a well-established suppressor of nausea.

Cinnamon: Adding a little cinnamon to food helps prevent spikes in blood sugar, says Richard Anderson, PhD, United States Department of Agriculture.

"Cinnamon can help normalize blood sugar by making insulin more sensitive and efficient," he finds. He isolated cinnamon's most active ingredient—methylhydroxy chalcone polymer (MHCP). The cinnamon compound increased the processing of blood sugar by about 2,000 percent or 20-fold in test tube studies. Cloves, turmeric, and bay leaves also energize insulin, but are much weaker. Using cinnamon could be especially important for type 2 diabetics, says Dr. Anderson, and could help prevent onset of the disease. In animals, low steady insulin levels are a sign of slower aging and greater longevity.

Hot Chile Peppers: If you have asthma, emphysema, chronic bronchitis, sinusitis, congestion from a cold or the flu, or other breathing problems, eat hot peppers and hot sauce, advises Irwin Ziment, MD, professor of medicine at UCLA. He says hot peppers work like expectorants to trigger a flash flood of fluids in the air passages, breaking up mucus, flushing out the sinuses, and washing away irritants. "When you're congested," Ziment says, "it's better to eat salsa than to suck on a menthol cough drop."

Hot peppers can also suppress appetite and burn off extra calories. In a British study, eating three-fifths of a teaspoon of hot chile sauce increased average metabolism by 25 percent, burning off 45 calories in the next three hours. Canadian study participants who ate an appetizer with hot sauce consumed 200 fewer calories during the meal than did those not given hot sauce. Incidentally, chile peppers do not damage normal stomachs or cause ulcers or heartburn, but they can worsen existing heartburn.

> **WHEN PEPPERS** get too hot, try a chaser of yogurt, beer, whole milk, or ice cream. They are better than water or soft drinks at putting out fiery aftertastes.
>
> **tip**

Garlic: An ancient folk medicine, garlic has antibacterial, antiviral, anti-cancer, anti-blood clotting, anti-inflammatory, cholesterol-reducing, immune-boosting, and decongestive properties, according to modern research. The strongest evidence exists for its anticancer activity. A study of 42,000 older women in Iowa, for example, found that those who ate garlic more than once a week were about half as apt to develop colon cancer as were women who never ate garlic. In test tube studies, a specific garlic compound suppressed the growth of prostate cancer cells by about 25 percent, indicating garlic might help block cancer spread.

Garlic may kill viruses responsible for colds and flu, according to tests. UCLA's Dr. Ziment recommends garlic as a remedy for congestion from a flu or cold. He notes that garlic's alliin, which gives garlic its flavor, behaves like a decongestant, mimicking a drug widely used to break up mucus in the lungs. Other studies suggest garlic revs up immune functioning by stimulating the potency of infection-fighting T cells.

Raw or cooked? For antibacterial or antiviral effect, raw garlic is best. However, both raw and cooked garlic seems to have cardiovascular, decongestive, and anticancer benefits.

Too much? High doses of raw garlic (usually more than three cloves a day) have caused gas, bloating, diarrhea, and fever in some people. Cooked garlic is gentler on the stomach.

go easy on salt

AMERICANS EAT TWO or three times more sodium than is good for us. Here's how to cut back:

* Buy fresh, plain frozen, or canned "no-salt added" vegetables. Canned corn has 100 times more sodium than frozen. Regular canned tomatoes have ten times more sodium than "no-salt added" canned tomatoes. Look for "no-salt added" canned beans at health food stores and some supermarkets.

* Restrict cured meats (bacon, ham), foods packed in brine (pickles, olives, sauerkraut), condiments (MSG, soy sauce, mustard, catsup, barbecue and chile sauce).

* Use spices instead of salt to flavor foods.

* Drain and rinse canned foods, such as tuna and beans, to remove some sodium.

* Cook rice, pasta, hot cereals, beans, and vegetables without salt.

* Eat fewer frozen dinners and pizzas, packaged mixes, canned soups or broths, and salad dressings—often loaded with sodium. Or look for low-sodium versions.

Nuts:
The New Superfood

NOT LONG AGO, nuts were dismissed as "fattening snacks." Today, experts urge you to eat nuts to save your heart, reduce diabetes, ward off cancer, lose weight and perhaps fend off Parkinson's disease, and live longer. Nuts are definitely one of the primary ingredients of a healthy diet.

"Nuts are excellent substitutes for meat, cheese, and other fatty foods, and satisfy the craving for fat," says research by the late Gene Spiller, PhD, director of the Health Research and Studies Center in Los Altos, California. Sure, nuts contain a significant amount of fat, but it's mostly the good monounsaturated type that discourages disease. Walnuts also contain high levels of healthy omega-3 fats.

Nuts are also packed with fiber, vitamins, and minerals, including calcium, folate, potassium, magnesium, and vitamin E, and with cancer-fighting antioxidants such as quercetin and kaempferol. Nuts are rich in arginine, an amino acid that relaxes blood vessels, which helps to lower blood pressure and deter blood clots. Brazil nuts are also the richest source of selenium, thought to help improve mood and prevent certain cancers.

HOW NUTS KEEP YOU HEALTHY

Reduce heart disease: Consistently, studies find that nut eaters are from 30 to 50 percent less apt to develop or die of heart disease. In a pioneering study at Loma Linda University, eating two ounces of nuts four or five times a week slashed heart attack risk by 50 percent. A large Harvard study found heart attacks were one-third less likely among women who ate five ounces of nuts weekly, compared with women who ate nuts once a month. In fact, a diet high in fatty peanuts and peanut butter helps hearts and improves cholesterol more than does a typical low-fat regimen, says Penn State research.

The Food and Drug Administration now agrees that eating an ounce and a half of nuts (about one-third cup) a day, including almonds, hazelnuts, pecans, pistachios, walnuts, and peanuts, as part of a low animal fat diet, may reduce heart disease.

Lower cholesterol: In several studies, the consumption of almonds, walnuts, or macadamia nuts (two to three ounces a day) depressed bad LDL cholesterol by up to 29 percent, and in some cases raised good HDL cholesterol by up to 8 percent. In Loma Linda University research, walnuts even enhance the cholesterol-lowering power of a Mediterranean diet. Eating eight to eleven walnuts daily instead of other fats, such as olive oil, further lowered bad cholesterol about 6 percent. This reduced heart disease risk by 11 percent. A daily ounce of almonds was part of a low-fat Canadian diet that reduced cholesterol as effectively as a statin drug (Lipitor) did.

Combat diabetes: A long-term Harvard study of 83,000 women nurses, ages 34 to 59, found that nuts, including peanuts, significantly lower the risk of developing type 2 diabetes. Women who ate an ounce of nuts more than five times a week were nearly 30 percent less apt to have diabetes as those who never ate nuts or ate less than an ounce a week, regardless of weight or other risk factors for diabetes.

Further, women who ate peanut butter five times or more a week (equal to five ounces of peanuts) had a 20 percent lower risk of diabetes than did women who rarely or never ate peanut butter.

Reduce cancer risk: Nuts may lower the risk of colon, stomach, and prostate cancers. In India, eating cashews is linked to less colon cancer, says Bandaru Reddy of the American Health Foundation. Canadian research suggests eating nuts and seeds and beans can reduce risk of endometrial cancer.

Prevent Parkinson's disease: When Harvard researchers analyzed the diets of thousands of doctors and female nurses in the long-term ongoing studies, they found that nuts may protect against Parkinson's disease. Individuals who ate an ounce of nuts more than five times a week, compared with those who did so less than once a month, had a surprising 43 percent lower risk of developing Parkinson's disease.

Promote weight loss: Contrary to popular opinion, people who eat nuts are not fatter than those who don't. To the contrary, studies show nut eaters are apt to lose weight and keep it off. In a study at Boston's Brigham and Women's Hospital, dieters on equal calories lost more weight on a diet high in monounsaturated fat, including nuts, peanuts, and peanut butter, than did those on a very low-fat diet and kept it off longer. After 18 months, high-fat nut eaters had lost nine pounds; low-fat dieters had gained more than six pounds.

Possible reasons: Purdue University research found peanut butter dampened the appetite, staving off hunger for two and a half hours compared with a mere half hour for snacks such as rice cakes. Further, the fat in nuts is not totally absorbed. Peanuts have an extremely low glycemic index, meaning they don't spike blood sugar that leads to hunger and weight gain.

Sweet News about Chocolate

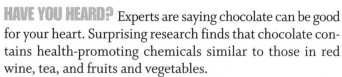

HAVE YOU HEARD? Experts are saying chocolate can be good for your heart. Surprising research finds that chocolate contains health-promoting chemicals similar to those in red wine, tea, and fruits and vegetables.

Even the prestigious *New England Journal of Medicine's Heart Watch* newsletter says "a sizeable chunk of research" suggests that cocoa bean compounds have modest "beneficial effects on specific factors linked to heart disease." The scientific *Journal of Nutrition* devoted an entire issue to an investigation of chocolate's "medicinal benefits."

HERE ARE THE WAYS CHOCOLATE GUARDS HEALTH

Provides antioxidants galore: Chocolate is rich in cell-protecting antioxidants. An ounce and a half of milk chocolate typically has 400 milligrams of antioxidants, about the same as a glass of red wine, reports chemistry professor Joe A. Vinson, of the University of Scranton, Pennsylvania. Dark chocolate has twice as much. White chocolate has none. Further, antioxidant activity jumped 31 percent in the blood of subjects two hours after eating 2.8 ounces of M&M's semisweet chocolate baking bits, according to research at the University of California–Davis. In another Italian study, eating dark chocolate boosted antioxidant blood levels more than milk chocolate did. Clearly, dark chocolate delivers the most antioxidants and greatest benefits.

Fights cholesterol: Antioxidants in chocolate help block chemical changes in bad LDL cholesterol that lead to clogged arteries. In fact, Vinson found chocolate's antioxidants more potent in detoxifying LDLs than is vitamin C. Additional research by Penny Kris-Etherton at Pennsylvania State University, shows that diets rich in dark chocolate or cocoa powder raise good HDL cholesterol. Previously, she found that eating a milk chocolate bar every day for a month (in place of another high-carb snack) did not raise bad LDL cholesterol in men.

Blocks blood clots: Chocolate's antioxidants act like aspirin to reduce blood platelet stickiness and clots that trigger heart attacks and strokes. In a study, 30 people drank either plain water, a caffeine drink, or a cocoa beverage containing one and a half times the antioxidants in a typical eight-ounce cup of hot cocoa. The cocoa significantly delayed blood clotting time.

Relaxes blood vessels: Good vascular function—how well blood vessels relax—helps prevent heart disease, particularly high blood pressure and artery clogging. Chocolate's antioxidants, called procyanidins, relax blood vessels by increasing concentrations of the chemical nitric oxide, according to studies at the University of California–Davis School of Medicine. UC research also shows that chocolate's antioxidants help suppress inflammatory processes, now recognized as a prime villain in cardiovascular disease.

TO GET THE most benefits, consume dark chocolate, which has more antioxidants than milk chocolate. White chocolate has none.

tip

Reduces blood pressure: When German study participants with mild high blood pressure ate a three-ounce dark chocolate bar daily for two weeks, their blood pressure sank. Systolic pressure (upper number) dropped an average 5.1 mm Hg and diastolic fell 1.9 mm Hg. Experts said the reduction was very similar to that produced by a low-salt diet.

QUESTIONING CHOCOLATE'S DARK SIDE

Won't chocolate make you fat? Since chocolate is packed with fat and sugar, overindulging is bound to put on pounds. But chocolate is not a

CHOCOLATE'S NEWLY discovered health benefits make it more than just an empty-calorie junk food, but nobody is saying it's okay to eat five to nine chocolate bars a day instead of apples and carrots. Chocolate is still a high-fat, sugary occasional indulgence, not an everyday healthy staple like fruits and vegetables.

prime cause of obesity, according to worldwide studies. The Swiss, for example, eat twice as much chocolate per person as do Americans—about 22 pounds a year—but still have one of the lowest rates of obesity.

Isn't chocolate full of artery-clogging fat? About 60 percent of chocolate's fat is saturated—and a typical chocolate bar contains 8 grams of saturated fat, so binging on chocolate drives up saturated fat intake. But moderate amounts of chocolate do not appear to be harmful. Extensive Harvard research found that women who ate a chocolate bar three to four times a week were no more likely to have heart disease than women who rarely ate chocolate.

Isn't the sugar in chocolate unhealthy? In excess, yes, however, a chocolate bar's glycemic index—the ability to drive up blood sugar—is lower than that of sugary cereals and bagels.

What about chocolate's caffeine? A dark chocolate bar's 10 to 30 milligrams of caffeine is modest compared with the 100 milligrams in a cup of coffee.

Cancer-Proof Your Barbecue, and Other Meaty Advice

THERE'S MOUNTING EVIDENCE that eating meat can have serious health consequences. Heavy meat eaters tend to have more heart disease, cancer, and other chronic diseases and a shorter life expectancy. "Eating substantial amounts of red meat may increase the risk of colorectal, pancreatic, breast, prostate, and renal cancer," the National Cancer Institute has declared. However, you can dramatically reduce the danger by eating less red meat (substituting poultry, fish, and other protein sources) and cooking meat in ways that minimize formation of carcinogens.

STUDIES UNCOVER CANCER RISK

Men and women who ate the most red meat (average three ounces daily), especially well done and/or fried, doubled their risk of colon cancer compared with those who ate the least (less than half an ounce daily), says a study by the National Institute of Environmental Health Sciences.

Breast cancer risk was twice as high in postmenopausal women who ate three ounces or more of red meat a day, compared with women who consumed an ounce or less daily, according to a study at the Portland, Oregon VA Medical Center. Odds of breast cancer jumped 85 percent in premenopausal women who ate the most red meat, compared to those eating the least, says a German study. Vanderbilt University investigators determined that women who ate the most deep-fried, well-done meat had nearly twice the odds of developing breast cancer as did those who ate the least.

The odds of pancreatic cancer doubled in people who ate the most grilled or barbecued red meat (ranging from three to twenty-one ounces a week) compared to non-red-meat eaters, finds a University of Minnesota study.

HIGH-HEAT HAZARDS

Much of the danger depends on how meat is cooked. Heat reacts with a protein in meat muscle (as well as in poultry and fish to a lesser degree) to form cancer-promoting chemicals called *heterocyclicamines* (HCAs). The higher and more prolonged the heat, as in grilling and frying, the greater the amounts of HCAs formed. Moreover, the carcinogenic HCAs are embedded deep in the meat, so you can't scrape them off the surface as you can the char from barbecue. Poultry and fish, although they, too, may contain HCAs, do not appear to be nearly as dangerous as red meat.

WAYS TO REDUCE THE THREAT

Substitute fish or poultry for red meat: Fish is safest, tests show, and may even discourage breast cancer risk. Women who ate fish three or more times weekly had a 30 percent lower breast cancer risk than did women who ate fish once a week in the study at Portland, Oregon VA Medical Center. In another study, eating chicken baked, broiled, or barbecued did not raise colon cancer risk. However, panfrying chicken boosted odds by 50 percent. You can also substitute turkey, chicken, or veggie burgers for beef burgers.

Cook smart: You can dramatically reduce dangerous HCAs by microwaving, poaching, stewing, and roasting meat, poultry, and fish. Prolonged cooking at high temperature, such as barbecuing and frying burgers, chicken, and chops well done, produces the most HCAs. Consistently eating crispy bacon and beef steak very well done, instead of rare or medium, boosted women's breast cancer risk nearly five times, in a University of Minnesota study.

Best way to cook meat: in the oven and simmering on the top of the stove—and best of all, in the microwave, where internal temperatures are no more than that of boiling water. Contrary to popular opinion, microwaving is not a high-temperature way of cooking. Important: hamburgers must be cooked well done to kill infectious agents, such as E. coli. See barbecue tips for reducing the hazards in hamburgers on pages 52–53.

Eat less red meat: Use smaller portions as in stews, casseroles, and stir-frys, not as the centerpiece of a meal.

Avoid or restrict nitrite-cured meats: This includes ham, bacon, hot dogs, and cold cuts. Nitrite can react with other chemicals in the intestinal tract to form nitrosamines, a potent family of carcinogens linked to higher rates of stomach, pancreatic and brain cancer, and leukemia. Always microwave bacon; it reduces nitrosamines by about 90 percent.

CANCER QUESTIONS:

Is fish safer? In one study, fried fish had only 20 percent as many HCAs as fried chicken and beef. It's safest to poach, bake, or microwave fish.

Is it okay to grill vegetables? Grilling vegetables at high heat does not form HCAs, says researcher James Felton, because they do not contain the meat protein that produces HCAs.

What about roast turkey and meat loaf? There's little hazard from HCAs because of the usually low oven temperature of 350 degrees fahrenheit or so. Also, it's unlikely turkey gravy made from such drippings are high in HCAs.

TEN WAYS TO CANCER-PROOF YOUR BARBECUE

Scientists have come up with ingenious ways to dramatically reduce the formation of carcinogens in grilled meat. Here are ten tested ways to make your barbecue safer:

1 FLIP BURGERS OFTEN. Turning burgers once a minute and cooking over lower heat reduces formation of cancer-causing HCAs and kills potentially deadly E. coli bacteria, finds a study at Lawrence Livermore National Laboratory in California. Important: Use a meat thermometer to make sure a burger's internal temperature reaches 160 degrees Fahrenheit, needed to deactivate E. coli. Just because meat is brown doesn't mean it's thoroughly cooked.

2 USE THE RIGHT MARINADE. Slash HCAs by marinating raw meat in a thin, very liquid sauce for at least 10 minutes, or more to taste. The Cancer Research Center of Hawaii found that a teriyaki marinade reduced HCAs by 67 percent, and a turmeric-garlic sauce, 50 percent. (You'll find recipes for these marinades on page 270). The key is to use a watery sauce: when a thick, concentrated commercial barbecue sauce was used, it actually tripled HCAs. So dilute thick sauces.

3 MICROWAVE FIRST. Partially cook burgers, poultry, ribs, and fish in a microwave oven before grilling, and be sure to discard the juices. Microwaving a hamburger a couple of minutes, or a batch of ribs and chicken 5 to 15 minutes eliminates 90 percent of HCAs, says James Felton, PhD, at Lawrence Livermore Lab. Important: Be sure to drain off the microwaved meat juices that contain the raw material for formation of HCAs. Don't use them to make gravy or sauces.

4 ADD SOY PROTEIN. Mix half a cup of textured soy protein into a pound of ground meat (beef, pork, veal, lamb, turkey, or chicken) before grilling. This cuts 95 percent of the expected HCAs in burgers without appreciably affecting the taste, according to tests by John Weisburger, PhD, at the American Health Foundation.

5 ENHANCE WITH E. Adding vitamin E to raw ground meat hinders HCAs, says J. Ian Gray, PhD, of Michigan State University. His tests showed that 120 milligrams of vitamin E powder mixed into or sprinkled on 3.5-ounce patties can reduce HCA formation by as much as 72 percent. Just crack open a capsule of powdered vitamin E.

6 TRY A "FRUIT BURGER." Mixing a pound of ground meat with a cup of ground, dried tart cherries before grilling suppresses 90 percent of HCA formation, according to research at Michigan State. A possible reason: Cherries are high in HCA-blocking antioxidants. Researchers say other deep-colored fruits rich in antioxidants (red grapes, blueberries, plums) should work, too. (Check out my Blueberry Burger recipe on page 264).

7 ADD GARLIC AND HERBS. In tests, garlic, rosemary, and sage reduced HCAs, Gray says. Mix them into burgers, use them in marinades, or just eat them in a meal with grilled meat. Antioxidants in citrus fruits also block HCAs.

8 BEWARE OF WELL DONE. The longer meat is cooked at high temperatures (grilling and frying) the more HCAs are produced. Cooking steaks very well done, compared to simply well done, doubles HCAs. To minimize HCAs, grill beefsteaks and lamb rare or medium-rare. Always cook burgers, pork, and poultry well done to avoid food poisoning. Do not eat the charred skin of barbecued meat, poultry, or fish; it contains carcinogens.

9 WASH DOWN BARBECUED FOOD WITH TEA. Chemicals in black and green tea help detoxify HCAs, Weisburger says. He recommends drinking hot or iced tea brewed from bags or loose tea (not bottled teas or powdered instant teas) regularly—and especially with barbecue. Or marinate meat, poultry, and fish in concentrated tea. To make a tea marinade, let a tea bag steep in ¼ cup of hot water for 5 minutes.

10 SKIP THE MEAT—GRILL "GREEN." Fruits and vegetables don't contain the animal protein needed to make HCAs. Pineapple and peppers are great grilled. Also, eating antioxidant-packed fruits, vegetables, and green salads along with barbecued meat lessens the cancer hazard.

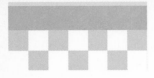

Tea: The Healthiest Drink

IT'S TIME TO pay serious attention to tea.

Research reveals some remarkable health properties of both black and green tea. Studies in leading medical journals have declared tea a potential heart-tonic, fat-buster, brain booster, cancer blocker, cavity-fighter, sight-saver, immune-stimulant, arthritis-soother, antiviral agent, cholesterol-suppressor, and detoxifier. That's not bad for a lowly shrub soaked in a little hot water.

"Tea is beating all scientific expectations as the most potent health beverage ever," says researcher John Weis-burger, of the American Health Foundation. "The many ways tea can promote health is truly astonishing." The bottom line is you should drink several cups of black or green tea, hot or iced, a day, advises Weisburger.

HERE'S HOW TEA BOOSTS HEALTH

Saves arteries: Drinking black tea helps prevent deadly artery clogging and reverses poor arterial functioning that can trigger heart attacks and strokes, according to two major studies. In a large ten-year Dutch study, men who consumed the amount of specific antioxidants called *catechins* in three cups of black tea a day were 50 percent less apt to die of ischemic heart disease, caused by narrowed clogged arteries, than did men consuming the catechins in about half a cup of tea a day.

In another test, Joseph Vita, MD, professor of medicine at Boston University School of Medicine, had heart patients drink either four cups of black tea daily or plain water for a month. Remarkably, impaired blood vessel functioning, a risk factor for heart attack and strokes, improved about 50 percent in the tea drinkers!

Moreover, a United States Department of Agriculture study found that drinking five cups of black tea daily (30 fluid ounces or slightly less than a quart) reduced bad LDL cholesterol by 11 percent within three weeks!

Inhibits cancer growth: Drinking tea has long been tied to a lower risk of certain cancers, notably, stomach, colon, and breast, although the connection is not proven. Now lab studies find that tea chemicals may actually stop cancer growth. Rutgers University researchers showed that TF-2, a compound in black tea, caused colorectal cancer cells to commit suicide; normal colon cells were unaffected. "The effect is quite dramatic," said Rutgers professor Kuang Yu Chen, who speculates the tea chemical might one day be made into an anticancer drug.

Tames inflammation: Chemicals in both black and green tea have anti-inflammatory activity that may combat arthritis. Case Western Reserve researchers gave arthritis-prone mice either green tea or water. The human equivalent of four cups of green tea daily cut the mice's risk of developing arthritis in half. Also intriguing, the anti-cancer compound TF-2 suppresses the Cox 2 gene that triggers inflammation, say Rutgers researchers. "the same way the drug Celebrex works to relieve arthritis," they point out. Investigators at UCLA report that drinking green tea reduced by half the risk of chronic stomach inflammation (gastritis), a prelude to stomach cancer, in a study of 600 Chinese men and women.

Wipes out viruses: Previous tests prove tea can neutralize a variety of germs, including some that cause diarrhea, pneumonia, cystitis, and skin infections. Research by Milton Schiffenbauer of Pace University in New York finds that black and green tea inactivates viruses, including herpes. He says when you drink tea, chances are good you wipe out viruses in your mouth. Flu viruses, too? Possibly. A Japanese study did show that gargling with black tea boosted immunity to influenza.

Burns off calories: Most surprising, green tea's antioxidant, EGCG, stimulates the body to burn energy, notably fat. In short, it converts flab to heat, getting rid of calories. So found Abdul G. Dulloo of the University of Fribourg in Switzerland. He gave men three capsules daily containing 270 mg EGCG—the amount in two to three cups of green tea. It caused them to burn 4 percent more energy—about 80 additional calories a day. Further, green tea did not increase heart rate, and the extra calorie-burning was not due to caffeine.

And still more: Researchers at McGill University in Canada blocked dental cavities in mice by giving them tea to drink instead of water. Eye researchers in India retarded progression of cataracts in rats by feeding them green or black tea extract. Israeli scientists blocked Parkinson's-like brain damage in mice by giving them green tea extract or pure ECGC, the tea's primary antioxidant.

the special magic of green tea

ALTHOUGH IT'S health-smart to drink any real brewed tea, including popular black tea, green tea appears superior, say studies. Commercial green teas average about twice the antioxidant activity as do black teas, according to a UCLA analyses. So you may have to drink twice as much black as green tea for similar benefits.

Moreover, green tea has higher concentrations of potent catechin antioxidants, mainly one called *epigallo-catechin-gallate* (EGCG). Here are some specific findings that make green tea a high priority:

* Consuming the EGCG in two or three cups of green tea helped block the spread of human lung cancer cells, in Japanese tests.

* The EGCG in three cups of green tea normalized vascular dysfunction (a condition that can trigger heart attacks) in patients with heart disease, says Boston University research.

* EGCG destroyed leukemia cells by disrupting their survival communication network, in a groundbreaking discovery at the Mayo Clinic.

* EGCG blocked expected alcohol-induced liver damage in rats, including fat accumulation, inflammation and necrosis (death) of liver cells, in University of North Carolina tests.

* EGCG inhibited growth of 80 percent of human breast cancer cells without damaging normal cells, report University of Alabama scientists.

* EGCG interfered with angiogenesis, formation of blood vessels that supply food to cancer cells, thus, starving the cancer, in Tufts University studies.

* Green tea extract strongly inhibited spread of infection by Helicobacter pylori bacteria that cause gastrointestinal ulcers and possibly stomach cancer in animals, find Japanese researchers.

2

VITAMIN ADVICE FROM THE EXPERTS

The Multivitamin Mineral Pill:
Why Everybody Needs One

VITAMIN/MINERAL SUPPLEMENTS give your body a "tune-up" and are insurance against health breakdown, says biochemist Bruce Ames, who wants everybody in the world to take a multivitamin/mineral pill. Ames, 76, is a world-renowned researcher on antioxidants and nutrients at the University of California–Berkeley and Children's Hospital of Oakland Research Institute. Because of poor diets, he says, widespread micronutrient deficiencies could condemn millions of Americans to poor health and substandard mental achievement.

In groundbreaking research, Ames and his group discovered a frightening picture of what happens to cells deprived of proper amounts of micronutrients. Their DNA (genetic material) and energy producing centers (mitochondria) are damaged. This damage could lead to cancer, brain cell decay and cognitive dysfunction, accelerated aging and degenerative diseases such as Alzheimer's and Parkinson's. Most astonishing, the nutrient-deprived cells look like they were exposed to radiation—as from atomic bomb fallout and X-rays—well documented as a cause of cancer. In short, being vitamin and mineral deficient is like being irradiated constantly. Who should worry? More than half of Americans, notably the young, the poor, the elderly, and the obese, may have at least one vitamin/mineral deficiency that can mimic radiation damage, says Ames.

Particularly worrisome: low levels of folic acid, zinc, B_{12}, B_6, and iron (in premenopausal women). The developing fetus and growing children are especially vulnerable. Note: In post-menopausal women and men age 18 and over, too much iron can accelerate aging and promote heart disease and cancer. Men and postmenopausal women should not take iron supplements, unless a doctor recommends or prescribes them.

WHY MULTIVITAMINS ARE GOOD FOR YOU

Heart disease: In a Swedish study, men who took multivitamins had a 20 percent lower risk of heart attacks, and women, a 35 percent lower risk, than those not taking supplements.

Infections: Taking multivitamins for a year boosted immune functioning and cut infections, such as the flu, 40 percent in diabetics and 50 percent in the elderly, compared with taking a placebo, according to tests at the University of North Carolina and Memorial University of Newfoundland.

Cancer: Harvard studies show that taking multivitamins containing folic acid cut the risk of colon cancer 50 percent in women with a family history of the disease.

Cataracts: Taking a multivitamin pill for more than ten years slashed the risk of cataracts by 60 percent, finds a study of 3,089 people ages 43 to 86, by ophthalmologists at the University of Wisconsin–Madison.

Kids' IQ: Ten out of thirteen studies show that giving children multivitamin/mineral pills raised their nonverbal IQ scores as much as 30 percent, reports British psychologist David Benton, University of Wales, Swansea. Benton estimates that one-third to one-half of all children have mild, unsuspected nutritional deficiencies that can be corrected by a multivitamin.

Even the conservative medical establishment now agrees that taking vitamins is essential. Writing in the *Journal of the American Medical Association*, two Harvard researchers advise all adult Americans to take a multivitamin supplement. They cite thirty years of studies showing the connection between low vitamin intake and increased risk of chronic diseases, such as cancer and heart disease.

Take Antioxidants To Stay Young

TAKING A LOW-DOSE multivitamin/mineral pill that provides 100 percent of the recommended daily allowances can fill in nutrient gaps, significantly boosting health. These doses, however, are not powerful enough to provide "optimal" protection for most people, especially as they grow older, according to compelling research. As you age, you need potent antioxidants that low-dose multivitamins lack. Antioxidants help neutralize cellular enemies called free radical chemicals that are considered a primary cause of accelerated aging and chronic disease. Start taking antioxidant supplements during your twenties, thirties, and forties when you're young and healthy, to stay that way, say leading researchers.

Chronic conditions like cancer and cardiovascular disease take decades to develop. So do wrinkles and fuzzy brains. That's why one of the world's leading authorities on antioxidants says no adult is too young to start taking these popular supplements.

After decades of research, Lester Packer, PhD, a molecular and cell biologist at the University of Southern California, worries that more than 70 percent of Americans will die prematurely from diseases caused by or compounded by deficiencies of antioxidants.

Packer insists that antioxidants "can make your heart strong, your mind sharp and your body youthful well into your seventies, eighties, nineties, and beyond. They can help prevent cancer, keep your skin supple and wrinkle-free, improve your sex life, and extend your life."

You'll find a list of twenty-one scientific studies showing why you need more than low doses of antioxidants, vitamins, and minerals to soften the threat of premature aging and chronic diseases.

HOW HIGH-POTENCY SUPPLEMENTS CAN SAVE YOU

1 VITAMINS E AND C PROLONG LIFE

Taking vitamin E and vitamin C (in higher doses than in a multi-vitamin) cut chances of death from all causes by 42 percent. Vitamin E users were 47 percent less apt to die of heart disease and 59 percent less likely to die of cancer, said the National Institute on Aging.

2 VITAMIN E BOOSTS IMMUNE SYSTEM

Taking 200 IU of natural vitamin E daily boosted immune functioning in older people, in Tufts University research. A supplement with only 60 milligrams of vitamin E daily did not improve immune functioning. Superior immune functioning lessens infections, and possibly cancer and heart disease.

3 ANTIOXIDANTS CUT DEATH RATES

Men who took a special antioxidant capsule for seven years had 31 percent less cancer and 37 percent lower death rates than did men getting a dummy pill or placebo, according to a French double-blind controlled study of 13,000 men and women aged 35 to 60. Doses in the daily capsule: 6 milligrams beta carotene, 120 milligrams vitamin C, 90 milligrams vitamin E, 100 micrograms selenium, and 20 milligrams zinc.

4 SELENIUM BOOSTS IMMUNITY AND MOOD

In a double-blind study of elderly people, researchers at the University of Brussels found taking 100 micrograms of selenium a day improved certain factors in immune functioning by 79 percent. One reason: The body needs selenium to produce a critical antioxidant enzyme that helps detoxify cellular fats that otherwise lower immunity, foster cancer and destroy arteries. A daily 100 micrograms of selenium also improved mood, in a British study.

5 VITAMIN C PREVENTS HEART ATTACKS

A Harvard study of 90,000 female nurses found that those who took 350 to 400 milligrams of vitamin C supplements daily for 16 years were 30 percent less apt to have a heart attack or other "coronary event" than non–vitamin C takers! Getting smaller amounts of vitamin C in foods did not prevent heart disease in the study. This surprising evidence that vitamin C in supplements gave the heart stronger protection than vitamin C in food provides "compelling evidence" for taking vitamin C, say experts.

6 VITAMIN E STOPS HEART ATTACKS

A daily dose of 400 to 800 IU of natural vitamin E cut subsequent heart attacks in men with heart problems by an astonishing 77 percent in British research at Cambridge University. Other research shows it takes 400 IU of vitamin E to squelch toxicity (oxidation) of LDL cholesterol.

7 VITAMIN C DROPS BLOOD PRESSURE

Taking 500 mg of vitamin C daily reduced blood pressure in type 2 diabetics, finds an Irish study. After only a month, systolic pressure (the upper number) dropped ten points—down from 142 to 132—and diastolic pressure fell about five points. Further, the vitamin C reduced the stiffness of arteries and the aorta, making them more flexible and able to dilate and contract properly.

8 B VITAMINS STOP STROKES

High doses of B vitamins decreased the amount of plaque in carotid (neck) arteries by 10 percent during a four-year study at the University of Toronto. Blocked carotid arteries can cause strokes. Plaque increased by 50 percent in non–vitamin B takers. Daily doses that reversed plaque: 250 micrograms B_{12}, 25 milligrams B_6, and 2500 micrograms folic acid. Researchers used the extra-high dose of folic acid, but said it may not be necessary. They said 800 micrograms of folic acid is effective for most people.

9 SELENIUM BLOCKS CANCER

In a groundbreaking study of 1,312 older people, taking 200 micrograms of selenium daily for seven years slashed overall cancer rates by 42 percent and cancer death rates in half, compared with those taking a dummy (placebo) pill, according to University of Arizona research. Specifically, taking selenium cut the occurrence of prostate cancer by 69 percent; colorectal cancer, 64 percent; and lung cancer, 39 percent.

10 VITAMINS REDUCE RISK OF OVARIAN CANCER

Taking vitamin C reduced risk of the most common form of ovarian cancer by 60 percent. Taking vitamin E reduced risk by 67 percent. Taking the two antioxidants together was most powerful, decreasing risk by 71 percent, according to a University of North Carolina study. Vitamin E and C in food alone did not deter the cancer. Daily protective dose (from food and pills) was more than 363 milligrams of vitamin C and more than 75 milligrams of vitamin E daily.

11 LYCOPENE SHRINKS PROSTATE TUMORS

Eating tomatoes, rich in the antioxidant lycopene, helps prevent prostate cancer, according to several studies. Taking lycopene supplements can shrink prostate tumors, too, according to Wayne State University investigators. They found that giving lycopene supplements to patients for only three weeks prior to surgery reduced prostate tumor size in 80 percent of men. More remarkable, the tumor did not spread beyond the prostate gland in 73 percent of men on lycopene; it did spread in 82 percent not getting lycopene.

12 VITAMIN E STOPS BLADDER CANCER

You're less likely to die of bladder cancer if you take vitamin E long term says a study by the American Cancer Society. Taking vitamin E supplements regularly (more than fifteen times a month) for more than ten years reduced the risk of death from bladder cancer by 40 percent. Taking the vitamin for a shorter time did not affect bladder cancer mortality.

13 VITAMIN C BUILDS BONES

Supplements of vitamin C stimulate the formation of collagen and bone, suggests research at the University of California–San Diego. Postmenopausal women who popped vitamin C pills for a dozen years or more had 3 percent higher bone mineral density

(BMD) at several sites, indicating stronger bones, than did nonusers. Women with the highest bone mineral density took 1,000 milligrams or more of vitamin C a day.

14 CALCIUM AND VITAMIN D PREVENT FRACTURES

Taking 500 milligrams of calcium and 700 IU of vitamin D daily for three years significantly cut the rate of bone loss and nonvertebral fractures in men and women older than age 65, reported Tufts University researchers.

15 ZINC FENDS OFF RHEUMATOID ARTHRITIS

A Mayo Clinic study found that older women who took various supplements were less apt to develop rheumatoid arthritis. Specifically, taking vitamin C or vitamin E cut risk by 30 percent. Taking zinc slashed risk by over 60 percent. Eating lots of fruits and cruciferous vegetables (cabbage, cauliflower, Brussels sprouts, and broccoli) also lowered risk of rheumatoid arthritis about 35 percent.

16 VITAMINS SLOW MENTAL DECLINE

Elderly women (ages 70 to 79) who were long-term, current users of vitamin E and vitamin C scored better on cognitive tests than were women who had never used vitamins E or C. In the large Harvard study, vitamin takers were better able to recall words and the contents of a short paragraph, and they had better verbal fluency and ability on a numbers-backwards test. Women who had taken the vitamins the longest tended to have the highest scores.

17 VITAMIN B$_{12}$ PROTECTS BRAIN

A United States Department of Agriculture study showed that 40 percent of Americans, ages 26 to 83, had "low normal" B$_{12}$ blood levels, sufficient to trigger neurological symptoms. A deficiency produces low cognitive performance in children and high rates of depression, dementia, and Alzheimer's disease in adults. Least deficient were those who took B$_{12}$ supplements, or ate the most dairy foods and fortified cereals.

If you're over 50, you should take a B$_{12}$ supplement, say experts. The low doses in "multis" help, but many older people need 500 or more micrograms daily. Three thousand micrograms a day is considered a safe dose at which no adverse effects have been reported.

18 VITAMINS PREVENT ALZHEIMER'S

Not a single older person who took separate doses of vitamin E (200 to 800 IU) or vitamin C (500 to1,000 milligrams) developed Alzheimer's disease during a four-year double blind study at Chicago's Rush Institute for Healthy Aging. Subjects who took multivitamin supplements with low doses of vitamin E (typically 30 IU) or vitamin C (60 milligrams) were not protected from Alzheimer's.

19 LUTEIN SAVES VISION

Taking ten milligrams a day of the antioxidant lutein actually reversed vision loss in patients with age-related macular degeneration, finds research at the Medical Center Eye Clinic and the University of Illinois in Chicago. After a year, the density of the macular pigment increased by 50 percent in the lutein takers. More remarkable, they improved in visual acuity, contrast sensitivity, and glare recovery. Adding other antioxidants to lutein improved vision even more.

20 VITAMIN C PREVENTS CATARACTS AND LOSS OF VISION

Women taking vitamin C supplements cut their risk of cataracts by 77 percent. In patients with early macular degeneration, taking daily doses of 500 milligrams of vitamin C, 400 IU vitamin E, 80 milligrams of zinc, 2 milligrams of copper, and 15 milligrams of beta carotene for eleven years slowed progression to the advanced stage of loss of vision, according to a major study by the National Institutes of Health.

21 VITAMIN C REDUCES INFLAMMATION.

Taking vitamin C (a daily dose of 515 milligrams) reduced blood levels of C-reactive protein (CRP), a marker of inflammation, by 24 percent, compared to taking a placebo, in a clinical trial of 160 subjects at the University of California–Berkeley. This is important, because chronic inflammation is now believed to be a major contributor to artery clogging and heart attacks, strokes, diabetes, and Alzheimer's disease. Using vitamin C to curb inflammation may help prevent such diseases, said researchers.

Vitamin C:
Facts and Fiction

CONFUSED ABOUT VITAMIN C? It's understandable. Much information about vitamin C is incomplete, misleading, or wrong. Here leading authority Balz Frei, PhD, director of the Linus Pauling Institute at Oregon State University, answers the most common questions about vitamin C.

WHAT IS THE MOST EXCITING NEW BENEFIT OF VITAMIN C?

Surprisingly, it's fighting heart disease. Vitamin C combats inflammation in blood vessels and helps stabilize plaque so it doesn't break off and create blockages. It also relaxes blood vessels, helping prevent high blood pressure, angina (chest pain), and mini-strokes. Several studies suggest that a high level of vitamin C in the blood lowers odds of heart disease by 25 to 60 percent. A likely effective dose: 200 to 500 milligrams of vitamin C daily. Taking 350 to 400 milligrams daily, in a Harvard study of women, slashed heart attack risk by one-third!

CAN VITAMIN C PREVENT OR CURE CANCER?

Vitamin C–packed fruits and vegetables appear to prevent cancer, but whether vitamin C is responsible is unclear. Using large oral doses of vitamin C to treat cancer failed, in a large Mayo Clinic Study. Infusions of extremely high concentrations of vitamin C, as the late Linus Pauling advocated, may be toxic to cancer cells, Frei speculates. Tests are being considered to find out. Some doctors discourage taking vitamin C during chemotherapy, but Frei considers the antioxidant—at least in daily doses up to 500—more beneficial than harmful to cancer patients.

DOES TAKING VITAMIN C CURE COLDS?

Popping high doses of vitamin C—1,000 milligrams or more—after you notice symptoms may cut the severity of a cold and its duration by a couple of days. There's no evidence, however, that regular megadoses of vitamin C actually prevent colds. Still Frei says, "I tell people, if it works for them, go ahead."

IS ESTER C™ A SUPERIOR FORM OF VITAMIN C?

"No. It's the most common question I get," says Frei. Contrary to advertising, your body doesn't know the difference between costly Ester C and plain old inexpensive ascorbic acid, a common form of vitamin C. "It's a marketing gimmick," says Frei.

HOW MUCH VITAMIN C CAN YOUR BODY USE?

In National Institute of Health studies, cells become "saturated" with vitamin C at daily doses of 200 milligrams to 400 milligrams, indicating that's the maximum humans can absorb. This research was conducted on healthy adults ages 25 to 30, so that's probably not an optimal dose for older people or those with infections, chronic inflammatory diseases, or cancer, Frei concludes. A safer daily dose to cover the uncertainties of aging is 500 to 1,000 milligrams, he says.

HOW SAFE IS VITAMIN C?

"It's impossible to overdose on vitamin C," says Frei. Excesses are simply excreted, although high doses can cause diarrhea. Also, occasional accusations that vitamin C supplements promote kidney stones, clogged neck arteries, or chromosome damage leading to cancer don't hold up. Since the body doesn't distinguish between vitamin C from pills and food, eating fruits and vegetables would cause the same harm, which is nonsensical.

Miraculous Magnesium

CHANCES ARE, YOU don't get enough magnesium. Americans' intake of magnesium dropped 50 percent in the last century, and the hidden health consequences are so alarming that most people would benefit from magnesium supplements, say experts.

A magnesium deficit underlies our epidemic of heart disease, high blood pressure, diabetes, and osteoporosis, declares Lawrence Resnick, MD, professor of medicine at Cornell Medical Center. When you lack magnesium, your heart beat irregularly, arteries stiffen, constrict and clog, blood pressure rises, blood tends to clot, muscles go into spasms, insulin grows weaker, blood sugar jumps, bones lose strength, and pain signals intensify.

how much?

MOST AMERICANS probably need to take 150 to 250 milligrams of magnesium daily, reported Dr. Seelig. Some need more—300 to 400 milligrams a day. Although magnesium is of low toxicity, it may cause diarrhea in some who can't tolerate high doses. Cut back or build the dose up gradually; your body usually adapts, advised Seelig. Warning: Don't take magnesium if you have kidney disease, without consulting with your doctor.

"Many people needlessly suffer pain—including fibromyalgia, migraines, and muscle cramps—because they don't get enough magnesium," in the words of the late Mildred Seelig, MD, formerly a leading magnesium researcher and adjunct professor, University of North Carolina.

Moreover, many people worsen the problem by loading up on calcium in efforts to combat osteoporosis. High calcium flushes magnesium from cells, creating electrical intracellular imbalances, a clear sign of many vascular diseases, says Dr. Resnick. To avoid this, he urges getting at least 1 milligram of magnesium for each 2 milligrams of calcium.

foods high in magnesium

* Almonds

* Cashews

* Peanuts

* Sunflower and pumpkin seeds

* Wheat bran cereals

* Wheat germ

* Spinach and other dark green leafy vegetables

* Legumes

* Tofu

TEN IMPORTANT WAYS MAGNESIUM HELPS:

1 HEART ARRHYTHMIAS: "People need to know that magnesium deficiency predisposes them to serious, even deadly, heart arrhythmias"—skipped, irregular and abnormally fast heart beats or atrial fibrillation—says cardiac specialist Michael Brodsky, MD at the College of Medicine of the Unversity of California–Irvine. In a British study, taking magnesium daily for six weeks reduced arrhythmias by 25 to 50 percent. In United States Department of Agriculture tests, women skimping on magnesium developed irregular heartbeats within three months. Magnesium supplements corrected the abnormality.

2 BLOCKED ARTERIES: High blood magnesium cuts your odds of dying from common ischemic heart disease (blocked or narrowed arteries) by one-third, say researchers at the Centers for Disease Control and Prevention. Other research shows that magnesium shortages lower good HDL cholesterol and accelerate atherosclerosis ("hardening of the arteries").

3 BLOOD PRESSURE: Cornell's Lawrence Resnick documented that the higher your magnesium inside your cells (intracellular), the more apt you are to have lower blood pressure, more elastic blood vessels, and a less enlarged heart. He calls magnesium a natural calcium-channel blocker (a blood-pressure drug), and says supplements can help normalize blood pressure.

4 DIABETES: "Diabetes is a magnesium deficiency state," says Jerry Nadler, MD, of the University of Virginia School of Medicine. He finds that 80 percent of diabetics have low intracellular magnesium. Indeed, research suggests low magnesium boosts your risk of developing type 2 diabetes by one-third. Nadler says magnesium supplements can improve insulin activity, and may cut the risk and complications of diabetes. Some specialists tell diabetics to take 400 milligrams magnesium daily.

5 STRONG BONES: Magnesium is as vital as calcium in building strong bones and preventing osteoporosis, said University of North Carolina's Mildred Seelig. "It's essential for normal bone metabolism." In a Swedish study, magnesium but not calcium helped prevent hip fractures in older women.

Tufts researchers found that high magnesium intake predicted higher bone mass and less bone loss in older people.

6 MIGRAINES: Half of migraine sufferers have low magnesium, and upping magnesium has reduced the duration, intensity, and frequency of migraines. Headache frequency dropped 42 percent in German adults who took 600 milligrams of magnesium daily for a month. Italian children given 122 milligrams to 366 milligrams magnesium daily had two-thirds fewer migraines after a month. Magnesium is now standard treatment at some headache clinics. One theory is that magnesium diminishes the brain blood vessel spasms involved in migraines.

7 SOUND SLEEP: Several studies show that a lack of magnesium can alter electrical activity in the brain, causing agitated sleep and frequent awakenings. "It looks like magnesium is important for a good night's sleep," says Forrest H. Nielsen, United States Department of Agriculture brain researcher.

8 SAFER PREGNANCY: Extensive research shows that magnesium lessens pre-eclampsia, in which blood pressure soars during late pregnancy, upping the risk of spontaneous abortions and premature, low-birth-weight babies. A large British study of 10,000 women in 33 countries confirms that taking magnesium sulphate supplements reduced the hazard by 50 percent.

9 PAIN RELIEF: If you have leg cramps or other muscle cramps, taking 100 milligrams to 400 milligrams of magnesium daily may bring relief, Seelig reported. Extra magnesium may also help prevent or relieve painful myalgias, including the syndrome known as fibromyalgia, chronic lower back pain, restless-legs syndrome, erythromelagia (a painful dilation of skin blood vessels), and chronic fatigue syndrome. Seelig reports that magnesium reduces a pain-transmitter in the nervous system called substance P.

10 EXTRA BENEFITS: Taking magnesium could help treat premature ejaculation, prevent death from a congenital condition called long QT syndrome, treat Tourette's syndrome, relieve certain PMS symptoms (premenstrual syndrome), and prevent permanent hearing loss due to loud noises and damage to the auditory nerve.

3

THE
RECIPES

Appetizers, Dips, Salsas, and Snacks

ALL TOO OFTEN, appetizers equal something fried. Dips usually come with lots of fat, and snacks often consist of something crunchy with lots of bad fat. It doesn't have to be that way. In the following section, you'll find plenty of wholesome appetizers, dips, salsas, and snacks that minimize the bad fats and maximize fiber, whole grains, lean protein, nuts, and vegetables.

ALMOND-CRUSTED SHRIMP
WITH APRICOT DIPPING SAUCE

12 large or jumbo shrimp, shelled and deveined, tails on
⅓ cup cornstarch
3 egg whites, beaten until frothy
1 cup sliced almonds
Olive oil or canola spray

Preheat oven to 400°F. Dredge shrimp in cornstarch, then in egg whites, then in almonds. Place on an oil-sprayed baking pan. Spray shrimp with olive or canola oil. Bake for about 10 minutes, or until shrimp are crusty and brown. Serve with Apricot Dipping Sauce.

SERVES 4 AS AN APPETIZER

PER SERVING: (3 shrimp) 252 calories, 15 g total fat (1.3 g saturated), 15 carbohydrate, 17 g protein, 1.2 g fiber, 115 mg sodium

APRICOT DIPPING SAUCE

½ cup apricot preserves
1 tablespoon reduced-sodium soy sauce
1 tablespoon rice vinegar or mirin

Place preserves in a small microwave-safe bowl and microwave on high until preserves are melted, about 3 minutes. Stir in soy sauce and vinegar.

SERVES 4

PER SERVING: 99 calories, 0 g total fat, 26 g carbohydrate, 0.5 g protein, 0.5 g fiber, 166 mg sodium

Antioxidant-rich almonds may help control weight gain by making you feel full and suppressing appetite, according to Purdue University studies.

SCIENCE SAYS

BLACK BEAN SALSA

1½ pounds tomatoes, diced

1 (15-ounce) can black beans, drained and rinsed, or homecooked

1 cup cooked yellow corn kernels

1 medium jalapeño pepper, seeded and finely minced

½ cup chopped red onion

2 cloves garlic, chopped or crushed

1 cup minced fresh cilantro

1 tablespoon canola oil

2 tablespoons fresh lime juice

1 teaspoon honey

Hot sauce, cayenne pepper, and salt

Combine all. Refrigerate for 2 hours to let the flavors combine. Serve with baked tortilla chips or low-fat crackers.

MAKES ABOUT 4 CUPS

PER ½ CUP: 94 calories, 2.5 g total fat (0.3 g saturated), 16 g carbohydrate, 3.6 g protein, 3.8 g fiber, 99 mg sodium

SCIENCE SAYS
Eating lycopene-rich tomatoes suppresses thickening of artery walls and blood clots that promote heart attacks.

CHEESY ARTICHOKE DIP

2 (9-ounce) packages frozen artichoke hearts
1½ cups fat-free cottage cheese
4 ounces herbed goat cheese (chèvre)
1 tablespoon plus 1 teaspoon Dijon mustard
3 tablespoons fresh lemon juice
2 garlic cloves, crushed
1 tablespoon Worcestershire sauce
⅓ cup light mayonnaise, such as Hellmann's
⅓ cup fat-free half-and-half
1 cup chopped chives
Salt and black pepper
¼ cup grated Parmesan cheese

Preheat oven to 350°F. Cook artichokes according to package directions; chop coarsely. Set aside. In a food processor, mix all ingredients (except artichokes and Parmesan cheese) until smooth. Stir in artichokes. Pour mixture into a 9-inch baking dish. Sprinkle with Parmesan. Bake for 30 minutes. If top hasn't browned, put under broiler to brown. Let sit for 15 minutes before serving; it may be watery when first removed from the oven. Serve with toasted whole wheat pita chips.

MAKES 4½ CUPS

PER ½ CUP SERVING: 130 calories, 6.5 g total fat (3 g saturated), 8 g carbohydrate, 9 g protein, 3 g fiber, 427 mg sodium

Artichoke hearts have five times more antioxidant power per cup than does broccoli or carrots, according to United States Department of Agriculture tests.

SCIENCE SAYS

CHICKEN SATÉ WITH EASY PEANUT DIPPING SAUCE

1 pound boneless, skinless chicken breast, cut into 6 x 1-inch strips
Olive or canola oil

Thread chicken on 12 small skewers. Brush or spray with olive or canola oil. Grill or broil until done, about 7 minutes, turning once.

Serve with Easy Peanut Dipping Sauce.

MAKES 12 APPETIZERS

PER SERVING: 173 calories, 10 g total fat (1.6 g saturated), 3 g carbohydrate, 8.6 g protein, 1 g fiber, 248 mg sodium

EASY PEANUT DIPPING SAUCE

½ cup smooth peanut butter, preferably natural
¼ teaspoon red pepper flakes
1 tablespoon reduced-sodium soy sauce
1 garlic clove, crushed
1 teaspoon curry powder
¾ cup fat-free, reduced-sodium chicken broth

Combine all in a microwave-safe bowl. Microwave, covered, on high for 2 minutes or until smooth. If too thick, add more broth.

MAKES ABOUT 1½ CUPS

PER 1 TABLESPOON: 40 calories, 3 g total fat (0.7 g saturated), 1.4 g carbohydrate, 1.8 g protein, 0.4 g fiber, 82 mg sodium

SCIENCE SAYS

Eating a tablespoon of peanut butter (or nuts) five times a week reduced women's odds of diabetes by 20 percent, in Harvard research.

CURRIED HUMMUS

2 (15½-ounce) cans chickpeas, rinsed and drained

2 tablespoons olive oil

3 garlic cloves, crushed

1 tablespoon plus 1 teaspoon curry powder

6 tablespoons fresh lemon juice

½ cup water

Salt

Hot sauce, such as Tabasco

Put all ingredients in a food processor and blend until smooth.

MAKES ABOUT 2 CUPS

Serve with toasted whole wheat pita chips, trans-fat-free crackers, and fresh vegetable crudités.

PER 2 TABLESPOONS: 56 calories, 2.6 g total fat (0 g saturated), 6 g carbohydrate, 2 g protein, 0 g cholesterol, 2 g fiber, 61 mg sodium

why it's good for you:

- Garlic is high in antioxidants.
- Curry powder contains curcumin, which fights cancer and protects the brain.
- Chickpeas and lemon juice suppress blood sugar rises.

Eating lots of garlic significantly cut the risk of colon, ovarian, kidney, esophageal, larynx, and oral cancers, in several Italian studies.

SCIENCE SAYS

FRESH SPRING ROLLS WITH THAI DIPPING SAUCE

6 spring roll wrappers (available in Asian markets)
12 medium shrimp, cooked and peeled
1 cup shredded lettuce
⅓ cup chopped fresh cilantro
½ cup peeled, seeded, chopped cucumber
1 medium carrot, julienned

In a bowl of cool water, soak a wrapper until it is limp. Lay wrapper out flat. Place one-sixth of each ingredient down middle of wrapper with lettuce first. Fold over each end, then roll wrapper around contents, as if making a burrito. Moisten at seam and press to close. Slice in two. Repeat with the remaining wrappers and filling ingredients. Serve with Thai Dipping Sauce.

MAKES 6 APPETIZER-SIZE ROLLS

PER SERVING: 49 calories, 4 g total fat (0.1 g saturated), 7 g carbohydrate, 4 g protein, 0.7 g fiber, 75 mg sodium

THAI DIPPING SAUCE

1 tablespoon reduced-sodium soy sauce
1 tablespoon white wine or rice vinegar
3 tablespoons mirin (sweetened rice wine)
¼ teaspoon grated fresh ginger (optional)

Combine all ingredients in a small bowl.

MAKES ABOUT ⅓ CUP

SCIENCE SAYS Shrimp is a good low-fat, high-protein alternative to meat and does not raise cholesterol.

GORGONZOLA-TOFU DIP WITH WALNUTS

8 ounces soft tofu, mashed

3 tablespoons soft or crumbled Gorgonzola

3 tablespoons chopped walnuts

¼ cup finely chopped onions

¼ cup fat-free sour cream

Salt

Combine all. Serve with apple wedges or sesame flatbread.

MAKES 1½ CUPS

PER TABLESPOON: 16 calories, 1 g total fat (0.2 g saturated), 1 g carbohydrate, 1 g protein, 0 g fiber, 14 mg sodium

Women who ate 25 grams of soy protein such as tofu and soy milk, daily for six weeks showed improved functioning of arteries and less inflammation.

SCIENCE SAYS

LIGHT SALMON MOUSSE

1 (14¾-ounce) can red or pink salmon, drained (reserve liquid)
1 cup plain fat-free yogurt
1 cup fat-free cottage cheese
1 packet unflavored gelatin
¼ cup chopped fresh dill
Freshly ground black pepper
1 cup thinly sliced, peeled cucumber

Place salmon in large bowl. Remove skin. Mash fish, including bones. In a blender or with a mixer, combine yogurt and cottage cheese. Add salmon and chopped dill. In a small saucepan, soften gelatin in reserved salmon liquid. Stir over low heat until dissolved, about 2 minutes. Add to salmon; mix thoroughly.

Line bottom of 3 to 4-cup mold, bowl, or loaf cake pan with cucumber slices. Pour in salmon mixture. Chill for 2–3 hours until set. Unmold and serve with crackers or bread.

SERVES 10–12 AS APPETIZER

PER SERVING: 77 calories, 12.3 g total fat (0.5 g saturated), 3 g carbohydrate, 0.6 g protein, 0.2 g fiber, 264 mg sodium

SCIENCE SAYS Eating fatty fish (salmon, tuna, sardines, or herring) twice a week cut endometrial cancer risk 40 percent in women. Lean fish did not.

NUTTY BROCCOLI APPETIZERS

¼ cup finely chopped onions
4 cloves garlic, crushed
1 tablespoon extra-virgin olive oil
1 (10-ounce package) frozen chopped broccoli
1 cup bread crumbs, preferably whole wheat
¼ cup chopped walnuts
¼ cup freshly grated Parmesan cheese
½ teaspoon dried oregano
½ teaspoon dried basil
2 eggs or ½ cup egg substitute, slightly whipped
Salt and freshly ground black pepper

Preheat oven to 400°F. Sauté onions and garlic in olive oil. Cook broccoli according to package directions; squeeze out excess water. Cool slightly. Combine with remaining ingredients. Form into balls 1½ inches in diameter. Place on nonstick baking sheet. (You also can spread mixture in a shallow pan, bake, and cut into squares.) Spray balls with olive oil or canola spray. Bake in oven for 20–30 minutes, or until browned. Serve warm or at room temperature.

MAKES 24 BALLS

PER BALL: 33 calories, 1.9 g total fat (0.4 g saturated), 3 g carbohydrate, 1.9 g protein, 0.5 g fiber, 41 mg sodium.

As a dip for the balls, you can use Thai Dipping Sauce (page 82) or Easy Peanut Dipping Sauce (page 80).

why it's good for you:

- Broccoli, garlic, and onions contain high amounts of antioxidants.
- Walnuts provide magnesium and other nutrients.
- Olive oil provides good fat.
- Plus: broccoli helps fight cancer.

Five to six daily servings of vegetables cut stroke risk by one-third. Most potent are leafy greens, such as broccoli and spinach.

SCIENCE SAYS

OYSTERS ROCKEFELLER

1 tablespoon extra-virgin olive oil
2 cloves garlic, crushed
1 (10-ounce package) frozen chopped spinach, thawed and squeezed very dry
¼ cup fat-free cream cheese
¼ cup fat-free half-and-half
Salt and freshly ground pepper
Pinch of ground nutmeg
1 pint shelled oysters, drained, rinsed, and patted dry
¼ cup grated Parmesan cheese
Hot pepper sauce

Preheat oven to 400°F. In a small skillet, sauté garlic in oil until soft; add spinach, cream cheese, and half-and-half. Sauté, stirring, until blended, about 5 minutes. Stir in salt, pepper, and nutmeg. Spread spinach mixture over bottom of 10-inch pie plate or ovenproof dish. Top with oysters; sprinkle with cheese and hot sauce. Bake for 15 minutes. If needed, briefly broil to brown.

SERVES 6

PER SERVING: 168 calories, 8 g total fat (2 g saturated), 11 g carbohydrate, 13 g protein, 2 g fiber, 336 mg sodium

SCIENCE SAYS

Women who ate foods highest in zinc, such as oysters, were one-third as likely to have breast cancer as were women who ate foods lowest in zinc, finds a German study.

PASTA APPETIZER WITH BRAZIL-NUT SAUCE

4 ounces dry spaghetti

2 large cloves garlic, crushed or minced

3 tablespoons extra-virgin olive oil or macadamia nut oil

½ cup chopped fresh parsley

½ cup sliced black olives

2 tablespoons capers (optional)

2½ ounces Brazil nuts, coarsely ground in a blender

Salt and freshly ground pepper

Cook spaghetti until al dente. While pasta is cooking, sauté garlic in oil over medium heat. Add oil and garlic to drained pasta. Stir in parsley, olives, capers, half the ground nuts, and season with salt and pepper. Transfer to plates and top with remaining nuts.

Note: The ground nuts have the appearance and texture of grated Parmesan cheese.

SERVES 4 AS AN APPETIZER

PER SERVING: 336 calories, 24 g total fat (4.5 g saturated, 13 g monounsaturated), 26 g carbohydrate, 7 g protein, 4 g fiber, 152 mg sodium

High blood selenium helps prevent polyps leading to colon cancer. Brazil nuts are exceptionally rich in selenium.

SCIENCE SAYS

QUICK GUACAMOLE

1 medium, ripe Hass avocado, mashed
1 teaspoon fresh lemon or lime juice
1 large garlic clove, crushed
Hot sauce, such as Tabasco
Salt and freshly ground black pepper

Mix all the ingredients. Serve with baked tortilla chips

SERVES 2

PER SERVING: 166 calories, 15.4 g total fat (2.5 g saturated), 8 g carbohydrate, 2.1 g protein, 2 g fiber, 16 mg sodium

SCIENCE SAYS   Men who ate lots of avocado's monounsaturated-type fat had a 20 percent drop in inflammation.

SCALLOP-AVOCADO APPETIZER

1 pound dry-pack scallops (16–20 count)
1 cup chopped tomato
1 cup sliced green onions with green tops
1 ripe Haas avocado, cubed
1 cup chopped cilantro
Juice of 2 limes (6 tablespoons)
1 tablespoon olive oil
½ teaspoon hot pepper flakes, or to taste
Salt

In a small pan, bring 4 cups of water to a boil. Add scallops, reduce heat, and simmer for 1½ minutes. Do not overcook. Refrigerate for 2 hours. Cut in small (about 1-inch) pieces. Combine all ingredients. Serve in cocktail glasses.

SERVES 6

PER SERVING: 159 calories, 8g total fat (1g saturated), 9 g carbohydrate, 14 g protein, 3 g fiber, 23 mg sodium

A small Haas avocado has eight times more antioxidant activity than does a medium raw tomato and the same type of monounsaturated fat as olive oil, finds United States Department of Agriculture tests.

SCIENCE SAYS

SPICY MIXED NUTS

1 egg white
2 tablespoons cold water
⅔ cup each walnuts, pecans, and almonds
½ cup sugar
1½ teaspoons cinnamon
¼ teaspoon ground ginger
¼ teaspoon nutmeg

Beat egg white and water until frothy. Stir nuts into mixture to coat, then drain slightly in a colander, for 3 to 4 minutes. Mix sugar and spices in a plastic bag. Add nuts and shake to coat. Spread wet nut mixture in a single layer on a microwave-safe plate; microwave on high for 1½ minutes, or until mixture is bubbly. Stir. Microwave for another 1½ minutes. Remove from oven and stir to separate. Cool. Store in a sealed container.

MAKES 2 CUPS

PER ¼-CUP SERVING: 235 calories, 17 g total fat (1.6 saturated, 9 monounsaturated), 18 g carbohydrate, 5 g protein, 2 g fiber, 9 mg sodium

> **SCIENCE SAYS** Adding cinnamon to foods helps suppress blood sugar by boosting insulin activity and cells' ability to process glucose.

TERRIFIC TRAIL MIX

1 cup mixed diced dried fruit, such as prunes, apricots, pears, and apples

½ cup raisins and/or dried cherries or cranberries

1½ cups unsalted sunflower seeds

1 cup unsalted dry-roasted peanuts or honey-roasted peanuts, chopped walnuts, or unsalted almonds

Mix all ingredients.

MAKES 4 CUPS

PER ¼-CUP SERVING: 165 calories, 11.3 g total fat (1.3 g saturated), 14 g carbohydrate, 5.6 g protein, 1.4 g fiber, 2 mg sodium

Raisins are high in antioxidants and produce beneficial changes in the colon that may help protect against colon cancer.

SCIENCE SAYS

why it's good for you:

- High in fiber and protein.

- Lemon juice suppresses blood sugar rises.

- Plus: beans beat most fruits and vegetables in antioxidant activity.

ZESTY MEXICAN BEAN DIP

**2 (15-ounce) cans pinto beans, preferably no-salt added*,
    drained and rinsed**
1½ teaspoons ground cumin, or to taste
1 teaspoon chile powder, or to taste
2 tablespoons fresh lemon juice
Hot sauce, such as Tabasco, or jalapeño peppers
Salt

Place the beans and seasonings in a food processor or blender. Process until smooth and creamy. Serve with fresh vegetables, tortillas, or crackers.

MAKES ABOUT 3 CUPS

PER ¼-CUP SERVING: 41 calories, 0.4 g total fat, 7 g carbohydrate, 2.7 g protein, 2 g fiber, 117 mg sodium

*With no-salt-added beans, the sodium drops to 11 mg per serving.

SCIENCE SAYS — Dried beans pack more protein than any other plant food, plus fiber, B vitamins, zinc, potassium, magnesium, calcium, and iron.

Soups

SOUPS ARE A great vehicle to help you get in more of those fruit and vegetable servings so many of us fall short on. The soups in this section are loaded with antioxidants from vegetables, fruit, herbs, and spices, and most provide an excellent amount of fiber, too. Use them as an accompaniment for a meal or even as a main course.

CARIBBEAN BLACK BEAN SOUP

4 cups cooked no-salt-added black beans (3 [15-ounce] cans, drained and rinsed)

1½ cups fat-free plain yogurt, plus extra for garnish

1 (4½-ounce) can mild peeled green chiles

2 teaspoons ground cumin

½ teaspoon balsamic vinegar or lemon juice

Salt and freshly ground black pepper

1 tablespoon snipped chives or sliced scallion greens

In a blender or food processor, puree beans, yogurt, chiles, cumin, vinegar, salt, and pepper. Serve cold, topped with a dollop of yogurt and sprinkled with chives or scallions.

SERVES 4

PER SERVING: 292 calories, 1 g total fat, 51 g carbohydrate, 21 g protein, 16 g fiber, 337 mg sodium

SCIENCE SAYS

Beans (legumes) are heart food. Eating beans four times a week, compared with once a week, cut heart disease risk 22 percent, in a Tulane University study.

CHILLED CITRUS BORSCHT

1 (16-ounce) jar pickled beets
1½ cups orange juice
3 tablespoons lemon juice
1 cup low-fat sour cream
1½ cup plain fat-free yogurt
Salt and pepper
3 tablespoons chopped chives

why it's good
for you:
■ Beets and orange
  juice contain
  antioxidants.
■ Low in fat.
■ Yogurt contains
  good bacteria.

In a blender, puree beets, orange and lemon juices, sour cream, and
1 cup of the yogurt. Add salt and pepper. Chill for 2 hours or more.
Serve with a dollop of the remaining yogurt, topped with chives.

SERVES 4

PER SERVING: 221 calories, 0.5 g total fat (0 g saturated), 44 g carbohydrates,
12 g protein, 2 mg cholesterol, 2 g fiber, 304 mg sodium

Orange juice helps block formation of kidney stones, builds
stronger bones, and may even ward off cancer, suggest several
studies.

SCIENCE
SAYS

COLD AVOCADO SOUP

1 medium, ripe Hass avocado, cut into chunks

1 tablespoon fresh lemon juice

1½ cups fat-free, reduced-sodium vegetable or chicken broth

¾ cup fat-free sour cream

1 teaspoon ground cumin

Salt

Dash of hot chile sauce, (optional)

Chopped fresh cilantro or parsley, for garnish

Tomato salsa or diced fresh tomatoes, for garnish

Combine avocado, lemon juice, broth, sour cream, cumin, salt, and chile sauce in a blender; puree until smooth. Chill for 1 to 2 hours. Serve garnished with chopped fresh cilantro and salsa.

SERVES 2

PER SERVING: 287 calories, 15.6 g total fat (2.5 g saturated), 29 g carbohydrate, 9.6 g protein, 2.1 g fiber, 274 mg sodium

SCIENCE SAYS Eating one-half to one and a half small avocados a day for three weeks reduced cholesterol 8 percent in Australian studies.

CORN CHOWDER WITH SHRIMP

1 medium yellow onion, chopped

1 red or green bell pepper, seeded and diced

1 tablespoon extra-virgin olive oil

2½ cups fat-free milk

1½ cups evaporated fat-free milk (1 [12-ounce] can)

2 medium baking potatoes, peeled and diced

2 cups frozen or canned yellow corn kernels

1 pound large or medium shrimp, peeled and deveined

Salt and freshly ground black pepper

⅓ cup chopped fresh cilantro

In a large pot, sauté onion and pepper in olive oil until soft, about 12 minutes. Add milk, evaporated milk, potatoes, and corn. Cover. Slowly bring to a boil and simmer over low heat until potatoes are tender, about 10 minutes. Add shrimp and cook for about 3 minutes, or until shrimp turns pink. Do not overcook shrimp. Add more skim milk if needed. Season with salt and pepper. Ladle into bowls and top with cilantro.

SERVES 6

PER SERVING: 278 calories, 4.2 g total fat (0.8 g saturated), 38 g carbohydrate, 24 g protein, 2.7 g fiber, 224 mg sodium

Starting a meal with chunky soup curbs appetite. Women in a Penn State study ate 27 percent fewer calories after a soup first course.

SCIENCE SAYS

CREAMY BROCCOLI SOUP

1 (10-ounce) package frozen chopped broccoli, or 2 cups fresh florets
2 cloves garlic, halved
1 medium onion, chopped
1 (15-ounce) can fat-free, reduced-sodium chicken broth
2 tablespoons fresh lemon juice
1 cup fat-free sour cream
½ cup fat-free milk
½ teaspoon ground nutmeg
Salt and freshly ground black pepper
Croutons (optional)
Freshly grated Parmesan (optional)

Place broccoli, garlic, onion, and 2 tablespoons chicken broth in a microwave-safe dish. Microwave, covered, on high until onions are soft (10–12 minutes), stopping once to break up the frozen broccoli. Put the vegetables, lemon juice, and remaining broth in a blender; puree. Blend in sour cream, milk, and seasonings. Chill.

Serve topped with croutons or Parmesan cheese.

SERVES 4

PER SERVING: 105 calories, 0.9 g total fat, 16 g carbohydrate, 6.5 g protein, 2 g fiber, 364 mg sodium

SCIENCE SAYS

Broccoli is packed with a unique antioxidant—sulforaphane glucosinolate—that boosts your body's ability to detoxify cancer-causing agents.

CURRIED LENTIL SOUP

1 tablespoon canola oil

1 cup chopped onion

2 cloves garlic, crushed

2 tablespoons curry powder

4 cups fat-free, reduced-sodium chicken broth

2½ cups water

2 cups chopped canned tomatoes, with liquid

2 cups dried lentils

1 cup finely chopped carrots

½ cup red wine (optional)

1 cup chopped fresh parsley

Salt and freshly ground black pepper

Heat oil in a large saucepan over medium heat. Sauté onion and garlic until soft. Stir in curry powder; sauté 1 minute. Add broth, water, tomatoes, lentils, carrots, and wine. Simmer, covered, until lentils are cooked, about 30 minutes. Stir in parsley; simmer for 5 minutes. Season with salt and pepper. Serve with sourdough bread.

SERVES 8

PER SERVING: 218 calories, 2.6 g total fat (0.2 g saturated), 35 g carbohydrate, 16 g protein, 7.6 g fiber, 378 mg sodium

Lentils are good diet food, because they control insulin and blood sugar rises that trigger hunger.

SCIENCE SAYS

CURRY-SQUASH-APPLE SOUP

1 (12-ounce) package frozen winter squash
2 cups fat-free, low-sodium chicken or vegetable broth
1½ cups unsweetened applesauce
2 teaspoons curry powder, or to taste
Salt
Fat-free sour cream, for garnish

In a microwave-safe dish, microwave squash on high power until mushy. Stir in broth, applesauce, curry powder, and salt. Microwave for 5 minutes, or until hot. Process in a blender for 15 seconds. Serve topped with a dollop of sour cream.

SERVES 4

PER SERVING: 98 calories, 0.3 g total fat (0.01 g saturated), 23 g carbohydrate, 3.2 g protein, 5 g fiber, 289 g sodium

SCIENCE SAYS   Apple antioxidants have aspirin-like anti clotting activity.

EYE-SAVING BEAN SOUP WITH KALE

1 tablespoon extra-virgin olive oil or canola oil

1 medium yellow onion, chopped

8 large cloves garlic, crushed or minced

4 cups chopped raw kale, or 1 (10-ounce) package frozen chopped kale, thawed and squeezed to remove excess water

4 cups fat-free, reduced-sodium chicken or vegetable broth

4 plum tomatoes, chopped

2 (15-ounce) cans white beans, such as cannellini or navy, undrained (about 3 cups)

2 teaspoons dried Italian herb seasoning, or 1 teaspoon each dried thyme and rosemary

Salt and freshly ground pepper

1 cup chopped fresh parsley

In a large pot, heat olive oil. Add onion and garlic, and sauté until soft. Add kale and sauté, stirring until wilted. Add 3 cups of broth, 2 cups of beans, and all of the tomato, herbs, salt, and pepper. Simmer for 5 minutes. In a blender or food processor, mix the remaining beans and broth until smooth. Stir into soup to thicken. Simmer for 15 minutes. Ladle into bowls; sprinkle with chopped parsley.

SERVES 8

PER SERVING: 133 calories, 2.4 g total fat (0.3g saturated), 23 g carbohydrate, 10 g protein, 6 g fiber, 283 mg sodium

---

why it's good for you:

- Provides a super dose (7 mg per serving) of the antioxidant lutein.

- Onions, tomatoes, garlic, and herbs are high in antioxidants.

- Beans are high in fiber.

- Very low in fat.

- Plus: beans discourage blood sugar rises, heart disease, diabetes, and cancer.

Kale is the richest source of antioxidant lutein, which reduces risk of cataracts, macular degeneration, blocked carotid (neck) arteries, and certain cancers.

SCIENCE SAYS

GINGER-CARROT SOUP

2 large yellow onions, chopped (2 cups)
1 tablespoon extra-virgin olive oil
1 pound carrots, cut into chunks
2 cups fat-free, reduced-sodium chicken broth
2 tablespoons minced crystallized ginger, or 2 teaspoons ground ginger
1 teaspoon ground cinnamon
1½ cups orange juice
½ cup fat-free half-and-half
Fresh chives, for garnish

In a large pot, sauté onions in olive oil until soft. Add carrots, broth, ginger, and cinnamon; simmer until carrots are thoroughly cooked. Transfer mixture to a blender or food processor and process until smooth. Stir in orange juice and half-and-half. Serve warm or chilled, garnished with snipped chives.

SERVES 4

PER SERVING: 207 calories, 3.8 g total fat (0.5 g saturated), 33 g carbohydrate, 4 g protein, 5 g fiber, 364 mg sodium

SCIENCE SAYS

Ginger's active component, gingerol, when fed to laboratory mice, blocked the development and growth of tumors, in University of Minnesota research.

GRILLED VEGETABLE GAZPACHO

1 red bell pepper, halved, seeded, and grilled

1 yellow bell pepper, halved, seeded, and grilled

1 large red onion, halved or sliced, grilled

1 large red tomato, unpeeled

1 large yellow tomato, unpeeled

1 (11½-ounce) can "spicy" V-8 juice

1 tablespoon chopped fresh basil

1 teaspoon balsamic vinegar

Dash of hot sauce

Chop all vegetables. Put half in blender with the V-8 juice and seasonings. Blend until smooth. Add remaining chopped vegetables. Chill and serve.

SERVES 6

PER SERVING: 49 calories, 0.3 g total fat, 11 g carbohydrate, 1.9 g protein, 2.2 g fiber, 176 mg sodium

NOTE: *This is an excellent way to use leftover grilled vegetables.*

In a University of North Carolina study, drinking V-8 juice daily reduced lung cell DNA damage in those exposed to air pollution. SCIENCE SAYS

why it's good for you:

- Peppers, tomatoes, onion, and basil, are high in antioxidants.

- Very low in calories and fat.

HEARTY ASIAN MUSHROOM SOUP

4 cups fat-free, reduced-sodium chicken broth

2 tablespoons reduced-sodium soy sauce

2 teaspoons grated fresh ginger

3 cloves garlic, crushed

3 cups assorted sliced or diced mushrooms, such as white button, stemmed shiitake, portobello, cremini, or oyster

1 cup thinly sliced carrots

3 cups white cabbage, cut into small wedges

2 cups shredded or cubed cooked chicken breast

2 cups fresh or cooked udon noodles (or substitute 2 cups cooked linguine)

1 cup thinly sliced scallions with some green tops

2 cups sliced raw spinach or whole baby spinach leaves

Freshly ground black pepper

1 tablespoon mirin (sweetened rice wine) (optional)

In a large pot, combine broth, soy sauce, ginger, garlic, mushrooms, carrots, cabbage, and chicken. Cover, bring to a boil and simmer until mushrooms are soft, about 5 minutes. Stir in noodles, scallions, and spinach; simmer until greens are wilted, about 2 minutes. Season with pepper. For a little sweetness, stir in mirin.

SERVES 6

PER SERVING: 163 calories, 2.6 g total fat (0.5 g saturated), 16 g carbohydrate, 19 g protein, 3 g fiber, 860 mg sodium

SCIENCE SAYS

Portobello, shiitake, cremini, button, and large white mushrooms contain estrogen-reducing chemicals that may help ward off breast cancer.

MEXICAN POTATO SOUP

1 large baking potato, peeled and cubed

1 cup corn kernels (fresh preferred)

½ small red bell pepper, finely chopped

2 teaspoons minced jalapeño, seeds and veins removed

2 cups fat-free half-and-half

½ cup water

1½ teaspoons ground cumin, or to taste

½ teaspoon chile powder, or to taste

Salt and freshly ground black pepper

Hot sauce, such as Tabasco

1 cup chopped fresh cilantro

In a medium saucepan combine potatoes, half-and-half, corn, red pepper, cumin, chile powder, salt, and pepper. Simmer, covered, until potatoes are done, 15–20 minutes. Remove from heat. Add cilantro. Ladle into bowls.

SERVES 4

PER SERVING: 153 calories, 0.7 g total fat (0 g saturated), 28 g carbohydrate, 2.5 g protein, 2 g fiber, 134 mg sodium

Eating hot chile pepper may help fight diabetes by reducing the amount of insulin needed to control blood sugar rises, especially in overweight individuals, finds Australian research.

SCIENCE SAYS

OLD-FASHIONED VEGETABLE-BARLEY SOUP

1 tablespoon extra-virgin olive oil

1 medium yellow onion, chopped

2 large cloves garlic, crushed or minced

¾ cup sliced carrots

1 cup cauliflower, cut into thick slices or chunks

2 cups canned no-salt-added diced tomatoes

4 cups fat-free, reduced-sodium chicken or vegetable broth

1 cup pearl barley

1 cup fresh spinach leaves, torn into pieces

5 drops hot chile sauce (optional)

Salt and freshly ground black pepper

In a large saucepan, heat oil. Add onions, garlic, and carrots to the pan, stirring until onions begin to soften, about 3 minutes. Add cauliflower, tomatoes, barley, and broth. Simmer, partially covered, for 20 to 25 minutes. Stir in spinach and seasonings, and simmer for an additional 5 minutes.

SERVES 6

PER SERVING: 188 calories, 2.9 g total fat (0.4 g saturated), 35 g carbohydrate, 7 g protein, 7.4 g fiber, 409 mg sodium

SCIENCE SAYS

Eating barley, a whole grain, lowered bad LDL cholesterol and blood pressure, in United States Department of Agriculture tests.

OUT-OF-THIS-WORLD THAI CRAB SOUP

1 (14-ounce) can light coconut milk
½ cup creamy peanut butter, preferably natural
4 small ripe bananas, sliced
6 cups bottled clam juice or homemade fish stock
2 cups dry white wine
8 scallions, thinly sliced with green tops
3 tablespoons reduced-sodium soy sauce
2½ tablespoons hot chile paste, or to taste
12 ounces fresh bean sprouts
1 pound backfin crabmeat*
1 cup chopped fresh cilantro
Juice of 1 lime

In a blender, puree coconut milk, peanut butter, and bananas. Transfer to a large pot; add clam juice, white wine, scallions, soy sauce, and chile paste. Cover and simmer 5 minutes. Add bean sprouts, crabmeat, ½ cup of the cilantro, and lime juice. Simmer for 5 minutes, covered. Add remaining ½ cup cilantro just before serving.

 * You can substitute 2½ cups less expensive imitation crabmeat or other whitefish.

Serves 12 as an appetizer soup, 8 as a main dish

PER SERVING AS AN APPETIZER: 204 calories, 8.8 g total fat (2.3 g saturated), 15 g carbohydrate, 13 g protein, 1.7 g fiber, 595 mg sodium

why it's good for you:

- Scallions contain anticancer agents.
- Bananas are high in vitamin B_6 and potassium.
- Very low in fat.
- Crab is high in protein.

Eating crab helped lower blood cholesterol, in University of Washington studies.

SCIENCE SAYS

SHRIMP BISQUE

1 tablespoon extra-virgin olive oil
1 medium red bell pepper, chopped
½ cup chopped yellow onion
½ pound cooked or raw shrimp, tails discarded, cut into pieces
2 cups fat-free half-and-half
1 cup no-salt-added tomato sauce
¼ teaspoon hot sauce, such as Tabasco, or to taste
Salt and freshly ground black pepper
1 teaspoon butter
¼ cup grated fresh Parmesan cheese

In saucepan, heat olive oil. Add red pepper and onion; sauté over low heat until soft, 15–20 minutes, stirring occasionally. Add shrimp, half-and-half, tomato sauce, salt, and pepper. Bring to a boil, reduce heat and simmer for 5 minutes. Add butter.

Put half of the hot mixture in a blender and process at high speed for about 10–15 seconds, or until no large pieces remain. (Be careful that hot liquid does not overflow.) Transfer bisque to soup bowls.

Repeat with remaining mixture. Sprinkle with Parmesan cheese.

SERVES 6

PER SERVING: 162 calories, 5 g total fat (2 g saturated), 14 g carbohydrate, 13 g protein, 76 mg cholesterol, 1 g fiber, 290 mg sodium

SCIENCE SAYS Compounds in olive oil may help protect your bones from osteoporosis, declare French scientists.

SNAPPY GAZPACHO

1 small cucumber, peeled and sliced

1 medium bell pepper, preferably red, cored, seeded, and cut into chunks

1 small zucchini, peeled and cut into chunks

1 medium onion, chopped

2 medium tomatoes, peeled and quartered

2 cloves garlic, minced or crushed

3 cups tomato juice, preferably low-sodium

¼ cup chopped fresh cilantro

½ teaspoon hot sauce, such as Tabasco

2 tablespoons distilled white vinegar or fresh lemon juice

Put all ingredients in a blender or food processor and process until chunky. Chill and serve. If you like, garnish with croutons.

SERVES 6

PER SERVING: 56 calories, 0.4 g total fat, 13 g carbohydrate, 2.4 g protein, 3 g fiber, 448 mg sodium

why it's good for you:

- Cucumber, peppers, zucchini, onion, tomatoes, and cilantro contain antioxidants.

- Very low in calories and fat.

Eating raw onions raised good HDL cholesterol in three out of four heart patients, in Tufts University research.

SCIENCE SAYS

TOMATO BISQUE IN A BLENDER

2 (14½-ounce) cans no-salt-added diced tomatoes, or 4 cups peeled fresh tomatoes
1 cup fat-free plain yogurt
¼ teaspoon hot sauce, such as Tabasco
2 large cloves garlic, crushed
1¼ teaspoons prepared horseradish
Salt and freshly ground black pepper
1 ripe Hass avocado, cubed (optional)

Put all ingredients but the avocado in a blender or food processor. Puree until smooth. Serve chilled or at room temperature, ladled over avocado cubes, if desired.

SERVES 4

PER SERVING: 77 calories, 0.6 g total fat (0.1 g saturated), 14 g carbohydrate, 5 g protein, 1.4 g fiber, 84 mg sodium

SCIENCE SAYS

Cooked and canned tomatoes have much greater amounts of bioavailable (absorbable) antioxidant lycopene than do raw tomatoes.

Side Dishes

IN THE FOLLOWING pages, you'll find a number of high-fat, high-calorie, blood-sugar-boosting traditional side dishes here made healthy, including the potato salad and coleslaw that you bring to your annual fourth of July picnic. You'll also find plenty of great, delicious, quick, and easy ways to sneak more vegetables, beans (featured in many of these recipes), and other foods onto your dinner plate. Note that side salads, featuring leafy greens, are in the section immediately following.

BLACK BEANS WITH MINT AND FETA

AN EASY
MICROWAVE DISH

2 (15-ounce) cans black beans, rinsed and drained (preferably no-salt added)*
½ cup chopped red onion
4 ounces feta cheese, crumbled
2 tablespoons extra-virgin olive oil
2 tablespoons fresh lemon juice
½ cup tightly packed fresh mint leaves, chopped

Toss together all the ingredients. Refrigerate for 30 minutes before serving.

SERVES 4

PER SERVING: 278 calories, 14 g total fat (5.3 g saturated), 26 g carbohydrate, 13 g protein, 8.5 g fiber, 672 mg sodium

With no-salt-added beans, the sodium drops to 353 mg per serving.

SCIENCE SAYS

Eating one and a half cups of cooked dried beans daily lowered cholesterol an average 19 percent after three weeks, in University of Kentucky tests.

BROCCOLI SLAW WITH LEMON DRESSING

4 cups "broccoli slaw," available packaged in most produce sections

8 ounces fat-free lemon yogurt

1 tablespoon reduced-sodium soy sauce

¼ cup fresh lemon juice or white rice vinegar

¼ cup toasted sesame seeds

1 red apple, cored and chopped (optional)

Toss all ingredients together and serve.

SERVES 4

PER SERVING: 143 calories, 5 g total fat (1.7 g saturated), 19 g carbohydrate, 7 g protein, 4 g fiber, 306 mg sodium

Eating lots of broccoli, cabbage, kale, Brussels sprouts, and cauliflower (brassica vegetables) reduces the risk of lung, stomach, colon, and rectal cancer, studies find.

SCIENCE SAYS

CARROT-PINEAPPLE SALAD

3 cups shredded or grated carrots (4 large carrots)
1 cup canned, crushed pineapple in juice
2 teaspoons fresh lemon juice, or to taste
¼ cup chopped walnuts (optional)

In a bowl, combine all ingredients and toss.

SERVES 4

PER SERVING: 73 calories, 0.2 g total fat, 18 g carbohydrate, 1 g protein, 3 g fiber, 30 mg sodium

SCIENCE SAYS Eating five large carrots a week cut the risk of stroke by 68 percent in a large group of female nurses, compared with eating no carrots or eating carrots only once a month.

CINNAMON-CRANBERRY APPLESAUCE

**3 pounds cooking apples, such as McIntosh or Rome, cored and sliced
(do not peel)**

1½ cups cranberry juice cocktail

⅔ cup red hot cinnamon candies (available in cake-decorating aisle)

In a large pot, combine all ingredients. Bring to a boil. Cook over medium heat, covered, for 15 minutes. Reduce heat; simmer for 20 minutes, or until apples are very soft. Cool slightly. Transfer to a food processor with the knife blade; process until smooth. Serve warm, chilled, or at room temperature.

SERVES 10

PER ½-CUP SERVING: 127 calories, 0 g total fat, 33 g carbohydrate, 0 g protein, 3 g fiber, 4 mg sodium

why it's good for you:

- Apples boost "memory" chemical.

- An apple a day cuts risk of various cancers.

- Apples improve breathing.

- Cranberry juice fights infections.

Cranberries have anti-inflammatory and antibacterial activity that can help ward off gum disease, report Canadian researchers.

SCIENCE SAYS

CONFETTI BEAN SALAD

2 cups red cabbage, shredded
1 (19-ounce) can cannellini beans, drained and rinsed
1 (11-ounce) can mandarin oranges, drained
⅓ cup walnuts, toasted
2 large scallions, sliced, with green tops
3 tablespoons extra-virgin olive oil
2 tablespoons balsamic vinegar
2 tablespoons orange juice
Salt and freshly ground black pepper

Put first five ingredients in a bowl. Whisk together oil, vinegar, and juice. Toss all. Serve.

SERVES 6

PER SERVING: 196 calories, 11 g total fat (1 g saturated), 19 g carbohydrate, 5 g protein, 5 g fiber, 118 mg sodium

SCIENCE SAYS Red cabbage raw or cooked, and Brussels sprouts, inhibited precancerous growths in laboratory animals, in Austrian studies.

CORN-ONION PUDDING

2 tablespoons extra-virgin olive oil

1 very large yellow onion, sliced thinly

1½ cups whole kernel yellow corn (fresh or frozen)

1 cup finely chopped bell pepper

3 eggs

1 cup fat-free half-and-half

Salt and pepper

½ cup grated Parmesan cheese

why it's good for you:

- Corn, onions, and peppers contain antioxidants.

- Eggs contain brain-boosting choline.

- A great low fat alternative to usual high-fat scalloped corn.

Preheat oven to 400°F. Heat oil in large skillet. Add onion; cook over low heat, stirring regularly, until golden and slightly caramelized, about 20 minutes. Place onion in a shallow 9 x 9-inch ovenproof dish. Add corn and bell pepper. Beat eggs; stir into half-and-half. Pour egg mixture over casserole, add salt and pepper, and stir. Sprinkle cheese on top.

Bake at 400°F for 30 to 35 minutes until firm. Brown top under a broiler. Let cool for 10 minutes. Cut into squares and serve.

SERVES 9

PER SERVING: 204 calories, 8 g total fat (2 g saturated), 26 g carbohydrate, 8 g protein, 77 mg cholesterol, 3 g fiber, 184 mg sodium

Eating onions more than once a day cut the risk of colorectal cancer by 56 percent and esophageal cancer 88 percent, according to Italian research.

SCIENCE SAYS

CRANBERRY-FRUIT SAUCE

1 (12-ounce) bag fresh cranberries
½ cup water
3 medium apples, such as Gala, peeled and chopped coarsely
2 pears, such as Bartlett, peeled and chopped coarsely
4–6 tablespoons sugar or no-calorie sweetener, such as Splenda
1½ tablespoons ground cinnamon
½ cup walnut pieces (optional)

Combine all ingredients except nuts, in a saucepan. Cover and simmer, stirring occasionally, until cranberries pop (25–30 minutes). Cool to room temperature or chill. Stir in nuts. Makes 4 cups.

SERVES 12

PER SERVING: 66 calories, 0.3 g total fat, 17 g carbohydrate, 0.3 g protein, 3 g fiber, 0 mg sodium

SCIENCE SAYS

Cranberry antioxidants help prevent brain cell damage that can lead to mini-strokes, Alzheimer's, and Parkinson's, find Tufts University researchers.

FIERY BAKED BEANS

½ cup chopped onion

2 tablespoons real maple syrup

1 tablespoon Dijon mustard

1 tablespoon plus 1 teaspoon canned chipotle chile peppers in adobo
    sauce, finely chopped

2 (16-ounce) cans no-salt-added navy beans, drained

1 cup no-salt-added ketchup, such as Hunt's

1 teaspoon ground cinnamon

Salt and pepper

Cooking spray

Preheat oven to 350°F. In a large bowl combine all ingredients. Spray a 7 × 11-inch shallow baking dish. Add bean mixture. Bake for 45 minutes.

SERVES 8

PER SERVING: 149 calories, 1 g total fat (0 g saturated), 31 g carbohydrate, 7 g protein, 0 mg cholesterol, 7 g fiber, 79 mg sodium

why it's good for you:

- Beans are high in protein and fiber.

- Beans, chile peppers, ketchup, and onions are high in antioxidants.

- Beans are high in zinc, potassium, and magnesium.

- Chile peppers may boost metabolism.

- Warning: this baked bean recipe isn't for the timid.

Contrary to popular belief, eating hot chile pepper did not produce burning or irritation in hemorrhoid sufferers, according to Italian research.

SCIENCE SAYS

GREEN BEAN SALAD WITH FETA

4 cups mixed baby salad greens

½ pound fresh green beans, trimmed, cooked al dente, and cut in half (about 1½–2 cups)

2 ounces feta cheese, crumbled or in small pieces

2 tablespoons extra-virgin olive oil

1 tablespoon balsamic vinegar

1 tablespoon orange juice

½ teaspoon fennel seeds, or to taste

Salt and black pepper

⅓ cup dried cranberries (optional)

In a medium-size bowl, combine greens, green beans, and feta. Add oil, vinegar, orange juice, fennel seeds, salt, and pepper, and toss. Sprinkle with dried cranberries.

SERVES 6

PER SERVING: 84 calories, 6.7 g total fat (2 g saturated), 4.5 g carbohydrates, 2.4 g protein, 1 g fiber, 112 mg sodium

SCIENCE SAYS   Every extra fruit or vegetable you eat a day cuts your risk of heart disease by 4 percent, according to a large French study.

JOANNA'S CRANBERRY FANTASY*

3 cups canned whole cranberry sauce
1 cup canned crushed pineapple packed in natural juice
1 cup chopped walnuts

Mix all ingredients together and refrigerate for 2 hours before serving.

SERVES 10

PER SERVING: 217 calories, 7.2 g total fat (0.6 g saturated), 49.7 g carbohydrate, 2.5 g fiber, 26 mg sodium

why it's good for you:

- Cranberries, pineapple, and walnuts contain antioxidants.
- Walnuts have good short-chain omega-3 fat.
- Cranberries help prevent urinary tract infections.

Harvard research finds that women who eat the most fruits and vegetables are 10 percent to 15 percent less likely to develop cataracts than are women who eat the least.

SCIENCE SAYS

Contributed by singer Joanna Simon

NORTH AFRICAN LIMA BEANS WITH APPLE AND CINNAMON

1 tablespoon olive oil
1 large onion, chopped
1 large tart apple, diced
¼ teaspoon ground turmeric
½ teaspoon ground allspice
¼ teaspoon ground cinnamon
4 cups cooked lima beans

Place onions and oil in a large microwave-safe bowl and microwave on high until onions are soft, about 5 minutes. Add apple and seasonings; microwave on high for 3 minutes until apples are softened but not mushy. Stir in beans and microwave for a couple of minutes to heat beans through.

SERVES 8

PER SERVING: 144 calories, 2 g total fat, 26 g carbohydrate, 6 g protein, 5 g fiber, 15 mg sodium

SCIENCE SAYS
Apples and apple juice boost production of acetylcholine, a "memory chemical" in the brain, report University of Massachusetts researchers.

ORANGE–WHITE BEAN SALAD

3 cups cannellini beans, drained and rinsed
1 cup diced celery
1 cup chopped red onions
2 tablespoons white wine vinegar
2 tablespoons water
6 tablespoons orange juice concentrate
½ cup chopped fresh mint
½ teaspoon finely minced jalapeño pepper

Combine all. Serve chilled or at room temperature.

SERVES 5

PER SERVING: 173 calories, 1 g total fat (0.2 g saturated), 32 g carbohydrate,
10.7 g protein, 5 g fiber, 236 mg sodium

why it's good for you:

- Beans are high in fiber and folic acid.

- Celery, red onions, and orange juice contain antioxidants.

- Plus: beans are very low-glycemic, help control blood sugar, and lower cholesterol.

Orange juice is rich in the antioxidant hesperetin, which blocks specific enzymes from switching on cancer-causing agents in the body.

SCIENCE SAYS

POTATO-BASIL SALAD WITH MUSTARD DRESSING

2 pounds small red potatoes, unpeeled, cooked and cut in bite-size pieces
1 pint grape tomatoes, halved
1 cup sliced celery
1 cup sliced green onions, with green tops
1 cup basil leaves, shredded

MUSTARD DRESSING

3 garlic cloves, crushed
3 tablespoons white balsamic vinegar or other white vinegar
9 tablespoons extra-virgin olive oil
1 tablespoon Dijon mustard
Salt and freshly ground black pepper

In a large bowl, combine potatoes, tomatoes, onions, basil, and celery. In a small bowl, whisk together garlic, vinegar, oil, mustard, salt, and pepper. Add dressing to potatoes and toss. Refrigerate until ready to serve.

SERVES 10

PER SERVING: 163 calories, 9 g total fat (1 g saturated), 20 g carbohydrate, 2 g protein, 2 g fiber, 83 mg sodium

SCIENCE SAYS

Using vinegar in recipes with high-glycemic carbs, such as potatoes, helps curb appetite and possibly weight gain, find Swedish investigators.

RED CABBAGE–APPLE SLAW

4 cups red cabbage, shredded or sliced
2 apples, such as Gala, cored and diced
⅓ cup walnut pieces, toasted

DRESSING

1½ tablespoons extra-virgin olive oil
1½ tablespoons balsamic vinegar
⅓ cup frozen apple juice concentrate
Salt and freshly ground black pepper

Combine cabbage, apples, and walnuts. Whisk together oil, vinegar, juice, salt, and black pepper to make a dressing. Toss with cabbage mixture and serve immediately or refrigerate.

SERVES 6

PER SERVING: 138 calories, 7.8 g total fat (0.9 g saturated), 18 g carbohydrate, 1.8 g protein, 2.7 g fiber, 10 mg sodium

why it's good for you:

- Cabbage, apples, and juice contain antioxidants.
- Walnuts have good fats.
- Very low in sodium.

Eating cabbage and other cruciferous vegetables alters estrogen metabolism in ways that appear to help prevent breast cancer and prostate cancer.

SCIENCE SAYS

ROASTED MUSHROOM SALAD

1 pound white button mushrooms, halved or quartered, depending on size
1 tablespoon olive oil
1 teaspoon lemon juice
¾ cup finely chopped red bell pepper
½ cup fresh basil or mint leaves, torn into pieces
¼ cup pine nuts, toasted
4 large leaves Boston lettuce
Freshly ground pepper

DRESSING

2 tablespoons extra-virgin olive oil
1 tablespoon balsamic vinegar or lemon juice
1 large garlic clove, crushed
Salt

Preheat oven to 400°F. Toss mushrooms with olive oil and lemon juice. Spread mushrooms on a large baking sheet and bake for 15 minutes. Drain off liquid. Cool slightly. In a bowl, combine mushrooms, red pepper, basil, and pine nuts. Toss with dressing. Place lettuce on 4 individual salad plates and top each with one-quarter mushroom mixture. Grind on black pepper to taste.

SERVES 4

PER SERVING: 179 calories, 15 g total fat (2 g saturated), 9 g carbohydrates, 5 g protein, 3 g fiber, 0 g cholesterol, 7 mg sodium

SCIENCE SAYS

Italians who eat more than two and a half tablespoons of olive oil a day are 60 percent less apt to have peripheral vascular disease (PVD) caused by hardening of the arteries, finds a study.

SOUTHWESTERN COLE SLAW

4 cups chopped or shredded cabbage
1 medium red bell pepper, chopped (1 cup)
1 cup thinly sliced scallions
1 cup cooked corn kernels
½ cup chopped cilantro (optional)
1 tablespoon finely minced jalapeno pepper, seeds and veins removed
    (optional)
⅔ cup rice vinegar or other white vinegar
⅓ cup no calorie sweetener such as Splenda, or sugar
Salt and freshly ground black pepper

Combine all ingredients in a large bowl, toss well, and chill before serving.

SERVES 8

PER SERVING: 37 calories, 0 g total fat, 9 g carbohydrate, 1 g protein, 0 mg cholesterol, 2 g fiber, 12 mg sodium

Women who ate lots of raw cabbage—at least three servings a week—had lower chances of developing breast cancer, in a U.S.-Polish study.

SCIENCE SAYS

SWEET-AND-SOUR CUCUMBERS

2 large cucumbers, peeled and thinly sliced
3 scallions, sliced thinly, with 3 inches of green tops
⅔ cup rice vinegar
⅓ cup sugar or no-calorie sweetener such as Splenda

Combine all ingredients; marinate for at least half an hour. With a slotted spoon, serve as a salad or a garnish.

SERVES 4

PER SERVING: 47 calories, 0.2 g total fat, 12 g carbohydrate, 0.7 g protein, 1.2 g fiber, 4 mg sodium

SCIENCE SAYS Eating onions reduced the DNA (genetic) damage in the cells of Scottish subjects, indicating protection against cancer.

TANGY MANGO SLAW

1 small head cabbage, shredded (4 cups)
½ cup finely chopped red onion
1 fresh mango, cubed
½ cup walnut pieces
¾ cup white rice vinegar or other white vinegar
¼ cup no-calorie sweetener such as Splenda, or sugar

In a bowl combine cabbage, onion, mango, and walnuts. In a cup or small bowl, dissolve Splenda or sugar in vinegar. Add to cabbage and toss. Serve cold or at room temperature

SERVES 8

PER SERVING: 79 calories, 5 g total fat (0.5 g saturated), 8 g carbohydrate, 2 g protein, 0 mg cholesterol, 2 g fiber, 7 mg sodium

why it's good for you:

- Very low in calories.

- Cabbage, onion, mango, and walnuts contain antioxidants.

- Vinegar curbs blood sugar, suppressing appetite and weight gain.

British research finds that eating more than five fruits and vegetables a day slashes your chances of stroke by 26 percent; more than three a day cuts risk by 10 percent

SCIENCE SAYS

TOMATO-CORN-BEAN SALAD WITH BASIL

1 pint cherry tomatoes, yellow or red (or combination) halved
1 cup cooked corn kernels, fresh or frozen
1 (15-ounce) can no-salt added navy beans, drained and rinsed
½ cup chopped red onion
3 tablespoon extra-virgin olive oil
2 tablespoon balsamic vinegar
1 clove garlic, crushed
Salt and freshly ground pepper
1 cup torn fresh basil leaves

In a medium bowl, combine tomatoes, corn, beans, and onion. Whisk together olive oil, vinegar, garlic, and salt and pepper to taste. Toss with tomato mixture and marinate for half an hour. Stir in basil leaves, and serve.

SERVES 6

PER SERVING: 167 calories, 7.5 g total fat (1 g saturated), 21 g carbohydrate, 6 g protein, 6 g fiber, 18 mg sodium

SCIENCE SAYS

German research suggests that eating antioxidant-rich tomatoes, dark chocolate, pomegranates, fatty fish, and green tea may help protect your skin from sunburn and wrinkles.

VEGGIE POTATO SALAD
FOR A CROWD

3 pounds small red potatoes, unpeeled

2 cups chopped red onions

12 ounces (about 6 cups) fresh green beans, trimmed, cooked al dente

3½ cups coarsely chopped red cabbage

1 pint grape tomatoes, halved

3 tablespoons capers, drained

2 ounces (about 3 cups very loosely packed) basil leaves, trimmed and torn into large pieces

Salt and freshly ground black pepper

MUSTARD DRESSING

⅔ cup extra-virgin olive oil

3 tablespoons white balsamic or rice vinegar

1 teaspoon salt

1½ teaspoons Dijon mustard

3 cloves garlic, crushed

In a large pot, cook whole potatoes until done. Cool. Cut into bite-size pieces. In a very large bowl, combine all ingredients from potatoes through basil. Whisk together dressing ingredients. Toss with vegetables, and add salt and pepper to taste. Chill. Serve.

SERVES 24

PER ¾ CUP SERVING: 120 calories, 6 g total fat (1 g saturated), 14 g carbohydrate, 2 g protein, 0 mg cholesterol, 3 g fiber, 161 mg sodium

> Italians who eat more than two and a half tablespoons of olive oil a day are 60 percent less apt to have peripheral vascular disease (PVD) caused by hardening of the arteries, finds one study.
>
> **SCIENCE SAYS**

why it's good for you:

- Potatoes, onions, green beans, cabbage, tomatoes, and basil contain antioxidants.

- Olive oil contains the good monounsaturated fat.

- Vinegar cuts white potato's high glycemic index.

- A great low calorie alternative to typical high fat potato salad.

Side Salads

MOST PEOPLE DON'T come close to consuming the recommended five to nine daily servings of fruits and vegetables. One great way to meet your quota: have a salad for either lunch or dinner. The following side salads, nearly all of which feature leafy greens, are loaded with vegetables, beans, and other wholesome foods. Best of all: they're all quick and easy to make.

ANTIPASTO SALAD WITH BASIL

3 tablespoons extra-virgin olive oil
1 tablespoon balsamic vinegar
2 cloves garlic, crushed or minced
1 (2-ounce) can anchovies, chopped (optional)
6 plum tomatoes, chopped
1 cup chopped red onion
½ cup black kalamata olives, chopped
1 cup basil leaves, torn into pieces
½ cup flat-leaf parsley, chopped
Freshly ground black pepper
⅓ cup crumbled feta cheese (optional)

Pour olive oil and vinegar into a medium bowl; stir in garlic and anchovies. Add tomatoes, onion, olives, basil, and parsley; toss. Divide among six plates; top with pepper and cheese.

SERVES 6

PER SERVING: 140 calories, 11.8 g total fat (2.5 g saturated), 8 g carbohydrate, 2.3 g protein, 2 g fiber, 295 mg sodium

why it's good for you:
- Vegetables and herbs are high in antioxidants.
- Olive oil contains good fats.

Vinegar, particularly balsamic vinegar, helps reduce blood sugar surges, say Australian researchers, and may discourage weight gain.

SCIENCE SAYS

HONEYED PEARS ON GREENS WITH BLUE CHEESE

3 tablespoons extra-virgin olive oil

4 tablespoons fresh lemon juice or more, to taste

2 teaspoons honey

2 teaspoons fresh thyme

Pinch of salt

2 ripe but firm pears, cored, unpeeled, and cut in chunks (about 6 chunks per half pear)

3½ ounces greens, such as baby arugala or watercress

4 ounces blue cheese, crumbled

⅓ cup crushed honey-coated almonds (optional)

Sprigs of thyme (optional)

In a small saucepan, combine oil, lemon juice, honey, thyme, and salt. Add pears and bring to a rapid boil, while gently stirring pears. Simmer at high heat for 1 minute. Pears should hold their shape, not be mushy. Refrigerate until cool. To assemble salad, divide greens among salad plates. Top each with one-quarter of the pears, including liquid. Top with blue cheese and almonds. Garnish with a thyme sprig or extra chopped thyme.

SERVES 4

PER SERVING: 260 calories, 19 g total fat (6.8 g saturated), 18 g carbohydrate, 7 g protein, 2.5 g fiber, 437 mg sodium

SCIENCE SAYS

Eating lots of fruits and vegetables rich in vitamin C could reduce inflammation, linked to heart disease and cancer, as much as 45 percent, according to British research.

MEDITERRANEAN MEDLEY SALAD

4 cups coarsely chopped raw vegetables (such as carrots, red onions, cucumbers, tomatoes, celery, red and green bell peppers, zucchini)
2 ounces feta cheese, crumbled
¼ cup pitted kalamata black olives
½ cup fresh torn basil leaves
2 tablespoons extra-virgin olive oil
1 tablespoon balsamic vinegar
Salt and black pepper

Toss all ingredients together.

SERVES 4

PER SERVING: 161 calories, 13 g total fat (3 g saturated), 10 g carbohydrate, 4 g protein, 3 g fiber, 324 mg sodium

Extra-virgin olive oil is a strong anti-inflammatory similar to ibuprofen, making it superior to lesser grades of olive oil, say scientists at Monell Chemical Senses Center in Philadelphia.

SCIENCE SAYS

MIXED GREENS WITH BEETS, ORANGES, AND NUTTY DRESSING

3 medium beets (about 1½ pounds), trimmed and scrubbed
4 cups gourmet salad greens
2 oranges, peeled and sliced
¼ cup minced red onion
¼ cup feta cheese

Place whole beets in pot and cover with water, cook for about 40 minutes. Rub off skins and remove tops. Cut beets into slices or julienne. Divide salad greens among four plates. Top with beets, oranges, onions, and cheese. Drizzle 2 tablespoons of Nutty Dressing over each salad.

SERVES 4

PER SERVING WITH DRESSING: 261 calories, 17 g total fat (3 g saturated), 26 g carbohydrate, 5 g protein, 4.5 g fiber, 304 mg sodium

NUTTY DRESSING
½ cup chopped walnuts
½ cup extra-virgin olive oil
¼ cup balsamic vinegar
¼ cup orange juice

Put all ingredients in a blender or food processor; process to desired smoothness.

MAKES 1¼ CUPS

Per tablespoon: 69 calories, 7.4 g total fat (1 g saturated), 1 g carbohydrate, 0.5 g protein, 0.1 g fiber, 0 mg sodium

SCIENCE SAYS

Fruits and vegetables contain salicylic acid, aspirin's active compound. Vegetarians' blood has as much salicylic acid as that of aspirin-takers, enough to provide anti-inflammatory benefits.

MIXED GREENS WITH FIGS AND WALNUTS

4 cups mixed gourmet greens
1 large fennel bulb, sliced thinly
½ cup chopped red onion
8 fresh ripe figs, cut in halves or quarters
½ cup walnut pieces
½ cup crumbled feta cheese

DRESSING

3 tablespoons extra-virgin olive oil
1½ tablespoons balsamic vinegar
1 clove garlic, crushed
3 tablespoons orange juice
Salt and freshly ground black pepper

In a large bowl, combine salad ingredients and gently toss with dressing.

SERVES 6

PER SERVING: 235 calories, 15.8 g total fat (3 g saturated), 22 g carbohydrate, 4.8 g protein, 4.9 g fiber, 159 mg sodium

why it's good for you:

- Greens, onion, fennel, and figs are high in antioxidants.
- Olive oil and walnuts contain good fats.

Figs have anticancer compounds that have shrunk tumors in animals and humans, according to Japanese studies.

SCIENCE SAYS

- Watercress,
  oranges, and
  onions are super
  high in
  antioxidants.

- Olive oil contains
  good fat.

- Very low in calories,
  fat, and sodium.

ORANGE-WATERCRESS SALAD

1 bunch watercress, cleaned and trimmed (4–5 cups)
2 medium Valencia oranges, peeled, sliced thinly, seeds removed
¼ cup chopped red onion

DRESSING

2 tablespoons extra-virgin olive oil
2 tablespoons balsamic vinegar
2 tablespoons orange juice
Salt and freshly ground black pepper

Put watercress, oranges, and onions in a salad bowl. Combine oil,
vinegar, orange juice, salt, and pepper. Pour dressing over salad
ingredients and toss.

SERVES 6

SUBSTITUTIONS: *Instead of oranges, use grapefruit, avocado, or
mango slices, or 1 cup sliced strawberries or halved seedless grapes.*

PER SERVING: 68 calories, 4.7 g total fat (0.6 g saturated), 7 g carbohydrate,
1.2 g protein, 1.3 g fiber, 12 mg sodium

**SCIENCE
SAYS**
Watercress has the highest overall antioxidant activity of any
green leafy vegetable, including spinach.

PEAR-MINT SALAD
WITH PARMESAN SHAVINGS

1 pear (preferably red), quartered, cored and cut into thin lengthwise slices

1½ tablespoons balsamic vinegar

1 cup mixed greens, such as mesclun

3 tablespoons shavings of Parmesan or Romano cheese

2 tablespoons chopped fresh mint

1 tablespoon chopped walnuts (optional)

2 teaspoons extra-virgin olive oil

Marinate pear slices in balsamic vinegar for 5 minutes, tossing to coat. Drain pears, reserving vinegar. On two salad plates, place equal amounts of greens. Top with pears, cheese, mint, and nuts. Mix reserved vinegar with oil; drizzle over salad.

SERVES 2

PER SERVING: 140 calories, 7.9 g total fat (2.4 g saturated), 15 g carbohydrate, 4.9 g protein, 2.9 g fiber, 185 mg sodium

why it's good for you:

- Greens and pears are high in antioxidants.

- Mint has antibacterial properties.

- Plus: vinegar suppresses blood sugar rises.

Mint thwarts the growth of infectious bacteria, including E. coli, staphyloccocus, and Helicobacter pylori (implicated in ulcers), in Japanese tests.

SCIENCE SAYS

PEPPERY GREENS WITH WATERMELON

1 cup watermelon cut into 1-inch cubes
2 ounces firm feta cheese cut into ½-inch cubes.
2 tablespoons balsamic vinegar
½ teaspoon freshly grated black pepper, or to taste
1 tablespoon extra-virgin olive oil
2 cups arugula or gourmet mixed greens
Salt
2 tablespoons chopped toasted almonds or macadamia nuts

In a medium bowl, combine watermelon, cheese, balsamic vinegar, and pepper, and let marinate in the refrigerator for 15 minutes. Add olive oil, greens, and salt; toss. Serve sprinkled with nuts.

SERVES 2

PER SERVING: 216 calories, 17.6 g total fat (5.6 g saturated), 10 g carbohydrate, 7 g protein, 1.7 g fiber, 325 mg sodium

SCIENCE SAYS Watermelon is high in lycopene, a strong anticancer antioxidant identical to that in tomatoes.

ROMAINE WITH APPLES, PECANS, AND CREAMY BLUE CHEESE DRESSING

4½ cups hearts of romaine lettuce, torn into pieces
1 large unpeeled apple, such as Gala, chopped
1 ripe Hass avocado, cubed
¼ cup toasted pecans, broken into pieces
½ cup chopped red onions

In a large bowl, combine salad ingredients. Toss with ½ cup Creamy Blue Cheese Dressing, or more to taste.

SERVES 4

PER SERVING: Salad with dressing: 205 calories, 14 g total fat (2.7 g saturated), 17 g carbohydrate, 5 g protein, 3.8 g fiber, 119 mg sodium.

CREAMY BLUE CHEESE DRESSING

⅓ cup blue cheese (about 2½ ounces)
2 tablespoons white vinegar
1 teaspoon Dijon mustard
⅓ cup orange juice
8 ounces plain fat-free yogurt

In a small bowl, mash cheese with a fork. Add vinegar, mustard, juice, and yogurt; stir to combine thoroughly.

MAKES 1½ CUPS

---

why it's good for you:

- Lettuce, apples, avocado, onions, and pecans contain antioxidants.
- Pecans contain fiber.
- Yogurt has gut-protecting bacteria.

Eating the skin of apples provides about twice the anticancer activity as eating only the pulp, show Cornell University studies.

SCIENCE SAYS

SPINACH AND ARUGULA WITH RADISHES

6 cups mixed baby greens, including spinach, arugula, and lettuces
1 cup very thinly sliced red radishes
⅓ cup shredded mint leaves
¼ cup pine nuts, toasted

HONEY-MUSTARD DRESSING

1 tablespoon extra-virgin olive oil
1 tablespoon honey
3 tablespoons rice vinegar
2 teaspoons Dijon mustard
Salt and freshly ground black pepper

In a large bowl, combine greens, radishes, mint, and nuts. Whisk together oil, honey, vinegar, and mustard. Add to salad and toss lightly. Grind on black pepper.

SERVES 6.

PER SERVING: 88 calories, 5 g total fat (0.8 g saturated), 9 g carbohydrate, 3 g protein, 3 g fiber, 102 mg sodium

SCIENCE SAYS Women who ate the most spinach and other greens lowered their odds of breaking a hip by 30 percent, compared with women who ate the least. Leafy greens are high in bone-protecting vitamin K.

SPINACH AND BERRIES WITH FAT-FREE CURRY DRESSING

6 ounces fresh spinach (about 6 cups), washed, dried, and torn into
    bite-size pieces
1 cup thickly sliced strawberries
1 cup blueberries, any stems removed
1 small red onion, sliced thinly
½ cup chopped pecans

FAT-FREE CURRY DRESSING

    2 tablespoons balsamic vinegar
    2 tablespoons rice vinegar
    1 tablespoon plus 1 teaspoon honey
    1 teaspoon curry powder
    2 teaspoons Dijon mustard
    Salt and freshly ground black pepper

Whisk together dressing ingredients. Add to spinach and toss lightly. Add berries, onion, and pecans. Toss lightly and serve.

SERVES 6

PER SERVING: 117 calories, 6.4 g total fat (0.5 g saturated), 14 g carbohydrate, 2 g protein, 3 g fiber, 67 mg sodium

Blueberries stimulate the birth rate of new brain cells in the hippocampus—the region responsible for memory—of elderly rats, says Tufts University research.

SCIENCE SAYS

SPINACH WITH ORANGE AND GINGER DRESSING

4 cups baby spinach leaves, washed and dried

1 ripe Hass avocado, diced

1 large orange, peeled, sliced, and seeded

ORANGE AND GINGER DRESSING

1 tablespoon extra-virgin olive oil

¼ cup orange juice concentrate

1 teaspoon fresh lemon juice

2 teaspoons grated fresh ginger

Salt and freshly ground black pepper

Divide the spinach among four salad plates. Top with avocado and orange. Whisk together dressing; drizzle on each salad. Top with freshly ground black pepper.

SERVES 4

PER SERVING: 170 calories, 11.5 g total fat (1.7 g saturated), 17 g carbohydrate, 3 g protein, 3.5 g fiber, 50 mg sodium

SCIENCE SAYS

In Cornell tests, spinach topped other vegetables in retarding the spread of human cancer cells. Next in order: cabbage, red pepper, onion, and broccoli.

SPINACH WITH PEARS AND BLUE CHEESE

3 cups baby spinach, washed and dried

3 medium, ripe yellow pears, cored but not peeled, and cut lengthwise into slices

2 tablespoons crumbled blue cheese

1/4 cup chopped walnuts

DRESSING

2 tablespoons balsamic vinegar

3 tablespoons extra-virgin olive oil

3 tablespoons orange juice

1 clove garlic, crushed

Salt and freshly ground pepper

In a salad bowl, place spinach, pears, and cheese. Whisk together dressing ingredients and toss with salad. Toast walnuts for 5 minutes in 325°F oven. Sprinkle warm walnuts over salad. Serve.

SERVES 4

PER SERVING: 243 calories, 17 g total fat (2.6 g saturated), 24 g carbohydrate, 4 g protein, 5.7 g fiber, 93 mg sodium

The folic acid in only ¾ cup of spinach a day relieved depression in study participants, at McGill University.

SCIENCE SAYS

THAI GINGER-CABBAGE SALAD*

¾ cup pickled ginger (6-ounce jar or fresh from an Asian market)

4 cups shredded green or red cabbage

½ cup peanuts, crushed

¼ cup mirin (sweetened rice wine)

¼ cup rice vinegar

4 scallions, sliced

Combine all ingredients.

SERVES 6

PER SERVING: 178 calories, 6 g total fat (0.8 g saturated), 25 g carbohydrate, 4g protein, 3 g fiber, 198 mg sodium

SCIENCE SAYS Cabbage and other cruciferous vegetables fed to lab animals reduced the incidence and spread of breast cancers.

* Inspired by a salad at Spices Restaurant in Washington, D.C.

Good-for-You Low-Calorie Salad Dressings

I'VE PROVIDED YOU with suggested dressings for most of the salads recipes in this book. If you like to experiment with your own salad creations, I've included some additional salad recipes in the following pages to help you dress up just about any salad or fruit dish with something that's healthy and low calorie.

BANANA-ONION DRESSING

2 large ripe bananas, peeled and cut into chunks
¾ cup yellow onions, chopped
¼ cup frozen unsweetened apple juice concentrate
Hot sauce, such as Tabasco (optional)
Salt and freshly ground pepper

In a blender, process ingredients until smooth.

MAKES ABOUT 2½ CUPS

PER TABLESPOON: 10 calories, 0 g total fat, 3 g carbohydrate, 0.2 g fiber, 1 mg sodium

CREAMY GARLIC-BASIL DRESSING

1 cup fat-free plain yogurt
4 large cloves garlic, coarsely chopped
⅓ cup tightly packed fresh basil leaves
2 teaspoons frozen orange juice concentrate (optional)
Salt and freshly ground pepper

In a blender, process all ingredients until smooth.

MAKES ABOUT 1¼ CUPS

PER TABLESPOON: 9 calories, 0 g total fat, 1 g carbohydrate, 1 g protein, 0 g fiber, 9 mg sodium

HONEY-GINGER DRESSING FOR FRUIT

¾ cup fat-free vanilla yogurt
1 teaspoon honey
2 teaspoons minced crystallized ginger
⅛ teaspoon ground cumin
⅛ teaspoon cayenne pepper, or to taste

Whisk together all ingredients.

MAKES ABOUT ¾ CUP

PER TABLESPOON: 16 calories, 0 g total fat, 3 g carbohydrate, 0.7 g protein, 0 g fiber, 10 mg sodium

MINTY LIME YOGURT DRESSING

1 (6-ounce) container fat-free key lime yogurt
¼ cup fresh lime juice
¼ cup chopped fresh mint leaves
Salt and freshly ground pepper

In a blender, process all ingredients until smooth.

MAKES ABOUT 1 CUP

PER TABLESPOON: 11 calories, 0 g total fat, 2 g carbohydrate, 0.4 g protein, 0 g fiber, 6 mg sodium

ORANGE-YOGURT SALAD DRESSING

½ cup fat-free plain yogurt
¼ teaspoon pure vanilla extract
1 teaspoon honey
2 tablespoons frozen orange juice concentrate

Whisk together all ingredients.

MAKES ⅔ CUP

PER TABLESPOON: 14 calories, 0 g total fat, 3 g carbohydrate, 0.1 g protein, 0 g fiber, 9 mg sodium

POPPY SEED DRESSING

½ cup firm tofu
¼ cup frozen orange juice concentrate
¼ cup rice vinegar
1 clove garlic, crushed
2 teaspoons fresh lemon juice
2 teaspoons poppy seeds

Combine all ingredients in a blender and process until smooth.

MAKES 1 GENEROUS CUP

PER TABLESPOON: 20 calories, 0.9 g total fat (0.1 g saturated), 2 g carbohydrate, 1.4 g protein, 0 g fiber, 2 mg sodium

TANGY AVOCADO DRESSING

1 ripe Hass avocado, cut into chunks
2 tablespoons white wine vinegar
3 tablespoons lemon juice
2 teaspoons Dijon mustard
1 cup fat-free half-and-half
Hot sauce, such as Tabasco
Salt and freshly ground black pepper

In a blender, process ingredients until smooth and creamy

MAKES ABOUT 1½ CUPS

PER TABLESPOON: 18 calories, 1 g total fat, 1 g carbohydrate, 0 g fiber, 18 mg sodium

TOMATO-BASIL DRESSING

¾ cup tomato juice
10 large basil leaves, shredded
2 teaspoons fresh thyme or oregano
2 teaspoons prepared mustard
Salt and freshly ground pepper

In a blender, process ingredients until basil is finely chopped. Chill before serving.

MAKES ABOUT ¾ CUP

PER TABLESPOON: 4 calories, 0 g total fat, 1 g carbohydrate, 0 g protein, 0 g fiber, 66 mg sodium

Salad Main Courses

YOU'LL FIND EVERYTHING you need to make delicious and healthy main course salads. In the following pages, you'll discover my healthy makeovers of traditionally high-fat salads. You'll even find a salad that provides you with all of your vegetable servings—in just one daily meal.

CLASSIC "STONE-AGE" SALAD

5 cups mixed greens, such as mesclun, spinach, or dark green lettuce
1½ cups cooked chickpeas
½ cup red onion, chopped or sliced into rings
1 cup cooked cubed chicken breast
1 cup chopped cauliflower
½ cup walnut pieces
3 tablespoons chopped fresh herbs, such as parsley, basil, or cilantro

DRESSING

6 tablespoons orange juice
2 teaspoons balsamic vinegar
2 tablespoons canola oil or extra-virgin olive oil
2 cloves garlic, crushed
Salt and freshly ground pepper

In a large bowl, combine salad ingredients. In a small bowl, whisk dressing. Toss together.

SERVES 4

PER SERVING: 331 calories, 19.3 g total fat (1.8 g saturated), 22 g carbohydrate, 9.5 g protein, 6 g fiber, 182 mg sodium

SCIENCE SAYS

Eating greens, legumes, nuts, and low-fat animal protein, such as chicken, is more compatible with our ancient "stone-age" genes and more apt to promote health.

FRUITY CHICKEN CURRY SALAD

2 cups cooked chicken cut into bite-size pieces
1 (20-ounce) can chunk pineapple, drained
½ cup chopped celery
¼ cup fat-free sour cream
2 teaspoons curry powder
Salt and freshly ground black pepper

Combine all.

SERVES 4

PER SERVING: 224 calories, 5.4 g total fat (1.4 g saturated), 22 g carbohydrate, 22 g protein, 87 mg sodium

why it's good for you:

- Pineapple and celery contain antioxidants.
- Curry powder reduces inflammation.
- Chicken is a good lean source of protein.

In India, where curry powder is a staple, the rate of Alzheimer's disease is extremely low.

SCIENCE SAYS

GRILLED TUNA WITH AVOCADO AND MANGO

1 pound fresh tuna steak, 1 inch thick

SAUCE

2 tablespoons extra-virgin olive oil

3 tablespoons fresh lime juice

Grated zest of 2 limes

2 teaspoons reduced-sodium soy sauce

10 dashes of hot sauce, such as Tabasco

Salt and freshly ground black pepper

SALAD

¾ cup thinly sliced scallions, with some green tops

¾ cup diced red onions

2 ripe Hass avocados, diced

1 mango, diced, or substitute 1 cup drained mandarin oranges

¼ cup chopped fresh cilantro or basil

Brush olive oil on both sides of tuna and on grill rack. Sear tuna, about 2½ minutes on each side; it will be rare inside. Do not overcook. Remove and when cool, cut tuna into pieces about 1-inch square. Alternatively, sear tuna in a heavy nonstick skillet brushed with olive oil.

In a large bowl, whisk together olive oil, lime juice, zest, soy sauce, hot sauce, salt, and pepper. Add grilled or seared tuna, scallions, and onions; mix well and let sit for a few minutes. Add avocado and mango, and toss lightly. Alternatively, heap tuna on a platter and surround with avocado and mango. Sprinkle with fresh herbs and serve at room temperature or chilled.

SERVES 4

PER SERVING: 425 calories, 27 g total fat (4.7 g saturated), 22 g carbohydrate, 27 g protein, 3.7 g fiber, 177 mg sodium

SCIENCE SAYS

Eating tuna, salmon, and sardines at least once a week slowed artery clogging in women, according to Tufts University studies.

JEAN'S SUPER-NUTRITIOUS ENTRÉE SALAD

1 cup romaine, torn into bite-size pieces
1 cup fresh spinach, torn into bite-size pieces
½ cup cauliflower sliced into bite-size florets
½ cup chopped or thinly sliced red onion
½ cup shredded red cabbage
1 orange, peeled and sliced
½ cup strawberries
½ cup cooked chickpeas
2 tablespoons dry-roasted unsalted peanuts
¼ cup crumbled blue cheese or feta
2 ounces cooked chicken or turkey white meat, salmon, or tofu, 1 hard-
    boiled egg (optional)

GINGER-CITRUS DRESSING

½ cup orange juice
2 tablespoons rice or white vinegar
2 tablespoons extra-virgin olive oil
2 cloves garlic, crushed
1 teaspoon reduced-sodium soy sauce
1 teaspoon grated fresh ginger
¾ teaspoon ground cumin

Whisk dressing ingredients together in a small bowl. (Makes ¾ cup
[12 tablespoons]).

In a large bowl, toss salad ingredients with ¼ cup Ginger-Citrus
Dressing.

SERVES 1

PER SERVING: 630 calories, 30.4 g total fat (9.1 g saturated), 73 g carbohydrate, 25 g protein, 18 g fiber, 615 mg sodium

> Eating green leafy vegetables, beans, olive oil, nuts, and multi-
> grain bread—in short, wholesome foods—leads to smoother
> skin and fewer wrinkles when you are older, find Australian
> researchers.

SCIENCE SAYS

why it's good for you:

- Contains your daily quota of 8 servings of antioxidant-packed, anti-cancer fruits and vegetables.

- High in fiber—18 grams.

- Lots of nutrients but low in calories

- Olive oil contains good fat.

- Plus: ginger is an anti-inflammatory.

LOW-FAT TACO SALAD

4 corn tortillas, or substitute low-fat tortilla chips

4 cups shredded dark green lettuce, such as romaine

½ cup chopped red onion

2 ripe Hass avocados or 1 medium Florida avocado, cubed

1 (4½-ounce) can chopped green chiles

1 large tomato, chopped

1½ cups tomato salsa

1 (15-ounce) can black beans, drained, rinsed (preferably no-salt-added)*

½ cup fat-free sour cream

1 cup shredded low-fat cheddar cheese

Preheat oven to 425°F. Spray tortillas on both sides with canola oil. Cut into ½-inch-wide strips and spread on a baking sheet. Bake, turning strips once, until brown and crispy, about 8 minutes.

Combine lettuce, onion, avocado, chiles, and chopped tomato. Combine salsa and beans. Divide salad among four plates. Top with salsa mixture, cheese, sour cream, and tortilla strips.

SERVES 4

PER SERVING: 423 calories, 17.4 g total fat (5.4 g saturated), 53 g carbohydrate, 20 g protein, 8 g fiber, 1108 mg sodium

*With no-salt-added beans, the sodium drops to 949 mg per serving.

SCIENCE SAYS   All dark green lettuces contain a variety of antioxidants, including beta carotene and lutein.

MIXED GREENS WITH CUMIN-CRUSTED SALMON

SALAD

2 ounces pine nuts, toasted

5 cups mixed greens

1 (15-ounce) can black beans, drained and rinsed

1 cup sliced scallions

1 large orange, cut into 1-inch pieces

½ cup crumbled feta cheese

1 cup chopped fresh cilantro

DRESSING

2 tablespoons orange juice concentrate

4 tablespoons extra-virgin olive oil

½ teaspoon ground cumin

1½ tablespoons balsamic vinegar

2 cloves garlic, crushed

Salt

CUMIN-CRUSTED SALMON

1½ tablespoons ground cumin

2 teaspoons paprika

Salt and freshly ground black pepper

1 pound salmon fillet, skin removed

In a large bowl, place all salad ingredients (reserve half of the cilantro and half of the pine nuts for garnish).

In a separate bowl, whisk together dressing ingredients.

In a shallow dish, combine cumin, paprika, salt, and pepper. Cut salmon into 8 strips and coat with spices. Grill (or sear in a nonstick skillet brushed with canola oil) until crusty.

Toss salad and dressing; divide among 4 plates. Top with salmon and reserved cilantro and pine nuts.

SERVES 4

PER SERVING: 583 calories, 37 g total fat (8 g saturated), 28 g carbohydrate, 35 g protein, 6.6 g fiber, 683 mg sodium

The spice cumin is the richest source of a potent compound, farnesol, which suppresses pancreatic tumors in hamsters.

SCIENCE SAYS

SALADE NIÇOISE

5 ounces fresh baby spinach or large spinach leaves torn into bite-size
    pieces
1 (12-ounce) can water-packed light tuna, drained and separated into
    chunks
1 medium red onion, chopped
¾ pound small red potatoes, cooked and quartered
1 (10-ounce) package frozen green beans, cooked, preferably French-cut
1½ cups grape tomatoes or halved cherry tomatoes
16 small black olives, preferably oil-cured
⅓ cup crumbled feta cheese
Freshly ground black pepper

DRESSING

½ cup extra-virgin olive oil
2 teaspoons Dijon mustard
2 cloves garlic, crushed
Salt
3 tablespoons balsamic vinegar

Cover the bottom of a large, shallow salad bowl with spinach leaves.
In another large bowl, whisk together dressing ingredients. Add
tuna, potatoes, onion, and green beans, and toss to combine. Spoon
mixture over spinach leaves. Decorate with tomatoes and olives;
sprinkle on feta cheese. Top with freshly ground black pepper.

SERVES 8 AS LUNCHEON SALAD

PER SERVING: 260 calories, 16.5 g total fat (1.2 g saturated), 15 g carbohydrate, 14 g protein, 2.6 g fiber, 238 mg sodium

**SCIENCE
SAYS**

Greeks who eat a Mediterranean-style diet—high in fish, vegetables, olive oil, and salads—have lower blood levels of inflammation, fibrinogen, and homocysteine, which are all risk factors
for heart disease.

Vegetables

DO YOU HAVE a vegetable deficiency? Many people do. The more vegetables you eat, the more you'll improve your health and lengthen your life. Think of them as preventive medicine. They don't have to be boring, either. In the following pages you'll find plenty of ways to dress up veggies. Try these delicious vegetable recipes and you'll soon become a vegetable overachiever!

AN EASY

MICROWAVE DISH

ASPARAGUS WITH BALSAMIC DRESSING

24 medium stalks of green asparagus (about 1 pound)
3 cups gourmet Italian salad greens with radicchio
¼ cup chopped hazelnuts

BALSAMIC DRESSING

6 tablespoons balsamic vinegar
2 tablespoons extra-virgin olive oil
2 teaspoons Dijon mustard
1 teaspoons reduced-sodium soy sauce
2 tablespoons orange juice

Whisk together all ingredients except hazelnuts. Trim, peel, and rinse asparagus: do not dry. Place spears flat two or three deep in a glass pie plate or similar dish. Cover *very tightly* with microwavable plastic wrap, and microwave on high for 2½ to 5 minutes, depending on wattage. Whisk together dressing ingredients; pour over asparagus and marinate in refrigerator until cool. Divide greens among four salad plates; top each with six asparagus spears. Drizzle with equal amounts of dressing and top with hazelnuts.

SERVES 4

PER SERVING: 149 calories, 11 g total fat (1 g saturated), 8 g carbohydrate, 4 g protein, 2 g fiber, 137 mg sodium

SCIENCE SAYS

Asparagus is the highest plant source of glutathione, a master antioxidant that helps deflect the absorption of bad fats. It also helps to reduce your risk of cancer.

BEETS WITH ORANGE AND GINGER

6 medium beets
1 tablespoon cornstarch
1 cup orange juice
1 tablespoon white vinegar
2 tablespoons maple syrup
2 tablespoons chopped crystallized ginger
½ cup walnut pieces

Scrub beets, leaving on root and 1 inch of stem. Place beets in a large pot with water to cover. Bring to a boil, cover and simmer for 45 to 60 minutes, or until tender. Drain, rub off skins (or peel), and cut into wedges.

In a saucepan combine cornstarch, orange juice, maple syrup, vinegar, ginger, and walnuts. Bring to a boil and simmer until sauce has thickened. Add beets and toss to coat.

SERVES 6

PER SERVING: 193 calories, 6 g total fat (0.6 g saturated), 32 g carbohydrate, 4 g protein, 2.3 g fiber, 121 mg sodium

why it's good for you:
- Beets are high in antioxidants.
- Walnuts contain good fat.
- Plus: ginger is an anticoagulant and vinegar helps suppress blood sugar spikes.

Beets contain anticancer chemicals that inhibit skin, lung, and liver tumors in mice.

SCIENCE SAYS

BROCCOLI-CAULIFLOWER ROAST

2 cups broccoli florets, 1–2 inches in diameter
2 cups cauliflower florets, 1–2 inches in diameter
5 cloves garlic, peeled and halved
2 tablespoons extra-virgin olive oil
Salt and freshly ground black pepper
1 teaspoon grated Parmesan cheese

Preheat oven to 450°F. Toss broccoli, cauliflower, and garlic with olive oil. Spread on a baking sheet and bake for 20 minutes, or until browned and tender-crunchy. Stir once or twice. Season to taste with salt and pepper. Sprinkle with Parmesan cheese before serving.

SERVES 4

PER SERVING: 92 calories, 7.2 g total fat (1 g saturated), 6 g carbohydrate, 3 g protein, 2.3 g fiber, 36 mg sodium

SCIENCE SAYS Women who ate lots of broccoli were 38 percent less apt to die of heart disease, in a ten-year study of 35,000 older women in Iowa.

CRISPY CHEESE CAULIFLOWER

Olive oil spray

⅔ cup freshly grated Parmesan cheese

½ teaspoon ground cumin

Salt and freshly ground black pepper

⅛ teaspoon cayenne pepper, or to taste (optional)

½ large head cauliflower, broken into pieces

2 eggs, beaten

½ cup finely chopped parsley

1 lemon cut in wedges

Preheat oven to 450°F. Spray a cookie sheet with olive oil. In a small, shallow dish, combine cheese, cumin, salt and pepper, and cayenne. Dredge cauliflower pieces in egg, then in cheese mixture. Place on cookie sheet. Spray cauliflower with olive oil. Bake for 15 minutes. Transfer to plate; sprinkle with parsley. Serve with lemon wedges.

SERVES 4

PER SERVING: 141 calories, 9 g total fat (3.9 g saturated), 6.5 g carbohydrate, 11 g protein, 2.7 g fiber, 350 mg sodium

Every extra fruit or vegetable you eat a day cuts your risk of heart disease by 4 percent, according to a large French study.

SCIENCE SAYS

why it's good for you:

- Cauliflower provides antioxidants.

- Vegetables are low on the glycemic index.

- May help prevent certain cancers.

AN EASY

MICROWAVE DISH

CURRIED CHICKPEAS AND ONIONS

1 (15-ounce) can chickpeas, drained and rinsed
1 medium yellow onion, chopped
1 (8-ounce) can no-salt-added tomato sauce
1 tablespoon curry powder
1 teaspoon ground cumin
¼ teaspoon cayenne pepper, or to taste

In a medium microwave-safe bowl, combine all ingredients. Microwave on high, covered, for 10 minutes, or until onions are soft.

SERVES 4

PER SERVING: 161 calories, 2 g total fat (0 g saturated), 32 g carbohydrate, 7 g protein, 0 mg cholesterol, 7 g fiber, 327 mg sodium

SCIENCE SAYS Curcumin, a compound in curry powder, may reduce toxic plaque in brain cells, thought to be a cause of Alzheimer's.

CURRIED ROOT VEGETABLES WITH PINEAPPLE

4 cups assorted root vegetables (sweet potatoes, carrots, turnips, and/or parsnips), cut into 1-inch chunks
1 medium yellow onion, cut into 8 wedges
1 tablespoon curry powder
1 (8-ounce) can pineapple chunks in juice
Freshly ground black pepper
Fat-free plain yogurt, chopped cilantro and/or crushed peanuts, for garnish (optional)

In a large, microwave-safe bowl, combine all vegetables, curry, and pineapple chunks with juice, cover tightly, and microwave on high for 20 to 25 minutes or until vegetables are tender. Grind on fresh black pepper. Serve immediately. Top with yogurt, cilantro, and peanuts. You can also serve over brown rice.

SERVES 6 A SIDE DISH, 4 AS A MAIN COURSE

PER SIDE DISH SERVING: 91 calories, 0.4 g total fat, 22 g carbohydrate, 1.6 g protein, 3.8 g fiber, 28 mg sodium

AN EASY

MICROWAVE DISH

Sweet potatoes were first and carrots second among fifty-eight vegetables, in vitamins A and C, folate, iron, copper, calcium, and fiber, as ranked by the Center for Science in the Public Interest.

SCIENCE SAYS

GREEN BEAN CASSEROLE

1 (16-ounce) package frozen green beans, French-cut
½ cup fat-free cottage cheese
½ cup (about 3 ounces) chèvre (soft goat cheese) with garlic and herbs
½ cup toasted slivered almonds
¼ cup freshly grated Parmesan cheese
Freshly ground black pepper

Preheat oven to 375°F. Cook green beans according to package directions, and drain. In a blender, mix cottage cheese and chèvre. Combine green beans, blended cheeses, and almonds; turn into a baking dish. Top with Parmesan cheese and pepper. Bake for 20 minutes. To brown top, put under a broiler for 3 to 5 minutes.

SERVES 6

PER SERVING: 161 calories, 10 g total fat (3.4 g saturated), 9 g carbohydrate, 10 g protein, 2 g fiber, 205 mg sodium

SCIENCE SAYS Colon cancer risk decreases when you eat lots of green vegetables, according to numerous studies.

FRESH SPRING ROLLS with **THAI DIPPING SAUCE,** PAGE 82

SPINACH AND BERRIES WITH **FAT-FREE CURRY DRESSING,** PAGE 143

ASPARAGUS WITH **BALSAMIC DRESSING,** PAGE 160

PORTOBELLOS STUFFED WITH GREENS AND CHEESE, PAGE 172

QUICK TEX-MEX RICE CASSEROLE, PAGE 193

HOT PEPPER QUESADILLAS, PAGE 189

PEPPER, ONION, AND FETA PIZZA, PAGE 211

ZITI SPINACH ALFREDO, PAGE 217

FIESTA SEAFOOD CASSSEROLE, PAGE 223

SALMON WITH SCALLOPED SWEET POTATOES, PAGE 233

GREEK-STYLE TURKEY BURGERS, PAGE 267

THREE-BERRY TRIFLE, PAGE 296

CHOCOLATE CAKE WITH **RASPBERRY SAUCE,** PAGE 276

SAUCY SUMMER FRUIT SALAD, PAGE 294

GRILLED PEPPERS

4 large bell peppers (red, green, and/or yellow), cored and cut lengthwise into 1-inch-wide strips

2 tablespoons extra-virgin olive oil

Heat grill. Toss peppers with olive oil. Spread peppers on grill; cover grill if possible. Cook until peppers are thoroughly limp and slightly charred. Serve as a side dish or as a topping for bread or polenta.

SERVES 4

PER SERVING: 87 calories, 7 g total fat (1 g saturated), 6 g carbohydrate, 1 g protein, 1.6 g fiber, 2 mg sodium

Red bell peppers have the most vitamin C per calorie of any vegetable; green bell peppers are next.

SCIENCE SAYS

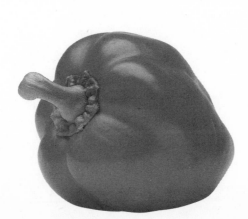

HERBED GRILLED TOMATOES

1 tablespoon extra-virgin olive oil

2 medium tomatoes, halved crosswise

2 teaspoons Dijon mustard

¼ cup bread crumbs

2 teaspoons freshly grated Parmesan cheese

4 large basil leaves, shredded

1 teaspoon fresh thyme, oregano, or rosemary, or ¼ teaspoon dried

Freshly ground black pepper

Brush half of oil over sides and bottoms of tomatoes. Brush tops with mustard. Combine cheese, bread crumbs, herbs; sprinkle on top of tomatoes. Drizzle on rest of oil to dampen bread-crumb topping. Add pepper. Put tomatoes on grill cut side up; cover. Grill until skins shrink from top of tomatoes and tomatoes are soft but not mushy, 10–20 minutes, depending on heat of grill. (Alternatively, roast in a 450°F oven for 15 to 20 minutes, or broil for 5 to 10 minutes.)

SERVES 4

PER SERVING: 75 calories, 4.4 g total fat (0.8 g saturated), 8 g carbohydrate, 2 g protein, 1.2 g fiber, 112 mg sodium

SCIENCE SAYS

Oregano oil is as effective as the common antibiotic drug, vancomycin, in treating staph infections in mice, says Harry Preuss, MD, Georgetown University.

LOW-FAT CREAMED SPINACH

2 small cloves garlic, crushed or minced
1 tablespoon extra-virgin olive oil
1 (10-ounce) package frozen chopped spinach, thawed and squeezed dry
¼ cup fat-free cream cheese
¼ cup fat-free half-and-half
Salt and freshly ground black pepper
Pinch of ground nutmeg

In a small skillet, sauté garlic in olive oil until soft but not brown; add spinach, cream cheese, and half-and-half. Cook, stirring, until blended and heated through, about 5 minutes. Stir in salt, pepper, and nutmeg, and serve.

SERVES 4

PER SERVING: 71 calories, 3.7 g total fat (0.5 g saturated), 5.6 g carbohydrate, 4 g protein, 1.5 g fiber, 135 mg sodium

why it's good for you:

- Spinach and garlic are super-high in antioxidants.
- Low in saturated fat.
- Low in calories.

Women who ate the most spinach and other greens reduced their odds of breaking a hip by 30 percent, compared with women who ate the least. Leafy greens are high in bone-protecting vitamin K.

SCIENCE SAYS

MEDITERRANEAN GRILLED VEGETABLES

1 small eggplant (or half of medium), cut into chunks
1 medium red onion, cut into wedges
5 ounces portobello mushroom, cut into 1-inch slices
2 small bell peppers (1 red, 1 green), cut into chunks or slivers
2 cups cherry or grape tomatoes

MARINADE

6 tablespoons extra-virgin olive oil
2 tablespoons balsamic vinegar
1 tablespoon reduced-sodium soy sauce
2 cloves garlic, crushed
¼ cup chopped fresh rosemary or basil

Prepare vegetables. Whisk together marinade ingredients in a large bowl. Add vegetables and toss to coat. Marinate for 1 hour. Put vegetables (except tomatoes) in grilling basket or on skewers. Grill, brushing with marinade and turning several times, for 15 minutes. Add tomatoes and grill for 5 minutes longer, or until all vegetables are as tender as desired.

SERVES 6

PER SERVING: 168 calories, 14.4 g total fat (2 g saturated), 11 g carbohydrate, 2.1 g protein, 2.5 g fiber, 180 mg sodium

SCIENCE SAYS

Eggplant contains a potent antioxidant—chlorogenic acid—known to kill germs (bacteria and viruses), fend off cancer, and reduce the "bad" LDL cholesterol, say USDA researchers.

OREGANO-BAKED ONIONS

4 medium yellow onions, peeled but not sliced
¼ cup balsamic vinegar
½ cup white wine, broth, or water
2 teaspoons dried oregano
¼ teaspoon salt
Freshly ground black pepper

Preheat oven to 425°F. Place onions upright in baking dish sprayed with oil. Mix vinegar, wine, and seasonings; pour over onions. Bake, covered, until onions are tender, about 45 minutes.

SERVES 4

PER SERVING: 72 calories, 0.6 g total fat, 16 g carbohydrate, 2 g protein, 2.7 g fiber, 150 mg sodium

Onions have potent antibacterial activity, destroying many disease-causing pathogens, including E. coli and salmonella.

SCIENCE SAYS

why it's good for you:

- Yellow onions are high in antioxidants.
- Plus: vinegar helps suppress blood sugar rises, and onions lower risk of prostate cancer.

PORTOBELLOS STUFFED WITH GREENS AND CHEESE

1 (10-ounce) package frozen collard greens or kale (about 2½ cups cooked)
2½ tablespoons extra-virgin olive oil
1½ tablespoons fresh lemon juice
2 large cloves garlic, crushed
1½ teaspoons dried thyme leaves
4 portobello mushrooms, stems removed
4 ounces Brie cheese, rind removed
Salt and freshly ground black pepper

Preheat oven to 350°F. Microwave greens according to package directions; drain and squeeze dry. Combine greens, oil, lemon juice, garlic, thyme, and salt. Put mushrooms, stem side up, in a baking dish. Fill hollows with greens. Top each with one-quarter of the cheese and freshly ground black pepper. Bake for 10 minutes. Broil to brown cheese, 2 minutes.

SERVES 4

PER SERVING: 228 calories, 17.1 g total fat (1.3 g saturated), 12 g carbohydrate, 11 g protein, 3 g fiber, 220 mg sodium

SCIENCE SAYS

Having high blood lutein from eating kale, spinach, and broccoli slowed thickening of neck arteries and stopped the progression of artery clogging, in a University of Southern California study.

QUICK PEANUT CABBAGE

4 cups thinly sliced cabbage

2 tablespoons chunky peanut butter, preferably natural

2 tablespoons frozen orange or apple juice concentrate

2 tablespoons balsamic vinegar

¼ teaspoon hot pepper flakes, or to taste

Put all the ingredients in a microwave-safe bowl. Cover and microwave on high for 4 minutes, or until the cabbage is limp and the peanut butter has melted. Stir to coat the cabbage with sauce, and serve.

SERVES 6

PER SERVING: 54 calories, 2.8 g total fat (0.5 g saturated), 6 g carbohydrate, 2 g protein, 1.3 g fiber, 11 mg sodium

why it's good for you:

- Cabbage contains anticancer chemicals.

- Orange juice provides antioxidants.

- Plus: Peanut butter helps control blood sugar and suppresses appetite.

AN EASY

MICROWAVE DISH

Eating cabbage and sauerkraut may slow estrogen activity and growth of estrogen-stimulated breast cancer cells, discouraging cancer spread, according to University of Illinois research.

SCIENCE SAYS

ROASTED SWEET POTATOES AND ONIONS

2 large sweet potatoes (about 2 pounds), peeled and cut into 1-inch chunks
2 medium Vidalia or other sweet onions, cut into 1-inch chunks
3 tablespoons olive oil
¼ cup Amaretto liqueur
1 teaspoon dried thyme
Salt and freshly ground pepper
¼ cup sliced almonds, toasted

Preheat oven to 425°F. Toss together all ingredients in a shallow medium-size baking dish. Bake for 45 to 50 minutes, or until tender. Sprinkle with toasted almonds.

SERVES 6

PER SERVING: 251 calories, 9 g total fat (1g saturated), 41 g carbohydrate, 4 g protein, 5 g fiber, 27 mg sodium

SCIENCE SAYS

Americans who eat the most onions and garlic have only half the chance of developing pancreatic cancer as those who eat the least, studies show.

SCALLOPED CORN WITH PEPPERS

1 (16-ounce) package frozen yellow corn kernels*

1 4-ounce can chopped green chiles

2 eggs, or ½ cup egg substitute

1 cup fat-free half-and-half

1 tablespoon butter or trans-fat free margarine

¾ cup crushed low-fat tortilla chips

Salt and freshly ground black pepper

Preheat oven to 400°F. Combine all ingredients. Put in a casserole, cover, and bake 20 minutes. Remove cover and bake for 15 more minutes, or until browned.

SERVES 6

PER SERVING: 205 calories, 9.5 g total fat (4.6 g saturated), 27 g carbohydrate, 6.8 g protein, 2.6 g fiber, 194 mg sodium

*NOTE: *frozen corn is much lower in sodium than canned corn.*

why it's good for you:
- Corn and chiles are high in antioxidants.
- Eggs contain choline and lutein.

Corn contains the highest amounts of zeaxanthin, an antioxidant that helps preserve good vision as you age.

SCIENCE SAYS

SPICY GREEN BEAN STIR-FRY

1 pound fresh string beans, stem ends removed
1 tablespoon canola oil
1 teaspoon Old Bay Blackened Seasoning
⅓ cup pecan pieces
Salt

Bring a large pot of water to a boil. Add green beans, return to a boil, and cook 1 minute; the beans should still be crisp. Drain the beans; don't rinse.

In a large skillet or wok, heat oil until very hot (the skillet is ready when a drop of water in the oil sizzles). Add beans and cook for about 1 minute, turning often with tongs or a spatula. Sprinkle on pecans and Old Bay. Turn beans and pecans to coat with oil and spices; cook for about 2 minutes more, or until beans and nuts are slightly browned. Salt to taste and serve.

SERVES 4

PER SERVING: 123 calories, 10 g total fat (1 g saturated), 9 g carbohydrate, 3 g protein, 0 mg cholesterol, 3 g fiber, 54 mg sodium

SCIENCE SAYS

People who eat the most vegetables are 42 percent less apt to have non-Hodgkin lymphoma than those who eat the least, finds a National Cancer Institute study.

STIR-FRIED BROCCOLI WITH ORANGE SAUCE

1 teaspoon sesame oil

1 teaspoon canola oil

2 cups bite-size broccoli florets

½ cup orange juice

2 teaspoons cornstarch

1 tablespoon reduced-sodium soy sauce

½ teaspoon no-calorie sweetener such as Splenda, or sugar

⅓ cup walnuts, toasted

In a small skillet, heat oils over medium-high heat. Add broccoli and stir-fry for 3 to 5 minutes. Combine orange juice, cornstarch, soy sauce, and sweetener. Add mixture to broccoli; lower heat and cook until sauce is thickened, about 1 minute. Stir in walnuts and serve.

SERVES 2

PER SERVING: 252 calories, 16 g total fat (1.5 g saturated), 9 g protein, 19 g carbohydrate, 4 g fiber, 345 mg sodium

Broccoli's main chemical, sulforaphane, performs wonders in preventing cancer in animals—slashing incidence by 60 percent and size by 75 percent.

SCIENCE SAYS

SUCCOTASH WITH ORANGE

AN EASY

MICROWAVE
DISH

why it's good for you:

- Beans are high in fiber.

- Corn, orange juice and cabbage contain antioxidants.

- Plus: beans hold down blood sugar rises.

1 (10-ounce) package frozen baby lima beans
1 cup frozen yellow corn kernels
1 cup orange juice
3 tablespoons rice vinegar or white wine vinegar
1½ cups shredded raw red cabbage

Combine first four ingredients in a large, microwave-safe bowl. Cover and microwave on high for 8 minutes, or until vegetables are cooked. Stir in cabbage. Serve warm or chilled.

SERVES 6

PER SERVING: 105 calories, 0.3 g total fat, 23 g carbohydrate, 4.6 g protein, 3.8 g fiber, 12 mg sodium

SCIENCE SAYS Foods, such as beans, that are low glycemic index (suppress blood sugar) are linked to a lower risk of colorectal cancer, says Harvard research.

SWEET-AND-SOUR BRUSSELS SPROUTS WITH TOASTED CASHEWS

1 pound fresh Brussels sprouts, trimmed and cut in half
2 tablespoons extra-virgin olive oil
2 tablespoons real maple syrup
2 tablespoons balsamic vinegar
1 teaspoon Dijon mustard
½ cup roasted cashews, toasted and broken into pieces*
Salt and pepper

In a medium saucepan, cook Brussels sprouts in ⅔ cup boiling water until crisp tender, about 8 minutes; test with a fork to be sure sprouts don't get soggy. Drain.

In a medium bowl, combine olive oil, maple syrup, vinegar, and mustard. Add Brussels sprouts and cashews, and toss.

   * Heat oven to 350°F. Place cashews in a pie pan and bake for about
     12 minutes or until slightly toasted, stirring once.

SERVES 4

PER SERVING: 225 calories, 15 g total fat (3 g saturated), 21 g carbohydrate, 6 g protein, 7 g fiber, 159 mg sodium

Three servings of green leafy and cruciferous vegetables a day slows loss of mental function by 40 percent, or by five years, compared with one serving a day, reports Rush University Medical Center in Chicago.

SCIENCE SAYS

AN EASY
MICROWAVE
DISH

SWEET-AND-SOUR RED CABBAGE

½ cup raisins

½ cup apple juice

½ large head red cabbage, coarsely shredded or sliced

2 tablespoons balsamic vinegar

1 tablespoon honey

¼ teaspoon ground cinnamon

½ cup chopped pecans (optional)

Soak the raisins in the apple juice for 2 hours, or until plumped. Place the cabbage in a large microwave-safe bowl. Add vinegar and stir. Cover and microwave on high for about 5 minutes. Add raisins, apple juice, honey, and cinnamon, and mix. Microwave, covered, on high for 3 to 5 minutes more. The cabbage should still be slightly crunchy. Sprinkle with pecans and serve.

SERVES 4

PER SERVING: 125 calories, 0.5 g total fat, 31 g carbohydrate, 2.6 g protein, 3.8 g fiber, 19 mg sodium

SCIENCE SAYS

Eating high amounts of fiber and lots of fruits and vegetables lowers risk of colon polyps that can lead to cancer, says National Cancer Institute research.

SWEET POTATO PUFF

3½ pounds sweet potatoes (4 large)

½ cup orange marmalade or apricot preserves

¼ cup brown sugar, or to taste

½ cup orange juice

2 teaspoons pure almond extract

3 egg whites

2 tablespoons almond slivers, toasted lightly

Cook sweet potatoes until tender (15–20 minutes in a microwave, 1 hour in a 450°F oven, or boiled for 25 minutes). Let cool. Preheat oven to 350°F. Peel sweet potatoes, place in a large bowl and mash. Add marmalade, sugar, orange juice, and almond extract; beat with mixer until smooth. In a separate bowl, beat egg whites to stiff peaks. Fold into potato mixture. Coat a 6-cup casserole with non-stick spray. Add sweet potato mixture and sprinkle with almonds. Bake until puffy and set, about 40 minutes.

SERVES 6

PER SERVING: 340 calories, 2 g total fat (0.2 g saturated), 76 g carbohydrate, 6 g protein, 6 g fiber, 71 mg sodium

why it's good for you:

- Sweet potatoes contain amounts of the super-antioxidant beta carotene.

- Orange juice and rind contains anti-cancer chemicals.

- Almonds have good fat.

Former or current smokers who ate ½ cup of sweet potatoes, carrots, or winter squash daily had half the lung cancer risk as those who ate none, says National Cancer Institute research.

SCIENCE SAYS

WARM MAPLED CARROTS WITH WALNUTS

4 cups carrots (1 pound), cut into ¼ to ½-inch slices
1 tablespoon trans-fat-free margarine or butter
2 tablespoons real maple syrup
2 tablespoons orange juice
¼ cup chopped walnuts, toasted
Pinch of ground cinnamon, or to taste
¼ cup dried cranberries (optional)
2 tablespoons chopped parsley for garnish (optional)

In a medium saucepan, combine carrots and ¾ cup water. Bring to a boil; cover and simmer until tender, about 15 minutes. Drain; place carrots in a large bowl. Add margarine, maple syrup, orange juice, walnuts, and cranberries. Toss. Serve warm, garnished with parsley.

SERVES 8

PER SERVING: 73 calories, 3.5 g total fat (0.5 g saturated), 10 g carbohydrate, 1 g protein, 2 g fiber, 32 mg sodium

SCIENCE SAYS Carrots are low glycemic; they discourage high blood sugar, cancer, and heart disease, studies show.

YOGURT VEGETABLE SALAD

2 cups low-fat or no-fat plain yogurt
1 large cucumber, peeled, seeded, and finely chopped
3 tablespoons finely chopped fresh mint leaves
Salt
1 cup chickpeas, drained
1 cup halved cherry tomatoes

In a medium bowl, combine yogurt, cucumber, mint, and salt. Stir in chickpeas and tomatoes. Garnish with fresh mint leaves

SERVES 4

PER SERVING: 138 calories, 3 g total fat (1.2 g saturated), 19 g carbohydrate, 9 g protein, 3 g fiber, 168 mg sodium

why it's good for you:

- Cucumber, chickpeas, and tomatoes contain antioxidants.
- Yogurt contains gut-protecting bacteria.
- Low in calories and fat.

Yogurt contains good bacteria that help ward off bad breath and gastrointestinal problems, research shows.

SCIENCE SAYS

Vegetable Main Courses

IF YOU THINK that you need meat to create a hearty, stick-to-your-ribs meal, think again. In the following pages, you'll find my favorite meat-free versions of many traditionally meat-centered dishes, such as stews, casseroles, chili, sloppy joe's and even shepherd's pie. These recipes deliciously use "meaty" ingredients such as soy, beans, and mushrooms to create the texture and taste of red meat without the cancer- and heart-disease-causing side effects.

CURRIED POTATO "KNISHES"

One large baking potato, peeled and cubed (2 cups)
½ cup reduced-sodium tomato juice
1 teaspoon extra-virgin olive oil
2 tablespoons uncooked oats
1 tablespoon curry powder
½ teaspoon ground cinnamon
⅓ cup raisins, plumped in hot water
1 cup frozen green peas
4 whole wheat tortillas

In a microwave-safe bowl, combine potatoes, juice, oats, and spices. Microwave covered on high for 5 minutes, until potatoes are softened. With a fork, mash about one-third of potatoes, leaving remainder in chunks. Mix in peas and raisins. Microwave, covered for 5 minutes.

Warm tortillas in skillet or oven. Open each tortilla onto a plate. Spread one-fourth of potato mixture over half the tortilla. Fold over the other half. Serve with chutney and raita.

SERVES 4

PER SERVING: 293 calories, 4 g total fat (0.7 g saturated), 58 g carbohydrate, 8.6 g protein, 6 g fiber, 430 mg sodium

why it's good for you:

- Potatoes, tomato juice, curry powder, raisins, and peas contain antioxidants.
- Whole-grain oats help reduce cholesterol.
- Cinnamon lowers blood sugar.

Among 1,000 older Asian men and women, those who ate curry once a month or even once in six months, did better on mental functioning tests than those who never ate curry.

SCIENCE SAYS

DOWN-HOME VEGETABLE FRITTATA

1 teaspoon extra-virgin olive oil

1 medium yellow onion, chopped

1 clove garlic, minced

1 green bell pepper, chopped

4 beaten eggs, or 1 cup egg substitute

2 tablespoons freshly grated Parmesan cheese

½ teaspoon chopped fresh rosemary or oregano, or ¼ teaspoon dried

Salt and freshly ground black pepper

1 large baking potato, cooked and cubed

1 medium tomato, chopped

Spicy tomato salsa, for garnish

Heat olive oil in a large nonstick skillet; sauté onion, garlic, and pepper until soft, about 3 minutes. Combine eggs, cheese, herbs, salt, and pepper in a bowl. Add potato and tomato to the skillet and immediately top with the egg mixture. Cook over low heat until nearly cooked through; top should be slightly uncooked. Transfer skillet to broiler for a minute, or until top is done and slightly browned. Loosen frittata around the edge with a narrow spatula and slide frittata from skillet to a plate. Cut into quarters. Serve with spicy tomato salsa.

SERVES 4

PER SERVING WITH EGGS: 209 calories, 7.3 g total fat (2.3 g saturated), 26 g carbohydrate, 1 g protein, 3 g fiber, 130 mg sodium.

SCIENCE SAYS Eating about three eggs a week as a teenager cut odds of breast cancer risk later in life by 18 percent, find Harvard researchers.

DR. JENKINS'S GREEK BEAN STEW*

3 large cloves garlic, minced

2 cups chopped onions

1 green bell pepper, diced

2 tablespoons extra-virgin olive oil

1 (28-ounce) can crushed tomatoes

4 cups white beans (navy, pea, or cannellini), drained and rinsed

2 bay leaves

1 teaspoon dried oregano

Dash hot chile sauce

½ cup pitted black Greek olives, preferably kalamata

In a large pot, sauté garlic, onions, and pepper in oil until soft, about 10 minutes. Add tomatoes, beans, bay leaves, oregano, and chile sauce; simmer, covered, for 30 minutes. Add olives and simmer for 5 minutes.

SERVES 6

PER SERVING: 294 calories, 8.5 g total fat (1 g saturated), 44 g carbohydrate, 13.7 g protein, 9 g fiber, 428 mg sodium

A diet rich in beans can control blood sugar, allowing some diabetics to reduce or discontinue their medication.

SCIENCE SAYS

Adapted, with permission, from a recipe by diabetes researcher David Jenkins, University of Toronto.

why it's good for you:

- Tomatoes, garlic, onions, pepper, and olives contain antioxidants.

- Beans are high in fiber.

- Oregano has antibiotic properties.

GOLDEN LENTIL SOUP WITH MINT PESTO

2 tablespoons olive oil

1 large yellow onion, chopped

1 cup chopped carrots

1 cup chopped celery with leaves

3 cloves garlic, crushed

7½ cups (2 [32-ounce] cartons) fat-free, reduced sodium chicken broth

2 cups dried lentils

2 bay leaves

1 tablespoon plus 1 teaspoon ground cumin

2 tablespoons tomato paste

Salt and pepper

1 cup chopped fresh parsley

2 tablespoons lemon juice

In a large pot, heat oil over medium heat. Sauté onion, carrots, celery, and garlic for about 5 minutes until softened. Add broth, lentils, cumin, bay leaf, tomato paste, salt, and pepper. Bring to a boil. Reduce heat and simmer until lentils are soft (30–40 minutes). Stir in parsley and lemon juice. Simmer for 2 minutes. Serve in bowls topped with a dollop of mint pesto.

MINT PESTO

¼ cup unsalted almonds

1 cup fresh mint

¼ cup freshly grated Parmesan cheese

⅓ cup extra-virgin olive oil

In food processor, pulverize almonds. Add mint and Parmesan, and process. Drizzle in olive oil and process until smooth.

SERVES 8 AS MAIN COURSE

PER SERVING: 360 calories, 16 g total fat (2.6 g saturated), 37 g carbohydrate, 20 g protein, 8 g fiber, 656 mg sodium

SCIENCE SAYS

Eating chunky soup before a meal suppresses appetite, leading to a lower calorie intake during the meal, according to Penn State research.

HOT PEPPER QUESADILLAS

2 large (10-inch) flour tortillas, preferably whole wheat
1½ cups (6 ounces) "light" shredded jalapeño or "Mexican" cheese, such as Sargento Light Mexican
1 cup minced red onions
⅓ cup canned sliced jalapeño peppers, drained
¼ cup oil-cured black olives, pitted and sliced
1 cup shredded fresh spinach

Preheat oven to 425°F. On a pizza pan or cookie sheet, place one tortilla. Sprinkle with half of the cheese, followed by all the onions, jalapeños, olives and spinach. Top with the second tortilla. Sprinkle with remaining cheese. Bake for 8 to 10 minutes, until cheese is melted and browned. Let cool for 5 minutes. Cut into 8 wedges and serve warm. Garnish with salsa, fat-free sour cream, minced onions, chopped cilantro, avocado slices, or guacamole.

MAKES 8 WEDGES

PER WEDGE: 120 calories, 5.7 g total fat (2.5 g saturated), 10 g carbohydrate, 7.8 g protein, 1 g fiber, 342 mg sodium

In tests, Canadians who ate capsaicin-packed hot chile sauce consumed 200 fewer calories a few hours later than did non–hot sauce eaters.

SCIENCE SAYS

"MEATY" PORTOBELLO STEW

12 ounces portobello mushrooms, cut into bite-size pieces

2 tablespoons canola oil

1½ cups canned black bean soup (use smooth, condensed soup; if beans are whole, run through a blender)

1 (14½-ounce) can fat-free, reduced-sodium vegetable broth

1 large baking potato, in chunks

1½ cups carrots, small or cut

2 medium yellow onions, quartered

2 bay leaves

½ teaspoon dried thyme

½ cup red wine (optional)

Salt and freshly ground black pepper

Sauté mushrooms in oil until brown and softened, about 5 minutes; set aside. In a large pot, combine bean soup, broth, potatoes, carrots, onions, and seasonings; simmer until vegetables are done, 20–30 minutes. Add mushrooms and red wine, if using. Heat through. Season with salt and pepper. Serve with brown rice.

SERVES 6

PER SERVING: 147 calories, 5.2 g total fat (0.5 g saturated), 22 g carbohydrate, 4.6 g protein, 4.5 g fiber, 626 mg sodium

SCIENCE SAYS

Beans are rich in folate, which helps prevent blood-clot type strokes, studies show.

MEDITERRANEAN VEGETABLE STEW

2 tablespoons extra-virgin olive oil

1 cup chopped red onions

1 cup coarsely chopped green pepper

2 large cloves garlic, crushed

1 cup sliced white button mushrooms

1 small eggplant (unpeeled), cut into 1–2-inch chunks
(about 12 ounces or 4 cups)

1 (28-ounce) can crushed tomatoes

1 (15-ounce) can chickpeas, drained and rinsed

½ cup kalamata olives, pitted and sliced

1 tablespoon chopped fresh rosemary

1 cup coarsely chopped fresh parsley

⅓ cup crumbled feta cheese (optional)

why it's good for you:

- Onion, pepper, garlic, eggplant, tomatoes, olives, parsley, and rosemary contain antioxidants.

- Olive oil has good fat.

- Chickpeas help suppress blood sugar spikes.

- Plus: white mushrooms have anticancer activity.

In a large skillet, heat 1 tablespoon of the olive oil. Sauté onions and green pepper until softened, stirring occasionally, about 10 minutes. Add the remaining 1 tablespoon olive oil, the garlic, mushrooms, and eggplant. Simmer, stirring occasionally, until eggplant is softened, but not mushy, about 15 minutes. Add tomatoes, chickpeas, olives, and rosemary. Simmer until heated through, about 10 minutes. Turn off heat and stir in parsley. Sprinkle with feta cheese. Serve over brown rice, polenta, or couscous.

SERVES 6

PER SERVING: 191 calories, 9 g total fat (1 g saturated), 24 g carbohydrate, 5.6 g protein, 6 g fiber, 507 mg sodium

Garlic is a natural expectorant and decongestant, good for treating common colds, says Irwin Ziment, MD, pulmonary expert at UCLA.

SCIENCE SAYS

MOROCCAN VEGETABLE DELIGHT

1 cup bulgur wheat

1 cup boiling water

1 medium yellow or red onion, chopped

1 tablespoon extra-virgin olive oil

2 large carrots, sliced into medium rounds

½ cup orange juice

1 (15-ounce) can chickpeas, drained and rinsed

3 tablespoons honey

2½ teaspoons ground cumin

⅓ cup slivered almonds, toasted

¼ cup raisins or currants

Pour bulgur into a small bowl. Add boiling water and set aside to soak for 30 minutes. Sauté onion in olive oil until soft. Simmer or microwave carrots in orange juice until tender. In a bowl, combine all ingredients. Warm in a microwave or serve at room temperature.

SERVES 6

PER SERVING: 316 calories, 8.7 g total fat (0.8 g saturated), 53 g carbohydrate, 10 g protein, 10 g fiber, 159 mg sodium

SCIENCE SAYS

Kids with low blood levels of beta and alpha carotene, found in carrots, and vitamin C, in orange juice, are at higher risk of asthma, studies show.

QUICK TEX-MEX RICE CASSEROLE

2 cups cooked brown rice

1½ cups tomato salsa

1 teaspoon chile powder

1 (15-ounce) can no-salt-added black beans, not drained

1 cup frozen yellow corn kernels

2 ounces reduced-fat sharp cheddar cheese, sliced ¼ inch thick

2 tablespoons sliced black or green olives (optional)

Combine rice, salsa, chile powder, black beans, and corn. Spoon into a 6 × 6-inch, shallow, microwave-safe casserole. Top with cheese slices, then olives. Microwave on high for 12 minutes, until heated through and cheese is melted.

SERVES 4

PER SERVING: 298 calories, 3.8 g total fat (2 g saturated), 51 g carbohydrate, 17 g protein, 8 g fiber, 674 mg sodium

AN EASY

MICROWAVE DISH

why it's good for you:

- Tomatoes and corn contain antioxidants.

- Beans contain fiber.

- Plus: brown rice is a whole grain that has been tied to less chronic disease.

Besides lycopene, tomatoes contain two other antioxidant carotenoids—phytoene and phytofluene—in the jellylike substance surrounding the seeds.

SCIENCE SAYS

SOY SLOPPY JOES

1 cup textured soy protein*
7/8 cup boiling water
1 tablespoon extra-virgin olive oil
1 green bell pepper, cored and diced
1 cup chopped yellow onions
1 cup strained no-salt-added tomatoes (Pomi) or tomato sauce
1 cup chile sauce or barbecue sauce
½ teaspoon chile powder, or more to taste
Salt and freshly ground black pepper

Add textured vegetable protein to boiling water; stir and let sit for 5 minutes or until needed. Heat olive oil a large skillet and sauté green pepper and onions until soft. Stir in tomatoes, chile sauce, textured vegetable protein, and chile powder. Simmer for 5 to 10 minutes or until heated through. Season with salt and pepper. Serve on whole wheat buns or bread.

SERVES 4

> *Textured soy protein, a flaky, dried soy product, is available in health food stores and some supermarkets. It is sometimes called textured vegetable protein (TVP).*

PER SERVING: 217 calories, 5.3 g total fat (0.5 g saturated), 29 g carbohydrate, 9.8 g protein, 5 g fiber, 923 mg sodium

SCIENCE SAYS Two to four servings of soy-protein foods a week are a healthful substitute for animal protein, says Harvard nutritionist Walter Willett.

SPINACH CHICKPEA CURRY

1 tablespoon canola oil
1 tablespoon curry powder
1 cup chopped yellow onion
2 cloves garlic, crushed
1 (10 ounce) package frozen chopped spinach, thawed, drained
1 (8-ounce) can tomato sauce
1 (19-ounce) can chickpeas, drained and rinsed
1 cup fat-free, reduced-sodium vegetable or chicken broth
Salt and freshly ground black pepper
Hot sauce or red pepper flakes (optional)

In a large skillet or saucepan, combine oil, curry powder, onions, and garlic; sauté for about 5 minutes. Add spinach, tomato sauce, and 1 cup of the chickpeas. In a blender, puree remaining chickpeas with broth. Add to vegetables. Simmer until heated through, about 10 minutes. Stir in seasonings. Serve over cooked brown rice or couscous.

SERVES 4

PER SERVING: 183 calories, 6 g total fat (0.4 g saturated), 26 g carbohydrate, 8 g protein, 7 g fiber, 609 mg sodium

Eating spinach three or four times a week reversed very early signs of macular degeneration, a potentially blinding eye disease.

SCIENCE SAYS

SPINACH-MUSHROOM FRITTATA PIE

1 (10-ounce) package frozen chopped spinach, thawed and squeezed dry
4 eggs, or 1 cup egg substitute
1 cup part-skim ricotta cheese
¾ cup freshly grated Parmesan cheese
¾ cup chopped mushrooms (white button, cremini, or portobello)
½ cup finely chopped scallions with some green tops (about 4 large)
¼ teaspoon dried Italian seasonings
Salt and freshly ground black pepper

Preheat oven to 375°F. In a large bowl, whisk together all ingredients until well mixed. Spray a 9-inch pie plate with cooking spray and fill with the spinach mixture. Bake for 30 minutes, or until browned and set. Let cool for 20 minutes; cut into wedges and serve.

SERVES 6

Per serving with eggs: 178 calories, 10 g total fat (5 g saturated), 6 g carbohydrate, 15.5 g protein, 1 g fiber, 358 mg sodium

SCIENCE SAYS Eating egg yolks spiked blood amounts of the antioxidant lutein 300 percent more than did eating lutein-rich spinach, in Tufts University tests.

SWEET POTATO STEW WITH BLACK BEANS

1 medium yellow onion, chopped (about 1 cup)

1 tablespoon chile powder

1 cup orange juice

1 tablespoon honey

Salt

2 large sweet potatoes (about 2 pounds),
    peeled and cut into 1-inch chunks

1 (15-ounce) can black beans, drained and rinsed

2 teaspoons butter, softened

2 teaspoons flour

¼ cup toasted almond slivers (optional)

Put onions, chile powder, orange juice, honey, salt, and sweet potatoes in a large, microwave-safe bowl. Cover and microwave on high power, stirring once, for about 20 minutes, or until potatoes are done but still hold their shape. Add beans. Blend butter and flour in a small bowl, and add to the mixture. Microwave on high for 5 minutes, or until beans are heated through and stew has thickened slightly. Sprinkle with almonds.

SERVES 6

PER SERVING: 212 calories, 2 g total fat (0.9 g saturated), 44 g carbohydrate, 5.2 g protein, 6 g fiber, 156 mg sodium

AN EASY

MICROWAVE DISH

Beans contain anticancer compounds called phytates and protease inhibitors.

SCIENCE SAYS

VEGETARIAN CHILI WITH BLACK BEANS

2 tablespoons extra virgin olive oil

1 cup chopped red onion

5 large cloves garlic, crushed or minced

2 tablespoons chile powder, or more to taste

2 teaspoons ground cumin

2 cups juicy chopped tomatoes, or 1 (14½ ounce) can no-salt-added diced tomatoes

1½ cups cooked black beans with ½ cup liquid, or 1 (15-ounce) can no-salt-added black beans, undrained

1 cup water or red wine

1 cup chopped bell pepper (any color)

1 cup chopped zucchini

1 cup yellow corn kernels

1 cup chopped white or portobello mushrooms

1 cup chopped fresh cilantro, packed

¼ teaspoon cayenne pepper, or more to taste

Salt and fresh ground black pepper

Optional garnishes: reduced-fat cheddar cheese, onion, fat-free sour cream, guacamole, fresh cilantro

Heat oil in medium pot. Add onion, garlic, chile powder, and cumin. Sauté over medium heat until onion is soft, about 5 minutes. Add remaining ingredients (except garnishes) and stir. Bring to a boil, then lower heat and simmer for 20 minutes, or until vegetables are soft. Add more liquid if needed.

Serve alone or over rice (preferably brown). Garnish if desired.

SERVES 6

PER SERVING: 173 calories, 6.3 g total fat (0.8 g saturated),26 g carbohydrate, 7 g protein, 5 g fiber, 55 mg sodium

SCIENCE SAYS

Eating legumes, such as chickpeas, lentils, and other dried beans, helps suppress blood sugar spikes, reducing the risk of diabetes and macular degeneration, find Tufts researchers.

VEGETARIAN SHEPHERD'S PIE

2 tablespoons extra-virgin olive oil

1 large yellow onion, coarsely chopped

4 cloves garlic, crushed

2 tablespoons curry powder

2 teaspoons ground cumin

1 small red pepper, coarsely chopped

1 small green pepper, coarsely chopped

1 medium eggplant, cubed, unpeeled (about 3 cups)

1 (15-ounce) can diced tomatoes with garlic

½ cup water, more if needed

10 small red potatoes, halved

½ cup fat-free half-and-half or milk

1 cup frozen or fresh peas

½ cup grated Parmesan cheese

Salt and freshly ground pepper

In a large skillet on medium heat, heat 1 tablespoon olive oil; add onion, garlic, curry powder, and cumin. Sauté until onions are soft, 5 minutes. Transfer to bowl.

Heat remaining olive oil in skillet; add peppers, eggplant, tomatoes, and ½ cup water. Sauté, stirring regularly, until vegetables are soft, about 20 minutes. Add more water if needed. Combine vegetables with onion and place in a shallow 8 × 8-inch baking dish.

Preheat oven to 400°F. In a saucepan, boil potatoes until done. Drain and smash. Stir in half and half, peas, salt and pepper, Spread potato mixture over vegetables and top with Parmesan and pepper. Bake for 15 minutes, uncovered. Brown in broiler. Serve.

SERVES 6

PER SERVING: 193 calories, 8 g total fat (2 g saturated), 22 g carbohydrate, 9 g protein, 7 g fiber, 390 mg sodium

Sticking close to a Mediterranean-style diet, rich in olive oil, vegetables, fruits, and whole grains, and low in meat, can cut your odds of developing Alzheimer's disease by 68 percent, concludes Columbia University research.

SCIENCE SAYS

Pizza, Pasta, and Grains

THE FOLLOWING RECIPES will help you to put the whole back into the grain. They'll also show you interesting ways to reduce the blood sugar impact of foods made from grain and flour.

BULGUR WITH ORANGES

1 cup raw bulgur wheat, cooked and drained

1½ cups coarsely chopped cabbage

¾ cup sliced scallions with green tops

½ cup chopped walnuts

1 large orange, cut into chunks with ½ cup orange juice, or 1 (11-ounce) can undrained mandarin oranges

2 tablespoons white vinegar

¼ teaspoon salt or to taste

Combine all ingredients in a large bowl. Chill several hours before serving.

SERVES 6

PER SERVING: 176 calories, 6.6 g total fat (0.6 g saturated), 27 g carbohydrate, 5 g protein, 6.7 g fiber, 105 mg sodium

why it's good for you:

- Bulgur wheat is high in fiber.

- Cabbage, onions, and oranges contain antioxidants.

- Walnuts provide good fat.

- Low in calories and saturated fat.

Eating bulgur and other whole grains can lower risk of colon and stomach cancer by as much as 50 percent, according to Italian researchers.

SCIENCE SAYS

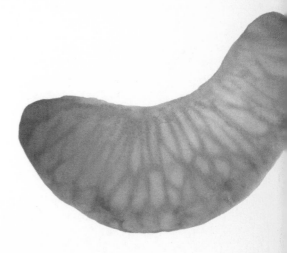

CRUNCHY TABBOULEH

1 cup raw bulgur wheat, cooked and drained
3 large tomatoes, diced
1 large cucumber, peeled and diced
1 large green bell pepper, diced
4 spring onions, sliced thinly
¼ cup fresh mint leaves, shredded
⅓ cup fresh lemon juice
2 tablespoons extra-virgin olive oil
Salt and freshly ground black pepper

Thoroughly combine all ingredients in a large bowl. Chill for several hours before serving.

SERVES 6

PER SERVING: 102 calories, 3.5 g total fat, (0.4 g saturated), 17 g carbohydrate, 2.6 g protein, 5.3 g fiber, 12 mg sodium

SCIENCE SAYS

Eating whole grains, such as bulgur wheat, cuts your risk of developing diabetes by 20 percent, finds University of Minnesota research.

FRUITY COUSCOUS SALAD

4 cups cooked couscous (1⅓ cups dry)*
⅔ cup slivered almonds
½ cup packed dried apricots, chopped
**⅔ cup Craisins or raisins, microwaved with ⅓ cup water for 1 to 2
    minutes to soften (discard any excess water)**
1 teaspoon ground cumin
3 scallions, thinly sliced with green tops
Salt and freshly ground black pepper

Prepare couscous according to package directions. Combine all ingredients, toss. Serve at room temperature or chilled.

SERVES 8

PER SERVING: 255 calories, 6 g total fat (0 g saturated), 45 g carbohydrate, 7 g protein, 0 mg cholesterol, 3.4 g fiber, 7 mg sodium

Using part or all orange juice instead of water or broth to cook couscous gives added flavor and nutrients.

People who ate at least three servings of fruit a day were less apt to develop shingles than were those who ate fruit less than once a week, finds British research.

SCIENCE SAYS

FETTUCCINE WITH FRESH TOMATO-BASIL SAUCE

5 medium, ripe tomatoes (1½ pounds), diced
1 medium red onion, chopped
1 clove garlic, crushed
¾ cup shredded fresh basil
1 cup chopped fresh parsley
⅓ cup coarsely crumbled feta cheese
3 tablespoons extra-virgin olive oil
2 teaspoons balsamic vinegar
Salt and freshly ground black pepper
1 pound dry fettuccine
¼ cup chopped black olives, preferably oil-cured (optional)

In a large bowl, combine tomatoes, onions, garlic, basil, parsley, cheese, oil, vinegar, salt, and pepper. In a large pot of boiling water, cook fettuccine until al dente. Drain pasta and combine with tomato mixture. Top with olives. Serve chilled or at room temperature.

SERVES 8

PER SERVING: 311 calories, 8.5 g total fat (2.4 g saturated), 49 g carbohydrate, 10 g protein, 3.2 g fiber, 129 mg sodium

SCIENCE SAYS
In studies of elderly Catholic nuns, those with the highest blood levels of lycopene (from eating tomatoes) had a lower risk of dementia.

LASAGNE WITH GREENS AND ONIONS

5 cloves garlic, crushed

2 cups chopped yellow onions

1 tablespoon extra-virgin olive oil

16 ounces frozen chopped kale, collard greens, or spinach

3 eggs, or ¾ cup egg substitute

32 ounces fat-free cottage cheese

1 teaspoon dried basil

1 teaspoon dried oregano

4 cups tomato pasta sauce, homemade or canned, low sodium, such as
   Classico Sweet Basil Marinara

9 lasagna noodles, cooked, or use no-boil lasagna noodles

1 cup freshly grated Parmesan cheese

Preheat oven to 350°F. Sauté garlic and onions in olive oil until soft, about 3 minutes. Cook greens as directed on package; cool. Squeeze out excess water with hands. If using whole eggs, whip lightly with a fork. In a bowl, combine eggs, cottage cheese, herbs, garlic, onions, and greens. Spread a thin layer of pasta sauce on bottom of a 9 × 13-inch baking dish. Lay 3 noodles in baking dish; top with half the kale mixture, followed by 3 more noodles, the remaining kale mixture, finishing with the last 3 noodles. Pour sauce on top; sprinkle with Parmesan. Bake, uncovered, for 45 minutes.

SERVES 8

PER SERVING: 392 calories, 9.6 g total fat (3 g saturated), 47 g carbohydrate, 29 g protein, 4.5 g fiber, 984 mg sodium

---

A daily fare of kale (lutein), tomato juice (lycopene) and sweet potatoes (beta carotene) boosted ability of immune responses to fight off viruses, in USDA test subjects.

SCIENCE SAYS

MACARONI-SALMON SALAD WITH CURRY DRESSING

1 (8-ounce) salmon fillet, skin removed, or 7½-ounce can red salmon

1 cup dry pasta, such as macaroni or small shells

½ cup minced red or yellow onion

1 cup diced celery

1 medium-to-large apple, such as Gala, diced

½ cup chopped walnuts or dry-roasted unsalted peanuts

Freshly ground black pepper

CURRY DRESSING

1 (6-ounce) carton (¾ cup) fat-free plain yogurt

2 tablespoons extra-virgin olive oil

1 tablespoon curry powder

2 teaspoons fresh lemon juice

2 cloves garlic, crushed

1 teaspoon Dijon mustard

½ teaspoon salt, or to taste

Poach or bake salmon, and cut into chunks. Cook pasta according to package directions; drain. In a large bowl, combine salmon and other salad ingredients. In small bowl, combine dressing ingredients. Pour dressing over salad and toss. Refrigerate or serve at room temperature.

SERVES 8

PER SERVING: 213 calories, 11 g total fat (1 g saturated), 18 g carbohydrate, 12 g protein, 2 g fiber, 208 mg sodium

NOTE: *You can also use this curry dressing for fish or salads. It is so good, you can eat it by the spoonful.*

SCIENCE SAYS

Celery contains an aromatic chemical—3-n-butyl phthalide—that lowered blood pressure in animals in doses comparable to their eating four stalks of celery daily, reports University of Chicago research.

GRANDMA'S TUNA-MACARONI SALAD

8 ounces dry macaroni, cooked and drained
1 (6-ounce) can light tuna in water, drained
⅔ cup sliced celery
3 scallions, with green, sliced
1½ tablespoons extra-virgin olive oil
1 tablespoon lemon juice
1 tablespoon balsamic vinegar
¼ cup capers, drained (optional)
Salt and pepper

Combine all ingredients in a bowl.

SERVES 4

PER SERVING: 318 calories, 6 g total fat (1 g saturated), 45 g carbohydrate, 19 g protein, 2 g fiber, 539 mg sodium

why it's good for you:

- Tuna contains omega-3 fat.

- Tuna is high in the mineral selenium.

- Scallions and celery contain antioxidants.

- Olive oil offers good fat.

Eating 2 ounces of fish a day cut heart attacks in elderly Japanese by 30 percent; 4 ounces a day, by 40 percent; and 6 ounces a day, by 65 percent.

SCIENCE SAYS

PASTA WITH QUICK ONION-PEPPER SAUCE

2 tablespoons extra-virgin olive oil

4 large cloves garlic, sliced thinly

½ cup coarsely chopped walnuts

10 cherry tomatoes, halved

2 medium bell peppers (green, red and/or yellow), cored and cut length-wise into ½-inch-long strips

1½ medium yellow onions, sliced thinly

1½ cups coarsely chopped fresh parsley

Freshly ground black pepper

3 cups cooked rotelle or other curly pasta (about 6 ounces dry)

Heat olive oil in large skillet over medium heat, add walnuts and garlic, and sauté about 3 minutes. Add tomatoes; cook until soft, about 5 minutes. Put peppers and onions in large, microwave-safe bowl; cover. Microwave on high until tender. Transfer peppers and onions to skillet and add parsley; stir to combine thoroughly. Put pasta in large shallow bowl and toss with onion-pepper sauce.

SERVES 4

PER SERVING: 367 calories, 17 g total fat (1.9 g saturated), 46 g carbohydrate, 9.6 g protein, 4.7 g fiber, 19 mg sodium

SCIENCE SAYS Your body absorbs two and a half times more antioxidant lycopene from cooked tomatoes as from raw tomatoes. Adding oil also improves absorption of lycopene.

PASTA WITH VEGETABLES AND CHICKPEAS

2 tablespoons extra-virgin olive oil

2 large cloves garlic, crushed

4 ounces ground turkey breast

1 (10-ounce) package frozen spinach, thawed, drained and squeezed dry

1 (8-ounce) can chickpeas, drained and rinsed

2 (14½-ounce) cans diced no-salt-added tomatoes

½ cup feta cheese (about 3 ounces), cubed or crumbled

1½ teaspoons fennel seeds

1 teaspoon dried oregano

¼ teaspoon hot pepper flakes, or to taste

Salt and freshly ground black pepper

8 ounces dry pasta, such as fettuccine or penne, cooked until al dente

In a large skillet, heat olive oil and sauté garlic for 30 seconds. Add turkey and sauté until slightly browned, about 4 minutes. Add spinach, beans, tomatoes, cheese, fennel, oregano, and pepper flakes, and simmer covered until heated through, about 10 minutes. Season with salt and pepper. Serve over cooked pasta.

SERVES 6

PER SERVING: 307 calories, 9.5 g total fat (2.9 g saturated), 41 g carbohydrate, 15.6 g protein, 4.2 g fiber, 264 mg sodium

Men who ate ten or more servings of tomatoes per week (raw tomatoes, tomato sauce, tomato juice, and pizza) cut odds of prostate cancer by 35 percent, reported Harvard research.

SCIENCE SAYS

PASTA SALAD WITH BEANS AND SMOKED SALMON

8 ounces corkscrew pasta

4 ounces smoked salmon (nova, not lox), cut into julienne strips

1 (16-ounce) can chickpeas, drained and rinsed

½ cup minced red onion

3 tablespoons capers, drained and rinsed

3 tablespoons chopped black olives, preferably oil-cured

1 cup finely chopped fresh parsley

DRESSING

¼ cup extra-virgin olive oil

2 cloves garlic, minced

2 tablespoons fresh lemon juice

Freshly ground black pepper

Whisk together the dressing ingredients. In a large saucepan of boiling water, cook pasta until al dente, drain, and put in a bowl. Add dressing and all other ingredients; toss. Serve at room temperature.

SERVES 6

PER SERVING: 320 calories, 13.5 g total fat (1.8 g saturated, 8.3 g monounsaturated), 39 g carbohydrate, 11.6 g protein, 3.6 g fiber, 498 mg sodium

SCIENCE SAYS   Black olives contain more antioxidants than green olives do.

PEPPER, ONION, AND FETA PIZZA

3 cups chopped mixed bell peppers, (red, green, yellow, and/or orange)

1 cup sliced yellow or red onions, separated into rings

3 cloves garlic, crushed

1½ teaspoons dried Italian herbs

Salt

¼ teaspoon dried red pepper flakes, (optional)

2 tablespoons extra-virgin olive oil

¾ cup crumbled herbed feta cheese

1 (12-inch) thin pizza crust, homemade or prepared (such as Boboli)

Preheat oven to 450°F. In a bowl, combine peppers, onions, garlic, seasoning and olive oil. Place crust on large pizza pan. Top with vegetable mixture. Sprinkle with cheese. Bake for 10 to 12 minutes. Cut into 6 slices.

PER SLICE: 258 calories, 11.6 g total fat (4 g saturated), 30 g carbohydrate, 8 g protein, 2 g fiber, 488 mg sodium

why it's good for you:

- Peppers, onion, garlic, and herbs contain super antioxidants.

- Plus: vegetables help lower blood pressure.

Garlic and other vegetables have diuretic properties that may help reduce high blood pressure, according to several studies.

SCIENCE SAYS

PICNIC RICE SALAD

4 cups cooked brown rice

1 (2½-ounce) can sliced black olives, drained

6 scallions, thinly sliced, including 3 inches green tops

1 cup cooked green peas

2 large tomatoes, chopped (unpeeled)

¼ cup shredded basil leaves

⅓ cup shelled salted sunflower seeds

¼ cup extra-virgin olive oil

1½ tablespoons balsamic vinegar

Salt and freshly ground black pepper

In a large bowl, combine rice, olives, vegetables, basil, and sunflower seeds. In a small bowl, whisk together oil, vinegar, salt, and pepper. Add to rice mixture and toss.

SERVES 6

PER SERVING: 293 calories, 15 g total fat (2 g saturated), 35 g carbohydrate, 6.3 g protein, 5 g fiber, 170 mg sodium

SCIENCE SAYS

In Harvard research, eating two and a half servings of whole grains daily, such as brown rice, slashed women's risk of heart disease by one-third to one-half.

PIZZA WITH MUSHROOM "SAUSAGE"

MUSHROOM "SAUSAGE"

3 cups chopped portobello mushrooms
2 tablespoons extra-virgin olive oil
3 cloves garlic, crushed
2 teaspoons fennel seed
1½ teaspoons dried Italian herbs
¾ teaspoon dried red pepper flakes
Salt and freshly ground black pepper

Combine all ingredients and set aside for 10–15 minutes to absorb flavors.

PIZZA

1 (12-inch) thin pizza crust, homemade or prepared (such as Boboli)
1 (8-ounce) can no-salt-added tomato sauce
1½ cups chopped green bell pepper
1½ cups chopped red onion
¾ cup shredded part-skim mozzarella cheese

Preheat oven to 450°F. Place crust on large pizza pan. Top with sauce, mushroom "sausage" mixture, green peppers, onions, and cheese. Bake for 10 to 12 minutes. Cut into 6 slices.

PER SLICE: 329 calories, 11.4 g total fat (3.4 g saturated), 45 g carbohydrate, 14 g protein, 4 g fiber, 482 mg sodium

Unique chemicals in mushrooms may boost immunity, helping fend off infections and even cancer, studies show. **SCIENCE SAYS**

SPAGHETTI WITH ROASTED RED PEPPERS, PARSLEY, AND WALNUTS

½ pound spaghetti or fettuccine

1 (7-ounce) jar roasted red peppers, drained and coarsely chopped, or 1 cup chopped, juicy, ripe tomatoes

2 cups chopped fresh parsley

¾ cup walnut pieces

3 tablespoons extra-virgin olive oil

1 clove garlic, crushed

Salt and freshly ground pepper

In a large pot of boiling water, cook pasta until al dente. While pasta is cooking, toss together red peppers, parsley, and walnuts. Combine cooked pasta with olive oil and garlic. Add parsley mixture, salt, and pepper, and toss again. Serve immediately at room temperature, or chilled.

SERVES 6

PER SERVING: 312 calories, 17 g total fat (1.9 g saturated), 35 g carbohydrate, 7.4 g protein, 3 g fiber, 55 mg sodium

SCIENCE SAYS Red peppers contain twice as much vitamin C and nine times more vitamin A than do green peppers.

SPAGHETTI AND TOFU IN SPICY PEANUT SAUCE

4 cups cooked whole-grain thin spaghetti, drained and rinsed

1 cup carrots, cut into matchsticks

8 ounces firm tofu, cubed

⅓ cup thinly sliced green onions

¼ cup chopped unsalted dry-roasted peanuts

SPICY PEANUT SAUCE

⅓ cup smooth peanut butter, preferably natural

⅓ cup fat-free, reduced-sodium chicken broth

1 tablespoon reduced-sodium soy sauce

1 tablespoon grated fresh ginger

1 teaspoon hot red pepper flakes

1 clove garlic, minced

1½ tablespoons orange marmalade

In a large bowl, combine Spicy Peanut Sauce ingredients. Add spaghetti, carrots, and tofu. Toss to coat with sauce. Sprinkle with green onions and peanuts.

SERVES 6

PER SERVING: 282 calories, 11 g total fat (2 g saturated), 35 g carbohydrate, 15 g protein, 5.9 g fiber, 217 mg sodium

why it's good for you:

- Carrots contain antioxidants.
- Tofu helps lower cholesterol.
- Ginger helps reduce blood clots.
- Whole grains discourage heart disease.
- Plus: peanut butter dampens blood sugar and appetite.

All onions and onion relatives (garlic, leeks, chives, and scallions) are rich in organosulfur compounds shown to help prevent cancer in lab animals.

SCIENCE SAYS

WILD RICE PILAF WITH WALNUTS AND CRANBERRIES

1 tablespoon extra-virgin olive oil
½ cup chopped onion
½ cup chopped celery
2½ cups no-fat, reduced-sodium chicken broth
1 cup uncooked wild rice
½ cup chopped walnuts
½ cup dried cranberries

In a medium saucepan, heat olive oil; sauté onion and celery until softened, about 5 minutes. Add broth and wild rice; bring to a boil. Reduce heat and cook at a rapid simmer for 50 to 60 minutes, or until rice is tender and liquid absorbed. Add walnuts and cranberries. Toss and serve warm. Or make ahead and reheat in microwave.

SERVES 9

PER SERVING: 148 calories, 6 g fat (0.6 g saturated), 5 g protein, 21 g carbohydrate, 2 g fiber, 166 mg sodium

SCIENCE SAYS Eating lots of magnesium in whole grains (such as wild rice), nuts, avocados and spinach, may help ward off prediabetes according to Northwestern University research.

ZITI SPINACH ALFREDO

8 ounces dry ziti or penne pasta
1 medium onion, chopped
2 large cloves garlic, crushed
1 tablespoon extra-virgin olive oil
2 tablespoons butter
3 tablespoons all-purpose flour
2½ cups fat-free half-and-half
1 cup grated Parmesan cheese
2 teaspoons dried Italian seasoning
Salt and freshly ground black pepper
1 (14½-ounce) can diced tomatoes with Italian herbs
1 (10-ounce) package frozen chopped spinach, thawed and drained

In a large pot of boiling water, cook pasta until al dente. In a small saucepan, sauté onions and garlic in olive oil until soft. In a large saucepan, melt butter; add flour and stir. Slowly add half-and-half and simmer, stirring constantly, until thickened. Add cheese and seasonings; stir until cheese melts. Add tomatoes, spinach, and onion mixture; heat through. Pour over warm pasta, toss, and serve.

SERVES 8

PER SERVING: 281 calories, 8 g total fat (4 g saturated), 38 g carbohydrate, 11 g protein, 2 g fiber, 436 mg sodium

Eating tomatoes may lower risk of prostate, lung, stomach, pancreatic, colorectal, esophageal, oral, breast, and cervical tumors.

SCIENCE SAYS

Seafood

YOU'LL FIND LOTS of salmon recipes in this section for good reason. Naturally high in the health-promoting omega-3 fats but lacking any significant amounts of contaminants such as mercury, salmon is one of the healthiest ocean foods you can eat. It's easy to make, too. You'll even find one recipe that will teach you how to cook it in the microwave. Now that's what I call *fast* food. In addition to salmon, you'll find plenty of other delicious and healthy fish and shellfish recipes in this section, including recipes for shrimp, scallops, and tuna.

ASIAN FISH WITH VEGETABLES

4 cups shredded savoy cabbage
1 medium red bell pepper, cut into slivers
6 scallions with green tops, sliced
2 (4-ounce) halibut or mahimahi fillets

SAUCE

2 large cloves garlic, crushed
⅓ cup dry-roasted unsalted peanuts, crushed in blender
2 tablespoons grated fresh ginger
⅓ cup water
1 teaspoon cornstarch
2 tablespoons reduced-sodium soy sauce
1 teaspoon sesame oil
1 tablespoon rice vinegar
1 tablespoon mirin (sweetened rice wine)

GARNISH

¼ cup chopped fresh cilantro or parsley
1 lime

Spread vegetables over bottom of shallow, microwave-safe dish. Top with fish. In a small bowl, combine sauce ingredients; pour over all. Cover tightly with microwave plastic wrap and microwave on high for 8 to 10 minutes. Vegetables will be crisp-tender. Place each fillet on a plate; spoon vegetables and sauce around fish. Garnish with cilantro and a squeeze of lime juice. Serve with brown rice.

Serves 2

PER SERVING (WITHOUT RICE): 375 calories, 15 g total fat (2 g saturated), 30 g carbohydrate, 32 g protein, 3.9 g fiber, 726 mg sodium

AN EASY
MICROWAVE DISH

People who ate fish or other seafood at least once a week were 34 percent less apt to develop Alzheimer's disease or other forms of dementia, says a French study.

SCIENCE SAYS

BAKED SALMON WITH COCONUT CRUST

4 (4-ounce) salmon fillets, skin removed
1 tablespoon lime or lemon juice
½ cup panko (Japanese breadcrumbs*)
¼ cup flaked sweetened coconut
Salt and freshly ground pepper
Cooking spray

Preheat oven to 425°F. Place salmon on a nonstick baking pan. Brush juice on salmon. In a shallow dish, combine coconut, panko, salt and pepper. Dredge each fillet in the mixture and return to baking pan. Spread leftover crumbs on top of fillets. Coat with cooking spray. Bake for 12 to 15 minutes. If desired, put under broiler for 30 seconds, or until crust is golden brown.

SERVES 4

PER SERVING: 272 calories, 16 g total fat (4 g saturated), 7 g carbohydrates, 24 g protein, 67 mg cholesterol, 0 g fiber, 101 mg sodium

Available in specialty markets or the ethnic section of supermarkets.

SCIENCE SAYS

Eating high-omega-3 fish, such as salmon, once a week or more cut chances of kidney cancer by an astonishing 74 percent over a 10-year period, reported Swedish researchers.

CHILLED SALMON WITH SUMMER TOMATO SALSA

4 (4-ounce) salmon fillets, skin removed
2 cups water

SUMMER TOMATO SALSA

1 cup chopped fresh tomato
½ ripe Hass avocado, chopped
1 clove garlic, crushed
1 tablespoon balsamic vinegar
1 teaspoon extra-virgin olive oil
½ cup cooked corn kernels
¼ cup minced red onions
¼ cup chopped fresh cilantro, plus sprigs for garnish
Salt and freshly ground black pepper
1 lime, cut into wedges

Place salmon in a shallow, microwave-safe bowl. Add water. Cover and microwave on high for 7 to 9 minutes, or until salmon is cooked as desired. Remove from water; refrigerate until cool. In a small bowl, combine all tomato salsa ingredients except lime. Refrigerate for 30 minutes. Serve salmon surrounded by salsa and lime wedges. Garnish with cilantro sprigs.

SERVES 4

PER SERVING: 275 calories, 16 g total fat (3 g saturated), 10 g carbohydrate, 22 g protein, 2 g fiber, 72 mg sodium

why it's good for you:

- Salmon is high in omega-3 fat.
- Tomato, avocado, corn, onions, and cilantro contain antioxidants.
- Avocado reduces inflammation.

Women with the highest omega-3 fish oil in breast tissue were about 70 percent less apt to have breast cancer than were women with the least omega-3.

SCIENCE SAYS

ELEGANT SHRIMP CASSOULET

3 cloves garlic, peeled and sliced thinly
1 cup chopped yellow onion
1 medium green bell pepper, chopped
1 tablespoon extra-virgin olive oil
2 (19-ounce) cans cannellini beans, drained and rinsed
1 (14½-ounce) can diced tomatoes
1 cup fat-free, reduced-sodium chicken or vegetable broth
½ teaspoon dried basil
½ teaspoon dried thyme
½ cup kalamata olives, pitted and halved
¾ pound large shrimp (raw or cooked), shelled, deveined, and halved
½ cup dry bread crumbs
¼ cup freshly grated Parmesan cheese
Salt and freshly ground black pepper

Preheat oven to 400°F. In large pan, sauté garlic, onion, and green pepper in oil over medium heat until soft, about 5 minutes. Add beans, tomatoes, broth, herbs, olives, salt, and pepper. Bring to simmer. Add shrimp; cook 3 minutes. Turn into large baking dish. Top with bread crumbs mixed with Parmesan. Bake until bubbly, about 20 minutes. Brown top under broiler if desired.

SERVES 8

PER SERVING: 239 calories, 6.7 g total fat (1.3 g saturated), 26 g carbohydrate, 18 g protein, 6.5 g fiber, 580 mg sodium

SCIENCE SAYS

Men who eat the most garlic, onions, and leeks—all members of the allium family—are much less apt to develop prostate cancer than are non-allium eaters.

FIESTA SEAFOOD CASSEROLE

2 tablespoons extra-virgin olive oil

4 large cloves garlic, crushed or minced

1 medium onion, chopped

1 medium green pepper, diced

2 (14½-ounce) cans diced no-salt-added tomatoes

1 tablespoon chopped fresh thyme, or 1 teaspoon dried thyme

16 ounces (2 cups) bottled clam juice or dry white wine

2 cups instant brown rice

1½ cups diced smoked turkey

12 uncooked jumbo shrimp, shelled and deveined, tails on (about 12 ounces)

8 ounces sea scallops, preferably dry pack, each cut in half horizontally

1 (10-ounce) package frozen peas

Salt and freshly ground black pepper

12 mussels in shells

2 canned roasted peppers, cut into strips about 5 inches long x 1 inch wide

why it's good for you:

- Garlic, onions, peppers, tomatoes, peas, and herbs contain antioxidants.

- High in low-fat, nonmeat protein.

- Shellfish lowers cholesterol.

- Plus: vegetables lower blood pressure and help prevent cancer.

Preheat oven to 350°F. In a large skillet, heat olive oil; sauté garlic, onion, and pepper until soft. Transfer to large shallow round or rectangular casserole. Stir in tomatoes, rice, turkey, scallops, shrimp, peas, salt, and pepper. Top with mussels (push mussels down into mixture slightly with tops protruding) and strips of roasted pepper. Bake for 30 minutes.

SERVES 7

PER SERVING: 320 calories, 7.6 g total fat (1.2 g saturated), 39 g carbohydrate, 27 g protein, 4.2 g fiber, 709 mg sodium

Eating a Mediterranean diet rich in seafood, fruits, vegetables, legumes, grains, and olive oil, and low in meat, resulted in 72 percent fewer heart attacks and 60 percent fewer deaths among French heart patients than did eating a standard low-fat diet.

SCIENCE SAYS

GINGERY FISH KABOBS WITH PINEAPPLE

1 tablespoon cornstarch

2 cups pineapple juice, preferably fresh

2 tablespoons reduced-sodium soy sauce

1½ tablespoons white vinegar

2 cloves garlic, crushed

3 tablespoons minced fresh ginger

1¼ pounds firm fish, such as salmon fillet, tuna steak, or halibut, cut into chunks*

4 cups fresh pineapple cut into large chunks, or canned unsweetened pineapple chunks

1 large onion, cut in wedges

In a small saucepan, dissolve cornstarch in pineapple juice. Add soy sauce, vinegar, garlic, and ginger, and simmer until slightly thickened, about 7 minutes. Let cool. Combine fish, pineapple chunks, and pineapple juice mixture in a shallow dish. Cover and marinate in the refrigerator for ½ hour. Thread fish, pineapple and onion onto skewers. Place skewers on a hot grill or under a broiler until fish has reached desired doneness. Serve with rice. If you like, bring the marinade to a boil and use as a sauce over fish and rice.

For variety, use more than one type fish.

SERVES 6

PER SERVING: 279 calories, 10.7 g total fat (2 g saturated), 25 g carbohydrate, 20 g protein, 1.3 g fiber, 250 mg sodium

---

SCIENCE SAYS

Eating fish only once a month reduces a man's chances of suffering as ischemic (blocked blood vessels) stroke, says a Harvard study.

GRILLED SALMON WITH ORANGE GLAZE

½ cup orange marmalade

2 teaspoons sesame oil

2 teaspoons reduced-sodium soy sauce

½ teaspoon grated fresh ginger

1 clove garlic, crushed

3 tablespoons rice vinegar or other white vinegar

1 pound boneless, skinless salmon fillet, cut into four pieces

6 thinly sliced scallions with some green (optional)

¼ cup toasted sesame seeds (optional)

Combine marmalade, oil, soy sauce, ginger, garlic, and vinegar. Heat grill. Brush orange glaze on each side of salmon and grill for about 5 minutes on each side. Top with scallions and sesame seeds before serving.

SERVES 4

PER SERVING: 226 calories, 8 g total fat (1.3 g saturated), 15 g carbohydrate, 23 g protein, 0.2 g fiber, 140 mg sodium

Eating fatty fish, such as salmon, could prevent an astounding 80 percent of sudden deaths from heart attacks, say Harvard investigators.

SCIENCE SAYS

MICROWAVE SALMON TERIYAKI

AN EASY

MICROWAVE DISH

¾ pound salmon fillet

2 heaping tablespoons frozen orange juice concentrate

2 cloves garlic, crushed or minced

1 teaspoon finely minced fresh ginger

2 tablespoons reduced-sodium soy sauce

3 scallions, sliced thinly, including 3 inches of green tops

2 tablespoons toasted sesame seeds

Place salmon fillet, skinside down, in a microwave-safe dish. Combine orange juice, garlic, ginger, and soy sauce; pour over fish. Microwave, covered, on high for 7 minutes. Test for doneness; cook longer if needed. Serve on platter or plates, covered with sauce and sprinkled with scallions and sesame seeds.

SERVES 2

PER SERVING: 351 calories, 14.7 g total fat (2.2 g saturated), 16.6 g carbohydrate, 37 g protein, 1 g fiber, 683 mg sodium

SCIENCE SAYS Eating the omega-3 fat in fish helps protect your skin from sunburn, find British researchers.

OLD-FASHIONED SALMON PATTIES

1 (14- or 15-ounce) can pink or red salmon*
8 low-fat or fat-free saltine crackers, crushed
2 beaten eggs, or ½ cup egg substitute
Ground black pepper (use cracked pepper for more bite)

Drain salmon; remove and discard skin. Mash salmon. Combine with crackers and eggs. Form into four patties; sprinkle with pepper. In a nonstick pan coated with canola oil, sauté over medium heat until patties are browned, 2–3 minutes per side. Serve with lime or lemon wedges. Or try this quick sauce: Combine ½ cup fat-free plain yogurt, 1 tablespoon prepared horseradish, and a dash of lemon juice.

*Pink and red salmon have equal amounts of beneficial omega-3 oils.

SERVES 4

SALMON PER PATTY: 190 calories, 7.7 g total fat (1.9 g saturated), 5 g carbohydrate, 24 g protein, 0.2 g fiber, 208 mg sodium

SAUCE PER TABLESPOON: 9 calories, 0 g total fat, 1 g carbohydrate, 0.9 g protein, 0 g fiber, 13 mg sodium

---

Omega-3 fats in fish act as a drug to suppress potentially fatal arrhythmias (irregular heart beats).

SCIENCE SAYS

---

why it's good for you:

- Salmon is a good source of omega-3 fat.
- Eggs are high in choline and lutein.

PECAN-CRUSTED BAKED SALMON

1 tablespoon Dijon mustard
1 tablespoon fat-free plain yogurt or extra-virgin olive oil
¾ pound salmon fillet or steak
¼ cup ground pecans
Freshly ground black pepper

Preheat oven to 450°F. Combine mustard and yogurt. Spread mustard mixture on top of salmon, then cover with pecans and pepper. Place on a baking pan sprayed with olive or canola oil. Bake for 12 to 15 minutes, or until fish flakes easily.

SERVES 2

PER SERVING: 404 calories, 26.2 g total fat (4.2 g saturated, 11.8 g monounsaturated), 2 g carbohydrate, 35 g protein, 1 g fiber, 368 mg sodium

SCIENCE SAYS   Yogurt helps suppress blood sugar, and may help lower risk of colon cancer.

PEPPER SALMON WITH TROPICAL FRUIT SALSA

8 (6-ounce) salmon steaks

2 teaspoons cracked black pepper (do not substitute regular black pepper)

Olive oil or canola spray

Salt

Press ¼ teaspoon cracked pepper into each side of steaks and spray with olive oil. Grill for 4 to 5 minutes on each side. Season with salt, if desired. Serve each steak with ¼ cup Tropical Fruit Salsa.

SERVES 8

PER STEAK: 254 calories, 12 g total fat (1.8 g saturated), 7 g carbohydrate, 33 g protein, 0.3 g fiber, 80 mg sodium

TROPICAL FRUIT SALSA

1 cup diced fresh pineapple

2 tablespoons fresh lemon juice

1 medium banana, diced

1 tablespoon apricot jam or orange marmalade

⅓ cup minced red onion

¼ teaspoon hot pepper flakes

2 tablespoons coconut flakes (optional)

Combine ingredients in a small bowl.

MAKES ABOUT 2 CUPS

PER ¼ CUP SERVING: 32 calories, 0.1 g total fat, 8 g carbohydrate, 0.3 g protein, 6 g fiber, 2 mg sodium

Omega-3 oils in fatty fish (salmon, tuna, sardines) may combat osteoarthritis by blunting inflammation and breakdown of cartilage, suggests a Welsh study.

SCIENCE SAYS

SALMON AND MASHED POTATO CASSEROLE

2 cups frozen mashed potatoes, made with fat-free milk
1 (6-ounce) can red or pink salmon, skin removed, flesh flaked
¾ cup fresh or frozen corn kernels
2 ounces canned chopped green chiles, drained
2 scallions, chopped
Salt and freshly ground pepper
½ cup shredded low-fat sharp cheddar cheese

Preheat oven to 400°F. With a fork, gently combine mashed potatoes, salmon, corn, chiles, and onions. Season with salt and pepper. Spray a pie pan with olive or canola oil. Spread potato mixture in pan. Sprinkle on cheese. Bake for 15 to 20 minutes. If desired, put under broiler until top is slightly browned.

SERVES 4

PER SERVING: 224 calories, 3.2 g total fat (0.8 g saturated), 30 g carbohydrate, 16 g protein, 3.5 g fiber, 501 mg sodium

SCIENCE SAYS Salmon, both wild and farmed, is high in good omega-3 fatty acids and very low in levels of methyl mercury, a potential toxin.

SALMON BOMBAY WITH BANANA RAITA

1 pound salmon fillet, skin removed
1 tablespoon lime juice
Cooking spray

SPICE MIXTURE

½ teaspoon ground ginger
½ teaspoon ground coriander
¼ teaspoon ground cumin
⅛ teaspoon ground cinnamon
⅛ teaspoon cayenne pepper, or to taste
Salt

GARNISH

½ cup chopped cilantro or parsley

Preheat oven to 425°F. Place salmon in a shallow baking dish coated with cooking spray. Brush salmon with juice. Combine spice ingredients in a small bowl. Sprinkle on spice mixture; lightly coat salmon with cooking spray. Bake for 10 minutes, or until done as desired. Serve with Banana Raita.

SERVES 4

PER SERVING: 196 calories, 12 g fat (2 g saturated), 0.5 g carbohydrates, 20 g protein, 0 g fiber, 62 mg sodium

BANANA RAITA

1 cup plain fat-free or low-fat yogurt
1 teaspoon lemon juice
¼ teaspoon grated fresh gingerroot
½ teaspoon ground cumin
1 large ripe banana, diced
1 teaspoon non-sugar sweetener such as Splenda, or sugar
2 tablespoons fresh cilantro leaves, chopped

In a small bowl, combine first 6 ingredients and let chill for an hour. Sprinkle on cilantro before serving.

SERVES 4–6

PER SERVING: 62 calories, 0 g total fat, 12 g carbohydrates, 3.6 g protein, 0.5 g fiber, 44 mg sodium

why it's good for you:

- Salmon is very high in omega-3 fat.
- Spices offer antibacterial properties.
- Ginger has anticoagulant activity.
- Yogurt boosts immune functioning.

Eating fish rich in DHA omega-3 fatty acids, such as salmon, at least once a week may cut your risk of developing Alzheimer's by 40 percent, concludes Tufts University research.

SCIENCE SAYS

SALMON ON SPINACH WITH LEMON-CHAMPAGNE SAUCE

4 5-ounce salmon fillets
2 (10-oz) bags fresh baby spinach.
2 tablespoons extra virgin olive oil.
Freshly ground black pepper

Coat fleshy side of fillet with black pepper and grill or panfry until done, turning once. Remove skin. Steam spinach in a large pot or in the microwave until just tender. Stir in olive oil.

On each of four plates, place a bed of spinach. Top with a salmon fillet. Drizzle fillet with ¼ cup Lemon-Champagne Sauce.

LEMON CHAMPAGNE SAUCE

2 eggs
4 tablespoons fresh lemon juice
⅓ cup dry white champagne or prosecco (Italian sparkling wine)
2 tablespoons chopped fresh dill
Salt and pepper

In a medium bowl, beat egg whites until frothy. Whisk in yolks and lemon juice. Transfer to a small pan and slowly add champagne, stirring constantly. Place over low heat, and stirring constantly, cook until sauce thickens. Do not boil. Remove from heat; stir in dill, salt, and pepper.

MAKES 1 CUP

PER SERVING, SALMON, SPINACH, LEMON SAUCE: 362 calories, 17.5 g total fat (3 g saturated), 32 g protein, 18 g carbohydrate, 8 g fiber, 359 mg sodium

SCIENCE SAYS

Salmon's omega-3 fatty acid DHA may discourage weight gain by suppressing development of fat cells, according to University of Georgia research.

SALMON WITH SCALLOPED SWEET POTATOES

3 medium sweet potatoes, peeled and sliced thinly (about 4 cups)

1 medium yellow onion, coarsely chopped

1 teaspoon grated fresh ginger

1 cup orange juice

3 tablespoons orange marmalade

2 tablespoons melted trans-fat-free margarine or butter

Salt

1¼ pounds salmon fillet, skin removed, cut into 6 pieces

Freshly ground black pepper

¼ cup almond slivers, toasted

¼ cup flat-leaf parsley sprigs

Preheat oven to 400°F. Combine sweet potatoes, onion, ginger, juice, 2 tablespoons of the marmalade, margarine, and salt. Place in a 9 × 13-inch casserole dish, sprayed with cooking spray. Cover and bake for 40 minutes. Remove from oven; top with salmon. Brush fish with the remaining 1 tablespoon marmalade; grind on pepper. Return to oven (uncovered) and bake for 10 to 12 minutes, until fish is done to your liking. Garnish with almonds and parsley.

SERVES 6

PER SERVING: 340 calories, 14 g total fat (2 g saturated), 27 g carbohydrate, 22 g protein, 5 g fiber, 90 mg sodium

Eating orange peel, as in marmalade, more than once a week cut odds of skin cancer by one-third, in a University of Arizona study.

SCIENCE SAYS

STIR-FRIED SCALLOPS WITH WALNUTS AND SNOW PEAS

2 teaspoons sesame oil mixed with 2 teaspoons canola oil

3 cloves garlic, crushed

8 scallions, including some green tops, cut into 1–2-inch long diagonal slices

1½ cups snow peas

1 cup walnut halves, toasted*

1¼ pounds sea scallops, preferably dry pack, halved horizontally

SOY-GINGER SAUCE

1 tablespoon cornstarch

¼ cup fat-free, reduced-sodium chicken or vegetable broth

2 tablespoons dry sherry

2 tablespoons reduced-sodium soy sauce

1 heaping teaspoon grated fresh ginger

¼ teaspoon hot pepper flakes, or to taste

To make the Soy-Ginger Sauce, combine cornstarch, broth, sherry, soy sauce, ginger, and pepper flakes; set aside.

Heat 2 teaspoons of the oil in a wok or large skillet, over medium high heat. Add garlic, scallions, and snow peas, and stir-fry 3 minutes or until they are crisp tender. Remove to a serving bowl. Add remaining oil. When hot, stir-fry scallops for 2 minutes. Stir in Soy-Ginger Sauce and cook until slightly thickened, about 2 minutes. Add scallions, snow peas, and toasted walnuts. Cook for about 1 minute—be careful to not overcook scallops. Serve at once with brown rice.

* *Toast walnuts in 350°F oven for 5 minutes.*

SERVES 6

PER SERVING: 258 calories, 14 g total fat (1.3 g saturated), 12 g carbohydrate, 20 g protein, 2.3 g fiber, 430 mg sodium

SCIENCE SAYS

Walnuts are a very high source of plant omega-3s, some of which which the body can convert to the long-chain omega-3's type found in fish.

TOMATO-RICH MEDITERRANEAN FISH STEW

3½ ounces sun-dried tomatoes, reconstituted in hot water*
2 tablespoons olive oil
1 large yellow onion, chopped (about 1 cup)
1 green bell pepper, chopped
2 (8-ounce) bottles clam juice
2 (14-ounce) cans diced tomatoes, no salt added
1 cup dry red wine, broth, or tomato juice
4 garlic cloves, crushed
4 tablespoons fresh herbs (such as thyme, rosemary, or basil), or 1½
    teaspoon dried
2 bay leaves
½ cup kalamata black olives, sliced
1 (15-ounce) can navy beans, drained and rinsed
1 pound firm fish, such as grouper, tilapia, or tuna, cut into 2–3 inch chunks
Salt and pepper
2 teaspoons fennel seeds, lightly crushed, or to taste
½ cup grated Parmesan cheese

In a pan, simmer sun-dried tomatoes in 1½ cups water until very soft; discard water. In a large pot, sauté onions and green pepper in oil, until softened. In a food processor or blender, process sun-dried tomatoes and 1 bottle clam juice until smooth; add to pot.

Stir in remaining clam juice, diced tomatoes, wine, garlic, herbs, bay leaves, and olives. Simmer for 20 minutes. Add beans, fish, salt, pepper, and fennel seeds. Simmer until fish is done, about 10 minutes. Remove bay leaves. Ladle into bowls; sprinkle with cheese.

SERVES 8

PER 1 CUP SERVING: 239 calories, 19 g protein, 8 g total fat (2 g saturated), 23 g carbohydrate, 6 g fiber, 519 mg sodium

Men who eat fish at least five times a week have a 40 percent lower risk of colorectal (colon) cancer than do men who eat fish less than once a week, according to Harvard research.

SCIENCE SAYS

TANGY FISHERMAN'S STEW

4 large cloves garlic, sliced thinly
1 small green bell pepper, diced
1 tablespoon extra-virgin olive oil
2 cups canned crushed tomatoes
2 cups water
2 medium potatoes (1 pound), peeled and cut into 2-inch chunks
½ teaspoon ground cumin, or to taste
⅓ cup chopped fresh parsley
¼ teaspoon hot pepper flakes, or to taste
1 pound firm fish (such as tuna, snapper, grouper, or sea bass), cut into 2-inch pieces
Salt and freshly ground black pepper

Sauté garlic and peppers in oil until tender. Add tomatoes, water, potatoes, cumin, parsley, and hot pepper flakes; bring to a boil. Simmer for 20 minutes, or until potatoes are tender. To slightly thicken stew, use the back of a spoon to mash some potatoes against the side of the pan. Add fish and simmer for 10 minutes, or until fish is done. Serve with warm Italian or French bread.

SERVES 4

PER SERVING: 297 calories, 9.4 g total fat (2 g saturated), 23 g carbohydrate, 30 g protein, 3 g fiber, 249 mg sodium

SCIENCE SAYS

Eating fish more than three times a week cut the progression of prostate cancer by 44 percent, compared with eating fish less than twice a month.

TROPICAL MAHIMAHI WITH PEANUTS

1 pound mahimahi, cut into 4 pieces, or substitute other white fish, such as bass, tilapia, or flounder.
1 banana, diced
1 (8-ounce) can crushed pineapple or tidbits, undrained
½ cup light coconut milk
1 tablespoon peanut butter, preferably natural
Dash of hot pepper sauce
Salt and freshly ground black pepper
¼ cup flaked sweetened coconut
⅓ cup crushed unsalted peanuts

Preheat oven to 350°F. Place fish in a small, shallow, microwave-safe dish or pie plate. Combine banana and pineapple. Microwave coconut milk for 1 minute; stir in peanut butter, hot pepper sauce, salt, and pepper. Add to fruit. Pour fruit mixture over fish. Top with flaked coconut. Bake for 15 minutes. Put under broiler to brown top if necessary. Serve with peanuts and brown rice.

SERVES 4

PER SERVING: 291 calories, 12 g total fat (3.5 g saturated), 22 g carbohydrate, 26 g protein, 2 g fiber, 123 mg sodium

Peanuts, like red wine, are rich in resveratrol, an antioxidant believed to discourage cancer and encourage longevity.

SCIENCE SAYS

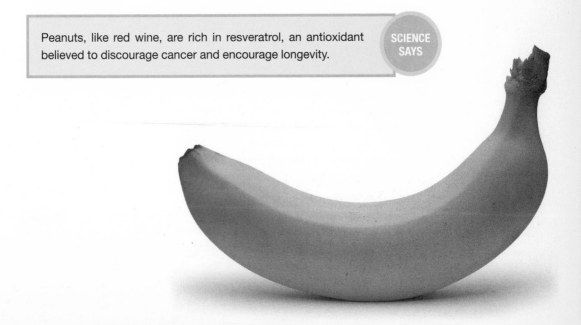

Poultry

IF YOU EVER think, "Not chicken again!" come dinnertime, you haven't tried these recipes. In the following pages, I show you innovative and delicious ways to make this suppertime staple. You'll see how to pair chicken and turkey with vegetables, herbs, spices, and other health-promoting ingredients. You'll also find delicious ways to substitute these naturally lean foods for red meat when making meat balls, stews, and other dishes.

BAKED CHICKEN
WITH BRUSSELS SPROUTS

1 tablespoon extra-virgin olive oil

1¼ pounds boneless, skinless chicken breast, cut into 8 pieces

1 pound fresh Brussels sprouts

1½ cups chopped yellow onion

2–3 tablespoons chopped fresh rosemary

1½ cups 99% fat-free chicken broth

Salt and black pepper

Preheat oven to 375°F. In a skillet, heat olive oil and brown chicken, Lay chicken in a shallow baking dish, and surround with Brussels sprouts. Sprinkle onions and rosemary over chicken. Add broth, salt, and pepper. Bake, covered, for 20 minutes. Uncover, increase oven temperature to 400°F and bake for 30 to 40 minutes, or until sprouts are cooked firm, not mushy. Serve.

SERVES 4

PER SERVING: 137 calories, 4 g total fat (1 g saturated), 8 g carbohydrate, 17 g protein, 3 g fiber, 286 mg sodium

why it's good for you:

- Brussels sprouts, onion, and rosemary contain antioxidants.
- Low in fat.

Indoles and other antioxidants in cruciferous vegetables, including Brussels sprouts, broccoli, cabbage, and kale, may help discourage breast cancer, several studies suggest.

SCIENCE SAYS

AN EASY

MICROWAVE DISH

CHICKEN, LENTIL AND VEGETABLE STEW

2 pounds boneless, skinless chicken thighs or breasts, cut into chunks
1½ cups thick-sliced carrots
2 cups fresh spinach, sliced into ribbons
1 (14½-ounce) can diced tomatoes with juice
1 cup dried lentils
1 cup fat-free, reduced-sodium chicken broth
1 teaspoon dried Italian herbs
1 teaspoon crushed fennel seed
8 cloves garlic, peeled and cut into chunks
Salt and freshly ground black pepper
Parsley sprigs, for garnish

Place all ingredients in a large, microwave-safe bowl. Stir to combine. Cover, microwave on high power for about 25 minutes, or until chicken and vegetables are done. Add more broth if needed. Garnish with parsley.

SERVES 6

PER SERVING USING CHICKEN THIGHS: 330 calories, 6.7 g total fat (1.6 g saturated), 27 g carbohydrate, 41 g protein, 6 g fiber, 353 mg sodium

SCIENCE SAYS

Eating lutein-packed spinach three or four times a week reversed very early signs of macular degeneration, a potentially blinding age-related eye disease.

COCONUT-PECAN CHICKEN "FINGERS"

1½ cups plain fat-free or low-fat yogurt
⅔ cup sweetened coconut flakes
⅔ cup panko crumbs (Japanese bread crumbs)
½ cup finely chopped pecans
1½ pound boneless, skinless chicken breast cut into 1-inch-wide strips

Preheat oven to 450°F. Put yogurt in a small bowl, and set aside. In a shallow pie plate, combine coconut, panko, and pecans. Dip chicken strips in yogurt to cover, then roll in panko mixture. Place strips on an oil-sprayed baking sheet. Spray top of chicken with oil. Bake for 15 minutes. Reduce heat to 350°F and bake for 15 more minutes. Check that coating browns but does not burn. Broil for 2 minutes for an even crunchier top.

SERVES 6

PER SERVING: 288 calories, 12 g total fat (3 g saturated), 31 g protein, 18 g carbohydrate, 67 mg cholesterol, 1 g fiber, 187 mg sodium

why it's good for you:

- Pecans contain antioxidants.

- A great low-fat substitute for deep-fried chicken fingers.

- Low in sodium.

Coconut oil contains luric acid, a type of fatty acid, which raised good HDL cholesterol, in tests.

SCIENCE SAYS

COMPANY GARLIC CHICKEN

2½ pounds boneless, skinless chicken breasts, cut into serving-size pieces
1 tablespoon canola oil
Salt and freshly ground black pepper
3 heads garlic, cloves separated but not peeled
1 tablespoon chopped fresh thyme, or 1 teaspoon dried thyme leaves
1 tablespoon chopped fresh rosemary, or 1 teaspoon dried rosemary
1½ cups dry white wine, or enough to cover chicken in casserole
¼ cup minced fresh parsley

Preheat oven to 350°F. In a large skillet, fry chicken in oil over medium-high heat until golden brown. Salt and pepper chicken. Layer chicken in 4-quart casserole. Put garlic cloves on top of and among the chicken pieces. Sprinkle with thyme and rosemary. Add wine to cover. Cover and bake for 1 hour, or until liquid is reduced and garlic is very soft. Before serving, sprinkle with parsley. Serve with toasted Italian or French bread (squeeze soft garlic onto bread).

SERVES 6

PER SERVING: 143 calories, 2.4 g total fat (0.4 g saturated), 2.2 g carbohydrate, 22.3 g protein, 0.2 g fiber, 153 mg sodium

SCIENCE SAYS

Eating a garlic clove (raw or cooked) or more a day cut odds of developing colon cancer by 30 percent, in University of North Carolina research.

15-MINUTE CHICKEN CHILI

1 tablespoon canola oil or extra-virgin olive oil

10 ounces boneless, skinless chicken breast, cut into bite-size pieces

1½ tablespoons chile powder

1½ tablespoons ground cumin

2 (14½-ounce) cans no-salt added diced tomatoes

1 (15-ounce) can no-salt-added black, kidney or red beans

1 (4½-ounce) can minced green chiles

1 cup yellow corn kernels, frozen or canned

Salt and cayenne pepper

In a large saucepan, sauté chicken in oil over medium-high heat for 3 minutes, or until white. Stir in chile powder and cumin to coat chicken. Sauté for 3 to 4 minutes. Add remaining ingredients; heat through.

SERVES 4

PER SERVING: 290 calories, 6 g total fat (0.6 g saturated), 36 g carbohydrate, 26 g protein, 9 g fiber, 244 mg sodium

why it's good for you:

- Corn contains the antioxidants lutein and zeaxanthin.

- Tomatoes contain the antioxidant lycopene.

- Beans are high in fiber.

- Low fat—only 20 percent of calories from fat.

- May help combat diabetes and heart disease.

- Plus: beans help suppress blood sugar rises and are high in antioxidants.

Corn is a prime source of zeaxanthin, a strong antioxidant linked to lower rates of macular degeneration and cancer.

SCIENCE SAYS

1 pound ground turkey breast

½ cup freshly grated Parmesan cheese

2 tablespoons fennel seeds

2 tablespoons olive oil

1 cup whole wheat bread crumbs

Combine all ingredients and form into small balls. Brown in a nonstick skillet. Use as you would beef, pork, or other meatballs—for example, in tomato sauce over pasta. Be sure turkey meatballs are cooked well done, with no pink.

SERVES 4

PER SERVING: 272 calories, 11.4 g total fat (3 g saturated), 7.6 g carbohydrate, 33.7 g protein, 2 g fiber, 310 mg sodium

SCIENCE SAYS   Substituting poultry for red meat lowers risk of colon, breast, and pancreatic cancers.

HONEY-MUSTARD GRILLED CHICKEN

1 boneless, skinless chicken breast (8–10 ounces), cut in half
2 tablespoons honey
2 tablespoons Dijon mustard
2 cloves garlic, crushed
1 teaspoon fresh thyme
Freshly ground black pepper

Microwave the chicken, covered, for 2½ minutes on high. Pat dry. Mix remaining ingredients and brush on both sides of chicken. Grill for 5 minutes on each side, or until done, brushing with more honey-mustard mixture if desired.

SERVES 2

PER SERVING: 222 calories, 2.4 g total fat (0.5 g saturated), 20 g carbohydrate, 30.5 g protein, 0.6 g fiber, 280 mg sodium

Honey contains antioxidants and natural antibiotics to fight germs, including E. coli. The darker the honey, the greater its potency.

SCIENCE SAYS

IN-A-HURRY CHICKEN CURRY

1½ tablespoons extra-virgin olive oil

1 boneless, skinless chicken breast (8 to 10 ounces), cut into bite-size pieces

1 medium yellow onion, chopped

1½ tablespoons curry powder

2 teaspoons cornstarch

1 cup fat-free, reduced-sodium chicken broth

¼ cup dried cherries or raisins

1 cup drained pineapple chunks

Hot red pepper flakes (optional)

In a large skillet, heat olive oil over medium heat. Add chicken and onion; sauté for 3 minutes. Add curry powder, stir to coat chicken, and sauté for 2 minutes. Blend cornstarch into chicken broth and add to skillet. Add cherries and heat until sauce bubbles. Add pineapple and pepper flakes. Simmer until pineapple is heated through and cherries are soft. Serve with brown rice.

SERVES 4

PER SERVING: 272 calories, 9 g total fat (1.7 g saturated), 19 g carbohydrate, 29 g protein, 2.5 g fiber, 261 mg sodium

SCIENCE SAYS   Curcumin, an antioxidant in curry powder, helped block development of cataracts in animals, in University of Texas research.

INDIAN CHICKEN STEW
WITH COCONUT MILK

1 pound boneless, skinless chicken breast, cut into bite-size chunks

1 medium yellow onion, chopped or sliced

1 cup peeled potatoes cut into 1-inch chunks

1 cup baby carrots, halved

1 (9-ounce) package frozen baby lima beans

1 (14½-ounce) can diced tomatoes

1 cup canned coconut milk

1 cup fat-free, reduced-sodium chicken broth

1 tablespoon ground cumin

1 tablespoon curry powder

Salt and freshly ground black pepper

¼ teaspoon hot sauce, such as Tabasco, or to taste

Fresh parsley or cilantro, for garnish

AN EASY
MICROWAVE
DISH

Put all ingredients in a large, microwave-safe bowl and mix thoroughly. Cover tightly and microwave on high for 30 to 40 minutes.

SERVES 6

PER SERVING: 276 calories, 10 g total fat (7 g saturated), 25 g carbohydrate, 24 g protein, 5 g fiber, 309 mg sodium

Coconut milk contains lauric acid, which raised levels of good HDL cholesterol in Dutch study participants.

SCIENCE SAYS

MEXICAN BAKE

3 cups cooked brown rice

1 pound boneless, skinless chicken breast raw or cooked, cut into bite-size pieces

2 (14½-ounce) cans no-salt-added tomatoes, diced or crushed

1 (15-ounce) can black beans, drained and rinsed, or 1½ cups home-cooked unsalted beans

1 cup frozen yellow corn kernels

1 cup chopped red bell pepper

1 cup chopped green poblano pepper or green bell pepper

1 tablespoon chile powder

1 tablespoon ground cumin

4 cloves garlic, crushed

1 cup shredded reduced-fat Monterey jack cheese

¼ cup jalapeño pepper slices (optional)

Preheat oven to 400°F. Spread rice in a shallow 3-quart casserole. Top with chicken. In a bowl, combine tomatoes, beans, corn, peppers, seasonings, and garlic; pour over chicken. Top with cheese and jalapeños. Bake for 45 minutes.

SERVES 6

PER SERVING: 378 calories, 6 g total fat (2.9 g saturated), 49 g carbohydrate, 33 g protein, 5.3 g fiber, 236 mg sodium

SCIENCE SAYS

Garlic may help prevent ulcers by destroying its prime cause, Helicobacter pylori bacteria, according to research at Bastyr University.

MOROCCAN CHICKEN WITH PRUNES

1 tablespoon canola oil

2 pounds boneless, skinless chicken breasts, cut into large chunks

1 cup fat-free, reduced-sodium chicken broth

1½ cups chopped onions

24 prunes (dried plums), preferably orange- or lemon-scented

1 cup prune juice

1 tablespoon ground cumin

2 teaspoons ground cinnamon

1 tablespoon reduced-sodium soy sauce

1½ tablespoons honey or brown sugar

⅓ cup whole raw unsalted almonds

Preheat oven to 375°F. Heat oil in a skillet and brown chicken. Transfer chicken to a large casserole. In a separate bowl, combine broth, onions, prunes, prune juice, spices, soy sauce, and honey. Cover and microwave on high for 5 minutes. Pour over chicken. Stir in almonds. Cover and bake for 45 minutes. Serve with brown rice.

SERVES 6

PER SERVING: 387 calories, 9 g total fat (1 g saturated), 39 g carbohydrate, 39 g protein, 5.3 g fiber, 370 mg sodium

why it's good for you:

- Prunes and prune juice are extremely high in antioxidants.
- Onions also have antioxidants.
- Low in saturated fat.
- Almonds contain magnesium.
- Plus: cinnamon helps suppress blood sugar.

Prunes contain a potent antioxidant—neochlorogenic acid—that can blunt artery damage from bad LDL cholesterol, finds University of California research.

SCIENCE SAYS

ONE-DISH CHICKEN CURRY WITH APPLES

1 tablespoon canola oil

Salt and freshly ground black pepper

2 pounds boneless, skinless chicken breast and thighs, cut into small serving pieces

3 medium Granny Smith apples, cored and chopped

2 large yellow onions, sliced thinly or chopped

6 large cloves garlic, minced or crushed

2 tablespoons curry powder, or more to taste

1½ teaspoons ground cumin

½ cup raisins

5 cups fat-free, reduced-sodium chicken broth

2 cups regular brown rice, uncooked (not instant)

In a large nonstick pot, heat canola oil. Salt and pepper the chicken, and brown it in oil. Remove chicken. Add apples, onions, garlic, curry, and cumin to skillet. Sauté, stirring, for 5 minutes. Add broth and raisins. Bring to a boil. Add rice and chicken. Cover, reduce heat, and simmer until rice is tender, about 1 hour. Serve with condiments such as chutney, chopped peanuts, toasted coconut, chopped cilantro, or sliced scallions.

SERVES 8

PER SERVING: 439 calories, 5.1 g total fat (0.8 g saturated), 62 g carbohydrate, 37 g protein, 5.4 g fiber, 120 mg sodium

SCIENCE SAYS Apples protect your lungs. Eating more than five apples a week improved breathing in middle-aged British men.

PEPPERY SOUP WITH TURKEY MEATBALLS

1 (14-ounce) can fat-free vegetable broth

1 (11½-ounce) can V-8 juice

1 medium yellow or red onion, chopped

1 large stalk celery, sliced

10 baby carrots cut in half

1 (15-ounce) can no-salt-added chickpeas or navy beans, undrained

1 cup dry pasta, such as rotelle or small shells

1 teaspoon coarsely ground black pepper

salt

⅛ teaspoon cayenne pepper, or to taste

1 tablespoon extra-virgin olive oil

TURKEY MEATBALLS

⅓ pound ground turkey breast

1 tablespoon fennel seeds

Salt

In a medium saucepan, combine first 9 ingredients (all except olive oil). Bring to a boil and simmer, covered, for about 10 minutes.

In the meantime, combine turkey, fennel seeds, salt, and pepper. Form into 12 small balls; heat oil in skillet and brown turkey on all sides. Add to soup and simmer for 10 minutes, covered, or until vegetables are soft. Serve with toasted whole-grain bread.

SERVES 4 AS MAIN COURSE

PER SERVING: 319 calories, 4.5 g total fat (0.6 g saturated), 21 g protein, 48 g carbohydrate, 9 g fiber, 381 mg sodium

why it's good for you:

- V-8 juice, onions, carrots, and legumes contain antioxidants.

- Low in saturated fat.

- Chunky soup helps suppress appetite.

Consuming any vegetable or fruit juice three times a week, compared with less than once a week, cut odds of Alzheimer's by 76 percent, say Vanderbilt University researchers.

SCIENCE SAYS

QUICK OLD-FASHIONED CHICKEN STEW

2 teaspoons canola oil

¾ pound boneless, skinless chicken breast, cut into bite-size pieces

1 medium baking potato, peeled and cut into chunks

1 medium yellow onion, cut into eighths

1½ cups sliced carrots, or baby carrots

1 cup sliced celery

1 cup mixed frozen vegetables, such as green beans, corn, peas or cooked leftover vegetables

2 teaspoons crushed fresh rosemary or thyme, or to taste

1 (12-ounce) jar fat-free chicken gravy (such as Heinz)

Salt and freshly ground black pepper

Heat oil in a small skillet and brown chicken, about 5 minutes. Put potato, onion, carrots, and celery into a large, microwave-safe bowl; cover and microwave on high for 12 minutes. Stir in chicken, chicken gravy, mixed vegetables, rosemary, and freshly ground pepper to taste. Cover and microwave on high for 10 minutes, or until vegetables are done and mixture is heated through.

Serve with low-fat biscuits.

SERVES 4

PER SERVING: 255 calories, 3.8 g total fat (0.5 g saturated), 28 g carbohydrate, 24.7 g protein, 5.2 g fiber, 617 mg sodium

SCIENCE SAYS Women who ate more canola oil and olive oil and less of other fats cut their risk of breast cancer in half, finds a large Swedish study.

SCALLOPED CABBAGE, FENNEL, AND TURKEY BREAST CASSEROLE

1½ pounds cabbage, shredded roughly (about 8 cups)
1 medium bulb fennel, chopped coarsely (about 2 cups)
½ pound smoked turkey breast, cut into ½-inch cubes
1 cup dried cranberries
1 tablespoon and 1 teaspoon fennel seeds
2 cups low-fat and reduced-sodium chicken broth (14½-ounce can)
½ cup "light" cranberry juice
1 tablespoon extra-virgin olive oil
Salt and black freshly grated black pepper

Preheat oven to 425°F. Place cabbage and fennel in a large shallow casserole. Sprinkle with turkey, cranberries, and fennel seeds. Top with chicken broth, cranberry juice, and olive oil. Add salt and black pepper. Bake, covered, for 30 minutes. Uncover, stir, and bake for 30 minutes.

MAKES 10½ CUP SERVINGS

PER SERVING: 122 calories, 4 g total fat (1 g saturated), 17 g carbohydrates, 6 g protein, 13 mg cholesterol, 3 g fiber, 403 mg sodium

why it's good for you:

- Cabbage, fennel, and cranberries contain antioxidants.
- Very low in fat and calories.
- Cranberry juice and cranberries help prevent infections.

> Women who eat more than 3 ounces of leafy vegetables a day cut their risk of asthma by 22 percent compared with those who eat only 1.4 ounces a day, according to the European Prospective Investigation into Cancer and Nutrition.

SCIENCE SAYS

SPICY MOROCCAN CHICKEN

2 teaspoons each cumin, cinnamon, coriander
½ teaspoon cayenne pepper, or to taste
Salt
1⅓ pounds boneless, skinless chicken breasts, cut into bite-size pieces
2 tablespoons olive oil
1 medium yellow onion, chopped
1 teaspoon grated gingerroot
3 garlic cloves, crushed
1 cup fat-free, reduced-sodium chicken broth
2 cups canned chopped no-salt-added tomatoes (such as Pomi)
1 (15 ½-ounce) can chickpeas (2 cups), drained and rinsed
¾ cup kalamata pitted olives, halved
½ cup raisins or dried cranberries
2 tablespoons honey
1 bay leaf
1 tablespoon ground cinnamon
½ lemon, seeded, cut into 4 wedges
⅓ cup chopped parsley, for garnish

In a shallow bowl, combine cumin, cinnamon, coriander, plus cayenne pepper and salt. Dredge chicken in spices.

In a large skillet, heat olive oil over medium heat. Add chicken; sauté until browned, turning once. Remove chicken. Add onion to skillet; sauté for 3 minutes. Add garlic, ginger, and broth; sauté for 5 minutes. Add all remaining ingredients and the chicken. Cover and simmer for 30 minutes.

Garnish with parsley. Serve in bowls, accompanied by toasted wedges of whole wheat pita bread.

SERVES 6

PER SERVING: 431 calories, 15 g total fat (2 g saturated), 45 g carbohydrate, 31 g protein, 59 mg cholesterol, 7 g fiber, 879 mg sodium

SCIENCE SAYS

Eating legumes, such as chickpeas, lentils, and other varieties of dried beans, helps suppress blood sugar spikes, lessening risk of diabetes as well as macular degeneration, find Tufts researchers.

STIR-FRIED CHICKEN WITH PINEAPPLE AND PEPPERS

1 pound boneless, skinless chicken breast, cut into 1-inch pieces

2 tablespoons canola or sesame oil

6 large scallions, with green tops cut into 2-inch diagonal pieces

2 cups fresh or frozen bell pepper strips (red, green, and/or yellow)*

1 (20-ounce) can chunk pineapple in juice

¼ cup sliced almonds (optional)

SAUCE

¼ cup reduced-sodium soy sauce

2 tablespoons white wine vinegar

2 tablespoons mirin (sweetened rice wine)

1 teaspoon grated fresh ginger

2 cloves garlic, crushed

1 tablespoon cornstarch

Combine sauce ingredients and stir to dissolve cornstarch. Set aside. In a large skillet, stir-fry chicken in hot oil until browned, about 5 minutes: remove chicken from the pan and set aside. Add scallions, peppers, and pineapple to the pan; stir until heated through. Pour in sauce and stir until thickened. Return chicken to skillet and heat through. Serve with brown rice. If you like, top with almonds.

SERVES 6

PER SERVING: 222 calories, 5.6 g total fat (0.9 g saturated), 23 g carbohydrate, 19 g protein, 1.7 g fiber, 454 mg sodium

Some frozen pepper packages contain onions, which is also okay to use.

Green peppers, pineapple, tomatoes, and carrots are tops in certain phenolic acids, which block formation of cancer-causing nitrosamines in the body.

SCIENCE SAYS

why it's good for you:

- Scallions, peppers, and pineapple contain antioxidants.

- Chicken breast is high in protein but low in fat.

- Plus: ginger fights inflammation and blood clots.

■ Beans fight cancer
and are packed
with antioxidants.

■ Beans discourage
blood sugar and
insulin spikes.

■ Tomatoes, parsley,
and cilantro
contain
antioxidants.

■ High in fiber and
low in sodium.

THREE-BEAN CHICKEN STEW

1 tablespoon canola oil

1¾ pounds boneless, skinless chicken breast or thighs, cut into chunks

1 large yellow onion, about 1½ cups

1 cup sliced celery

1 cup julienned or thinly sliced carrots

3 cups chopped no-salt-added tomatoes, canned or in carton (such as
    Pomi, 750 grams)

1 (14-ounce) can fat-free, less-sodium chicken broth

1 (15-ounce) can no-salt-added black beans, drained

1 (15-ounce) can no-salt-added navy beans, drained

1 (15-ounce) can no-salt-added kidney beans, drained

1 cup dry red wine

1 large bay leaf

1 tablespoon Italian herbs

1 cup chopped parsley

1 cup chopped cilantro

Salt and freshly ground black pepper

Heat oil in a large pot, and brown chicken. Remove chicken from
pan. Sauté onions, about 5 minutes, until soft. Add celery, carrots,
tomatoes, beans, wine, and seasonings. Bring to a boil and simmer,
covered, for about 40 minutes. Add chicken, parsley, cilantro, and
simmer for 5 minutes. Salt and pepper to taste.

SERVES 8

PER SERVING: 361 calories, 6 g total fat (3 g saturated), 32 g carbohydrate, 39
g protein, 75mg cholesterol, 12 g fiber, 267 mg sodium

SCIENCE SAYS

Cutting salt intake, especially in canned and processed foods,
can help control high blood pressure and reduce the need for
hypertension medication, says the American Medical Association.

TURKEY-APPLE PATTIES

1 pound ground turkey breast
1 Granny Smith apple, peeled, cored, and grated coarsely
2 cloves crushed garlic
1½ teaspoons ground sage
½ teaspoon dried thyme
¼ teaspoon dried oregano
1½ teaspoons anise (or fennel seeds)
2 tablespoons olive oil
½ teaspoon coarse black pepper
Salt

Thoroughly combine all ingredients. Form into small, thin patties, about 1 ounce each, 2 inches in diameter. Spray a skillet with oil or coat with canola oil. Sauté patties over medium heat until done and slightly browned.

SERVES 4, MAKES ABOUT 16 PATTIES

PER PATTY: 53 calories, 1.9 g total fat (0.3 g saturated), 7 g protein, 1.5 g carbohydrate, 0.2 g fiber, 14 mg sodium

Women who ate an apple a day were 28 percent less apt to develop type 2 diabetes than were women who ate no apples, according to Harvard research.

SCIENCE SAYS

TURKEY MARZETTI

1 tablespoon canola oil

1 medium onion, chopped

1 medium green bell pepper, diced

1 pound ground turkey breast

1 (26-ounce) carton no-sodium-added strained tomatoes (such as
    Pomi), or 2 (14½-ounce) cans no-salt-added diced tomatoes

1 (10-ounce) can diced tomatoes and green chiles (such as Ro-Tel)

1 (4½-ounce) can chopped green chiles

8 ounces dry noodles, cooked

1 cup shredded reduced-fat cheddar cheese

Salt and freshly ground black pepper

Preheat oven to 400°F. In a large skillet, heat oil. Sauté onion, pepper, and turkey for 10 to 15 minutes. Add tomatoes and chiles; simmer for 5 minutes. Spread cooked noodles over the bottom of a large, shallow casserole; add turkey mixture and stir to combine. Sprinkle cheese over top and bake for 20 minutes. Put under broiler for a few minutes to brown top, if desired.

SERVES 10

PER SERVING: 233 calories, 4.2 g total fat (1.6 g saturated), 29 g carbohydrate, 20 g protein, 3.4 g fiber, 288 mg sodium

SCIENCE SAYS

Veggies are bone-boosters. Eating onions, tomatoes, cucumbers, arugula, garlic, parsley, and dill increased bone mass, in animal studies.

TURKEY MEATLOAF WITH CARAMELIZED ONION-TOMATO GRAVY

1½ pounds ground turkey breast
1 medium green bell pepper, finely chopped (1 cup)
1 medium yellow onion, chopped
½ cup bread crumbs
2 eggs, beaten, or ½ cup egg substitute
1 tablespoon Worcestershire sauce
3 cloves garlic, crushed
⅔ cup chile sauce or ketchup (reserve 2 tablespoons)
Salt and freshly ground black pepper
¼ cup freshly grated Parmesan cheese

CARAMELIZED ONION-TOMATO GRAVY

1½ teaspoons extra-virgin olive oil
1 large onion, sliced thinly
1 cup stewed-type tomatoes
¾ cup fat-free half-and-half
1 tablespoon all-purpose flour
Salt and freshly ground black pepper

MEATLOAF: Preheat oven to 350°F. In a bowl, combine all ingredients except the cheese and reserved chile sauce. Form the mixture into one large loaf or two small loaves. Put in a shallow baking dish. Sprinkle reserved chile sauce and cheese on top. Cover and bake for 30 minutes. Remove cover and bake for 30 minutes more. Serve with gravy.

GRAVY: In a large skillet, heat olive oil; sauté onions until golden or caramelized, stirring frequently, 20–25 minutes. In a blender, combine tomatoes, half-and-half, and flour; pulse twice. Add tomato mixture to onions; stir over medium heat until slightly thickened, about 10 minutes.

SERVES 6

MEATLOAF PER SERVING: 253 calories, 4 g total fat, (1.3 g saturated), 18.6 g carbohydrate, 33 g protein, 1 g fiber, 652 mg sodium
GRAVY PER SERVING: 60 calories, 1.2 g fat (0.1 g saturated), 10 g carbohydrate, 0.9 g protein, 0.9 g fiber, 125 mg sodium

> Onions and garlic contain 30 different anticancer agents and are consistently linked to lower rates of various cancers.
>
> **SCIENCE SAYS**

why it's good for you:

- Peppers, onions, garlic, and tomatoes contain antioxidants.
- Turkey breast is high in protein but low in fat.
- Choline and lutein in eggs protect the brain and eyes.

TURKEY TORTILLA PIE

6 corn tortillas

1 tablespoon canola oil

1 medium yellow onion, chopped

1 medium green bell pepper, diced

2 cloves garlic, crushed

1 pound ground turkey breast

1 tablespoon chile powder

1 teaspoon ground cumin

2 (14½-ounce) cans no-salt-added diced tomatoes

1 cup frozen corn kernels

½ cup chopped green or black olives

1 (4½-ounce) can chopped green chiles, drained

1½ cups reduced-fat shredded cheddar or pepper jack cheese

Preheat oven to 400°F. Spray tortillas on both sides with butter-flavor oil spray. Cut into fourths. Spread on a baking sheet. Bake until crispy. (Do not turn off oven.)

In large skillet, heat oil. Add onion, green pepper, garlic, and turkey. Sauté until turkey is done and vegetables are soft, about 10 minutes. Add tomatoes, corn, olives, spices, and chopped chiles. Turn mixture into a shallow casserole dish. Crumble baked tortilla chips on top of pie. Sprinkle with cheese. Bake, uncovered, for 20 minutes, or until cheese melts.

SERVES 6

PER SERVING: 276 calories, 9.8 g total fat (4 g saturated), 16 g carbohydrate, 30 g protein, 5 g fiber, 638 mg sodium

SCIENCE SAYS

Eating lycopene-rich tomatoes discouraged thickening of artery walls that lead to blood clots, in Finnish men.

Great Burgers

THE TRADITIONAL BURGER presents you with a number of health challenges. First, the beef is generally high in artery-clogging saturated fat. Second, you need to cook your burger well done to ensure you kill any germs that could result in food poisoning. Yet, if you cook a burger to well done over high heat—usually a grill— you increase the carcinogens in the meat! In the following pages, you'll find a number of recipes that allow you to solve these problems, allowing you to enjoy your burger and your good health!

ANTICANCER
TRADITIONAL BEEF BURGERS

1 pound lean ground beef
½ cup textured vegetable protein (a soy protein sold in health food stores and some supermarkets)
2 tablespoons cold water
Salt and freshly ground black pepper

Put all ingredients in a large bowl. Knead until combined. Form into 4 patties. Grill, broil, or fry. Serve on whole-grain buns with sliced onion, for antioxidant protection.

SERVES 4

PER PATTY: 241 calories, 14.9 g total fat (5.9 g saturated), 3 g carbohydrate, 24 g protein, 2 g fiber, 63 mg sodium

---

SCIENCE SAYS Soy protein can help lower blood cholesterol, according to several studies and the Food and Drug Administration.

ASIAN SALMON BURGERS WITH DILLED YOGURT SAUCE

1 (14½-ounce) can pink or red salmon, skin removed
1 medium potato, baked or boiled, peeled
1 tablespoon reduced-sodium soy sauce
1½ teaspoons grated fresh ginger
2 cloves garlic, crushed
½ teaspoon cracked black pepper

Mash salmon and potato; mix in soy sauce, ginger, and garlic. Form into 4 patties. Sprinkle with cracked black pepper on one side. Spray with olive or canola oil and grill on each side for about 4 minutes. Serve on whole wheat buns with dilled yogurt sauce and shredded raw cabbage.

DILLED YOGURT SAUCE: Mix 1 cup fat-free plain yogurt with ⅓ cup chopped fresh dill. Add salt to taste.

SERVES 4

PER PATTY: 165 calories, 4.7 g total fat (1.3 g saturated), 10 g carbohydrate, 20 g protein, 0.7 g fiber, 570 mg sodium

Virtually all canned salmon is wild, not farmed. Both wild and farmed salmon have about the same concentrations of omega-3 fatty acids.

SCIENCE SAYS

BLUEBERRY BURGERS

1 pound ground turkey breast or lean beef
1 cup blueberries or pitted tart cherries, ground in a food processor
¾ teaspoon dried thyme
2 cloves garlic, crushed
Salt and freshly ground pepper

Combine all ingredients. Form into 4 burgers. Grill until well done.

SERVES 4

PER PATTY: 149 calories, 0.9 g total fat (0.2 g saturated), 6 g carbohydrate, 28 g protein, 1 g fiber, 58 mg sodium

SCIENCE SAYS

Eating blueberries reverses some of the deleterious effects of aging in the brains of old rats and may even help overcome a genetic disposition toward Alzheimer's disease, says James Joseph of Tufts University.

"CRAB" BURGERS

½ pound imitation crab (substitute real crab if desired), chopped
   coarsely
½ cup fine bread crumbs
2 tablespoons finely chopped green bell pepper
1 teaspoon crab seasoning, such as Old Bay
½ cup egg substitute, or 2 eggs

Combine all ingredients. Form into 4 patties. Spray both sides with olive or canola oil, and grill for 4 minutes each side. Serve on whole wheat buns with dill pickles, lettuce, or cabbage and one of the following sauces.

TARTAR SAUCE: Mix 2 tablespoons low-fat mayonnaise and 1 tablespoon pickle relish.

COCKTAIL SAUCE: Mix 3 tablespoons ketchup, 1 teaspoon prepared horseradish, and 1 teaspoon fresh lemon juice.

SERVES 4

PER PATTY: 116 calories, 2.2 g total fat (0.2 g saturated), 16 g carbohydrate, 10.7 g protein, 0.6 g fiber, 818 mg sodium

> Some older people need to eat more protein to help keep muscles strong, Tufts researchers find.
>
> SCIENCE SAYS

why it's good for you:
- High in protein.
- Low in fat and calories.
- Eggs contain antioxidants and choline.

GINGERED TUNA BURGERS

1 pound fresh tuna, chopped finely in food processor
2 large cloves garlic, crushed
1½ tablespoons reduced-sodium soy sauce
2 tablespoons grated fresh ginger

Combine ingredients and form into 4 burgers. Grill or fry in a heavy, nonstick, sizzling-hot skillet to desired doneness—about 1 minute on each side for rare, 4–5 minutes for well done. Serve on whole wheat buns topped with Yogurt-Cucumber Sauce and pickled ginger slices.

YOGURT-CUCUMBER SAUCE: Combine 1 cup fat-free plain yogurt with ⅓ cup peeled, chopped, and seeded cucumber. Add salt to taste.

SERVES 4

PER PATTY: 172 calories, 5.6 g total fat (1.4 g saturated), 2 g carbohydrate, 27 g protein, 1 g fiber, 270 mg sodium

SCIENCE SAYS

Eating fish oil lowered signs of inflammation in the blood or C-reactive protein (CRP), which is associated with a higher risk of heart disease, reports University of North Carolina research.

GREEK-STYLE TURKEY BURGERS

1 pound ground turkey breast
⅓ cup chopped fresh mint
3 scallions including 3 inches green tops, finely minced
⅓ cup freshly grated Parmesan cheese
2 cloves garlic, crushed

Combine all ingredients. Form into 4 patties. Grill until no pink remains. Serve on whole wheat buns with Yogurt Sauce.

YOGURT SAUCE: Mix 1 cup fat-free plain yogurt with ½ cup of a mixture of chopped mint, chopped tomato, and chopped peeled and seeded cucumber. Add salt to taste.

SERVES 4

PER PATTY: 171 calories, 3 g total fat (1.8 g saturated), 2 g carbohydrate, 32 g protein, 1 g fiber, 209 mg sodium.

Turkey is an excellent source of B vitamins, zinc, and selenium, and is linked to lower risk of heart disease and cancer.

SCIENCE SAYS

PORTOBELLO MUSHROOM BURGERS

⅓ cup minced onion
1 large clove garlic, crushed
1 tablespoon canola oil
6 ounces (3½–4 cups) diced portobello mushrooms
½ cup bread crumbs
1 beaten egg or ¼ cup egg substitute
Salt and freshly ground black pepper

In a large skillet over medium heat, sauté onion and garlic in oil for 2 minutes. Add mushrooms and cook, stirring frequently, until mushrooms are cooked down and liquid has disappeared, 15–20 minutes. Let cool. Combine with rest of ingredients; form into 2 patties. Sprinkle with black pepper. Grill on both sides until heated through. Serve on whole wheat buns.

SERVES 2

PER PATTY: 239 calories, 10.5 g total fat (1.6 g saturated), 27 g carbohydrate, 9.6 g protein, 3 g fiber, 270 mg sodium

SCIENCE SAYS
Extracts of mushrooms, including portobello, have curbed estrogen activity and proliferation of breast cancer cells, in tests at the Beckman Research Institute in California.

SPINACH-STUFFED TURKEY BURGERS WITH BLUE CHEESE

why it's good for you:
- Turkey is high in protein but low in fat.
- Spinach and garlic contain antioxidants.

1 pound ground turkey breast
1 (10-ounce) package frozen chopped spinach, thawed and squeezed dry
2 cloves garlic, crushed
¼ teaspoon hot red pepper flakes
Salt and freshly ground black pepper

Combine turkey, spinach, garlic, and pepper flakes. Form 4 patties. Sprinkle with salt and pepper. Grill until done (no pink), 4 to 5 minutes on each side. Serve on whole wheat buns with Blue Cheese Sauce and onion and tomato slices.

BLUE CHEESE SAUCE: Mix 2 tablespoons blue cheese with ½ cup fat-free sour cream.

SERVES 4

PER PATTY: 190 calories, 1.7 g total fat (0.8 g saturated), 9 g carbohydrate, 33 g protein, 2 g fiber, 173 mg sodium

Eating spinach, particularly cooked spinach, twice a week or more cut women's risk of cataract extractions by up to 38 percent.

SCIENCE SAYS

Anticancer Marinades for Grilled Meats, Poultry, and Fish

MARINATING RAW MEAT, poultry, or fish in a thin sauce before grilling can dramatically reduce the amounts of carcinogens (HCAs) formed when the meat cooks. In the following pages, I've include three sauces that have been tested and proved to remove from 50 to 67 percent of the carcinogens formed during cooking.

ROSEMARY-TEA MARINADE

1 teaspoon crushed rosemary
1 clove garlic, crushed
2 teaspoons honey
2 teaspoons reduced-sodium soy sauce
½ cup concentrated tea (2 bags black tea brewed in ½ cup hot water
    for 5 minutes)

Add rosemary, garlic, honey, and soy sauce to hot tea. Cool slightly. Pour over chicken, steaks, ribs, burgers, or fish and marinate for at least 10 minutes.

MAKES ½ CUP

TERIYAKI SAUCE

1 clove garlic, crushed
1 piece fresh ginger, minced
2 teaspoons brown sugar
½ cup reduced-sodium soy sauce
½ cup water

Combine ingredients. Pour over steaks, chicken, or ribs. Cover and marinate overnight (12–16 hours) in the refrigerator.

MAKES 1 CUP

TURMERIC-GARLIC MARINADE

2 teaspoons garlic powder
1 teaspoon ground turmeric
½ cup water or orange juice

Combine ingredients. Pour over steaks, chicken, or ribs. Cover and marinate in the refrigerator for several hours.

MAKES ½ CUP

Desserts

THE WORDS HEALTHY and *dessert* can indeed go into the same sentence. Although the vast majority of desserts combine three health evils—sugar, white flour, and fat—the desserts in this section minimize these ingredients whenever possible and maximize health promoting spices, herbs, and fruit. I'm confident that your taste buds won't feel deprived.

BRAZIL NUT–STUFFED PRUNES

20 orange- or lemon-scented pitted prunes (dried plums)
20 raw Brazil nuts
¼ cup sugar
1 teaspoon ground cinnamon

Insert a nut into each prune. Blend sugar and cinnamon. Roll prunes in spiced sugar. Serve as dessert or snack.

VARIATION: Stuff prunes with almonds or walnuts.

MAKES 20 STUFFED PRUNES

PER STUFFED PRUNE: 56 calories, 3.2 g total fat (0.8 g saturated), 7 g carbohydrate, 0.9 g protein, 1.2 g fiber, 1 mg sodium

Selenium, as found in Brazil nuts, boosts mood and reduces lung and prostate cancer.

SCIENCE SAYS

BLUEBERRY-LEMON PARFAIT

2 cups fresh or thawed frozen blueberries
2 (8-ounce) containers fat-free lemon yogurt
10 gingersnaps, crumbled

In each of four parfait glasses or tall wine glasses, put ½ cup blueberries, followed by ½ cup yogurt, then the crumbled gingersnaps. Serve.

SERVES 4

PER SERVING: 147 calories, 2.9 g total fat (0 g saturated), 15 g carbohydrate, 3.7 g protein, 2 g fiber, 160 mg sodium

SCIENCE SAYS Eating six ounces of yogurt a day reduced hay fever attacks and colds, in a University of California–Davis study.

CHOCOLATE ANGEL BITES

1 cup finely ground walnuts
½ cup unsweetened cocoa powder
1 cup sugar
3 tablespoons canola oil
8 egg whites beaten until stiff with ½ teaspoon salt
¼ cup confectioners' sugar

Preheat oven to 350°F. Combine nuts, cocoa, sugar, and oil. Fold in one-quarter of beaten egg whites. Fold in rest of egg whites. Spoon batter into nonstick or oiled minimuffin pans. Bake for 12 minutes. Cool for 5 minutes. Remove from pan and sprinkle with confectioners' sugar.

MAKES 4 DOZEN

PER MINI-CAKE: 31 calories, 1 g total fat (0.1 g saturated), 5 g carbohydrate, 0.8 g protein, 0.3 g fiber, 33 mg sodium

Eating three ounces of dark chocolate daily for two weeks lowered blood pressure in German study participants, about the same as going on a low-salt diet, said researchers.

SCIENCE SAYS

CHOCOLATE CAKE WITH RASPBERRY SAUCE

1½ cups semisweet chocolate chips
2 cups (19-ounce can) chickpeas, drained and rinsed
4 eggs, or 1 cup egg substitute
1 cup no-calorie sweetener such as Splenda, or sugar
½ teaspoon baking powder
1 tablespoon confectioners' sugar

QUICK MICROWAVE RASPBERRY SAUCE

½ cup seedless raspberry jam
2 teaspoons fresh lemon juice
1 pint fresh raspberries

CAKE: Preheat oven to 350°F. In a small bowl, melt chocolate in microwave, 2–3 minutes. In a blender or food processor, combine chickpeas and eggs; process until smooth. Stir in sweetener, baking powder, and melted chocolate; process again until smooth.

SCIENCE SAYS

Eating legumes, including chickpeas, once a week reduced risk of fatal pancreatic cancer by 40 percent, in Loma Linda University research.

Spray eight 4-ounce or 6-ounce ovenproof custard cups or ramekins with cooking spray. Divide batter evenly among baking dishes.

Bake for 25 minutes, or until a knife inserted comes out clean. Cool. Place cakes upside down on a large plate, and sprinkle with confectioners' sugar. Serve on individual dessert plates with raspberry sauce, if desired.

SAUCE: In a bowl, microwave jam until melted, 1 minute. Stir in juice and berries.

Note: If you are surprised at using legumes in a cake, be assured they make a very rich, moist chocolate cake that's excellent for those who cannot eat wheat flour.

SERVES 8

PER CAKE: 238 calories, 13 g total fat (6 g saturated), 28 g carbohydrate, 3.7 g fiber, 6.8 g protein
SAUCE PER SERVING: 64 calories, 0 g total fat, 17 g carbohydrate, 1.7 g fiber, 0.4 g protein, 8 mg sodium

CHOCOLATE FRUIT-NUT CLUSTERS

1 cup semisweet chocolate chips
½ cup walnut pieces
¼ cup raisins
½ cup raw oats

Microwave chocolate chips in a covered bowl on high until melted, 2–3 minutes. Stir until smooth. Add nuts, raisins, and oats; combine thoroughly. Drop by teaspoons onto waxed paper and cool in refrigerator or freezer until hardened.

MAKES 15 CLUSTERS

PER CLUSTER: 96 calories, 5.8 g total fat (2 g saturated), 12 g carbohydrate, 1.5 g protein, 0.6 g fiber, 1 mg sodium

Chocolate eaters seem to live a year longer than non-chocolate eaters, report Harvard researchers. Dark chocolate especially is high in antioxidants.

SCIENCE SAYS

CHOCOLATE-PRUNE SURPRISE

20 pitted prunes (dried plums)
20 whole almonds or walnut halves
1 cup semisweet chocolate chips

Stuff each prune with a nut. Microwave chocolate chips in a covered bowl on high until melted, 2–3 minutes. Stir until smooth. Using two forks, roll each prune in chocolate until lightly covered. Drop onto waxed paper and cool in refrigerator or freezer until hardened.

MAKES 20 PIECES

PER PIECE: 66 calories, 2.9 g total fat (1.4 g saturated), 11 g carbohydrate, 0.7 g protein, 0.7 g fiber, 1 mg sodium

SCIENCE SAYS

An ounce (about a handful) of almonds per day lowered bad LDL cholesterol, an average of 4.4 percent, in University of Toronto tests.

COCONUT-APRICOT TRUFFLES

1½ cups whole, unsalted almonds

2 cups dried apricots

2 teaspoons ground cinnamon

2 teaspoons pure almond extract

½ cup sweetened shredded coconut, such as Baker's Angel Flake

In a food processor with the knife blade, thoroughly process first four ingredients until mixture forms a ball. Using your hands, roll and press into 1-inch balls. Roll in coconut.

MAKES 3 DOZEN BALLS

PER PIECE: 55 calories, 3 g total fat (0.5 g saturated), 6 g carbohydrate, 1 g protein, 1 g fiber, 4 mg sodium

Coconut contains fatty acids that are anti-inflammatory, anti-bacterial, and antiviral, and may help fight heart disease, says Mary Enig, a leading authority on fats, previously at the University of Maryland.

SCIENCE SAYS

CURRIED FRUIT TOPPING

1 cup orange juice
1 tablespoon cornstarch
1 tablespoon curry powder
1 tablespoon non-calorie sweetener such as Splenda, or sugar
1 cup fresh blueberries
2 nectarines, sliced
1 banana, sliced
¼ cup toasted almonds

In a saucepan, combine juice, cornstarch, curry, and sweetener. Bring to a simmer. Add blueberries and nectarines; stir until sauce is slightly thickened. Add banana and almonds, then immediately remove from heat. Use warm or cold over angel food cake, ice cream, pancakes, or waffles.

SERVES 6

PER SERVING: (WITH SPLENDA): 172 calories, 4 g total fat (0 g saturated), 34 g carbohydrate, 3 g protein, 3 g fiber, 4 mg sodium

SCIENCE SAYS
Specific antioxidants in blueberries, raspberries, strawberries, and cranberries helped stop the growth of human prostate, breast, and colon cancer cells, in tests at UCLA.

DARK CHERRY GALETTE

1 refrigerator piecrust
2 (12-ounce) bags frozen dark sweet cherries*
1 tablespoon cornstarch
1 teaspoon pure almond extract

Preheat oven to 400°F. In a small saucepan, combine cherries, cornstarch, and almond extract. Bring to a boil and simmer until thickened, about 2 minutes. Let cool for 10 minutes. Roll pie crust to a 12-inch diameter; place on a pizza pan. Spread cherries in middle of crust; fold edges of crust up over cherries, to cover them partially. Bake for 30 minutes, or until crust is golden.

If you have too much fruit, save it as a topping.

SERVES 6

PER SERVING: 242 calories, 10 g total fat (4 g saturated), 37 g carbohydrate, 1.4 g protein, 1.7 g fiber, 128 mg sodium

You can substitute peaches, blueberries, or mixed berries.

Cherries have anti-inflammatory activity. In one study, eating 10 ounces of sweet cherries cut blood urate levels—a sign of gout—by about 15 percent in a group of women.

SCIENCE SAYS

FAT-FREE GINGER COOKIES

1 cup packed brown sugar
1 jar (2½-ounce) baby-food prunes
¼ cup molasses
¼ cup egg substitute
2¼ cups all-purpose flour
2 teaspoons ground ginger, or 2 tablespoons grated fresh ginger for a strong ginger taste
1 teaspoon ground cinnamon
1 teaspoon baking soda
¼ teaspoon ground cloves
¼ cup granulated sugar

In a large bowl, beat the brown sugar, prunes, molasses, and egg substitute until smooth. Combine the remaining ingredients except the sugar; thoroughly stir into the wet mixture. Cover and refrigerate for at least 2 hours, or overnight.

Preheat oven to 350°F. Spray a cookie sheet with canola or olive oil. Form the dough into walnut-size balls, roll in the sugar, and place 2 inches apart on the cookie sheet. Bake for 10 to 12 minutes. Cool on a wire rack.

MAKES 4 DOZEN

PER COOKIE: 43 calories, 0.1 g total fat, 10 g carbohydrate, 0.8 g protein, 0.2 g fiber, 31 mg sodium

---

SCIENCE SAYS Ginger has relieved arthritis pain and stiffness in patients better than aspirin and other NSAID drugs did, report Danish researchers.

GINGER-FRUIT SALAD

1 (8-ounce) can crushed pineapple

2 kiwis, peeled and sliced

1 apple, cored and diced

1 cup strawberries, sliced, or whole blueberries

½ cup orange juice

1 large banana, sliced

1 cup fat-free lemon yogurt

2 tablespoons chopped crystallized ginger

Toss fruits and juice together, adding banana just before serving. To serve, put in bowls or parfait glasses, top with yogurt and sprinkle on chopped ginger.

SERVES 4

PER SERVING: 209 calories, 0.6 g total fat, 51 g carbohydrate, 3.4 g protein, 4.3 g fiber, 37 mg sodium

why it's good for you:

- Pineapple, kiwi, apple, berries, and bananas are high in antioxidants.

- Kiwi is extra-high in vitamin C.

- Yogurt contains gut-protecting bacteria.

Pineapple and its juice are packed with the trace mineral manganese, which can help keep bones strong to prevent osteoporosis.

SCIENCE SAYS

INSTANT STRAWBERRY SORBET

1 pound frozen strawberries (about 3 cups)
1 banana, sliced and frozen
½ cup fat-free vanilla yogurt

Put all ingredients in a food processor fitted with the steel blade and process until smooth.

Serve immediately.

SERVES 4

PER SERVING: 90 calories, 0.3 g total fat (0 g saturated), 22 g carbohydrate, 2.3 g protein, 0.5 g fiber, 23 mg sodium

SCIENCE SAYS   Strawberries are antioxidant powerhouses and have prevented—and even reversed—aging changes in the brains of lab animals.

LIGHT HOLIDAY FRUIT CAKES

3 egg whites

1 cup unsweetened applesauce

¼ cup fat-free half-and-half

1 teaspoon pure vanilla extract

1 cup no-calorie sweetener such as Splenda

½ cup whole wheat flour

½ cup all-purpose flour

1 teaspoon baking soda

1 tablespoon pumpkin pie spice

1 teaspoon ground cinnamon

½ cup chopped dried pineapple

½ cup dried cranberries, preferably orange flavored

½ cup chopped almonds or walnuts

Confectioners' sugar for dusting (optional)

Preheat oven to 350°F. In a large bowl, beat egg whites until stiff. Fold in applesauce, half-and-half, and vanilla. In a separate bowl, combine sweetener, flour, baking soda, and spices. Fold dry ingredients into wet mixture. Fold in pineapple, cranberries, and nuts. Spoon batter into nonstick mini-muffin pans greased with cooking spray. Bake for 12 to 15 minutes. Remove, cool. Dust with confectioner's sugar.

MAKES 30 CAKES

PER CAKE: 56 calories, 1.2 g total fat (0 g saturated), 10 g carbohydrate, 1.3 g protein, 1 g fiber, 54 mg sodium

why it's good for you:

- Pineapple, cranberries, and applesauce are high in antioxidants.

- Very low in calories and fat.

- The whole wheat flour and nuts provide good amounts of fiber.

Eating cranberries helps prevent urinary tract infections by keeping bacteria from sticking to the walls of the bladder. In one test, Craisins worked as well as drinking cranberry juice.

SCIENCE SAYS

MAPLE-APPLE CRUNCH

4 cooking apples, such as Granny Smith or McIntosh (about 1½ pounds), unpeeled and sliced thinly
2 tablespoons fresh lemon juice
1 teaspoon ground cinnamon
½ cup raisins
¼ cup real maple syrup
Fat-free vanilla frozen yogurt (optional)

TOPPING

1 cup uncooked regular rolled oats
⅓ cup flour
½ cup sliced almonds
2 tablespoons canola oil
2 tablespoons real maple syrup
1 teaspoon pure almond or vanilla extract

Preheat oven to 350°F. In a bowl, combine apple slices, lemon juice, cinnamon, raisins, and syrup. In another bowl, combine topping ingredients. Spray a 9 × 13-inch baking dish with canola or olive oil cooking spray. Add apples, cover with foil, and bake till apples are softened, 30–40 minutes. Sprinkle with topping. Bake uncovered another 20 to 30 minutes until crisp. Serve warm with fat-free vanilla frozen yogurt.

SERVES 8

PER SERVING: 236 calories, 7.5 g total fat (0.7 g saturated), 41 g carbohydrate, 3.8 g protein, 3.6 g fiber, 4 mg sodium

SCIENCE SAYS

Men who eat oats and other whole-grain cereals have 20 percent lower death rates from all causes compared with men who eat refined-grain cereals, say Harvard studies.

MICROWAVE INDIAN PUDDING

1 cup fat-free half-and-half

3 eggs, or ¾ cup egg substitute

1 (15-ounce) can pumpkin puree

¾ cup cornmeal

½ cup molasses

¼ cup brown sugar

2 tablespoons white sugar (or non-calorie sweetener such as Splenda)

¼ cup raisins

¼ cup almond slivers

1 teaspoon ground cinnamon

½ teaspoon ground ginger

½ teaspoon ground cloves

Whisk together milk and eggs in a microwave-safe bowl. Add remaining ingredients and stir to blend. Microwave on high for 3 minutes; stir. Microwave for 3 more minutes, or until pudding is set (an inserted knife comes out clean). Serve warm alone or with fat-free or low-fat ice cream.

SERVES 8.

PER SERVING: 201 calories, 3 g total fat (0.5g saturated), 40 g carbohydrate, 6.2 g protein, 3 g fiber, 78 mg sodium

AN EASY MICROWAVE DISH

Eating cloves, the spice—one or two cloves daily for a month—cut blood glucose in diabetics by 33 percent and bad cholesterol by 17 percent, in USDA studies.

SCIENCE SAYS

MINT CHOCOLATE–PECAN CLUSTERS

1 cup semi-sweet chocolate chips
1 teaspoon mint extract
½ cup pecan pieces
⅔ cup oat-rings cereal such as Cheerios
⅓ cup M&Ms mini baking bits, or substitute raisins

Microwave chocolate in a bowl on high until melted, about 1½–2 minutes. Stir in mint. Thoroughly stir in remaining ingredients. Using a teaspoon, drop 1½-inch pieces on waxed paper. Cool in refrigerator until hardened.

MAKES 2 DOZEN CLUSTERS

PER PIECE: 68 calories, 4 g fat (2 g saturated), 7 g carbohydrate, 1 g protein, 1g fiber, 8 mg sodium

SCIENCE SAYS Antioxidants in chocolate may help block the occurrence and spread of prostate cancer, according to European animal studies.

ORANGE-FRUIT NUT TRUFFLES

1½ cups walnuts
1 cup orange-flavored prunes (dried plums)
½ cup dried cranberries
½ cup chocolate-covered raisins or plain raisins
1 teaspoon ground cinnamon
¼ teaspoon ground ginger
1 teaspoon pure vanilla extract
Walnut halves, for garnish (optional)

In a food processor with the knife blade, blend all ingredients until a ball is formed. Using your hands, form into 1-inch balls. Top each ball with a walnut half.

MAKES ABOUT 3 DOZEN BALLS

PER BALL: 62 calories, 3 g total fat (0.5 g saturated), 8 g carbohydrate, 1 g protein, 1 g fiber, 1 mg sodium

Consuming high amounts of fiber from prunes, other fruits and vegetables, whole-grains, and legumes reduces C-reactive protein (a blood marker of inflammation), as much as 63 percent in some studies.

SCIENCE SAYS

PEACH CRISP

1 (16-ounce) bag frozen peach slices, thawed
2 tablespoons brown sugar
½ teaspoon ground cinnamon
½ cup no-added-fat granola
Fat-free vanilla ice cream or frozen yogurt (optional)

Put fruit in a shallow, microwave-safe dish. Toss fruit with sugar and cinnamon. Top with granola. Microwave for 4 minutes on high, or until fruit is warm. Top with ice cream.

SERVES 4

PER SERVING: 138 calories, 2.6 g total fat (1.6 g saturated), 29 g carbohydrate, 2 g protein, 3.4 g fiber, 31 mg sodium

SCIENCE SAYS Cinnamon is also an antibiotic. In one test at Kansas State University, one teaspoon of cinnamon wiped out 99.5 percent of a million E. coli bacteria.

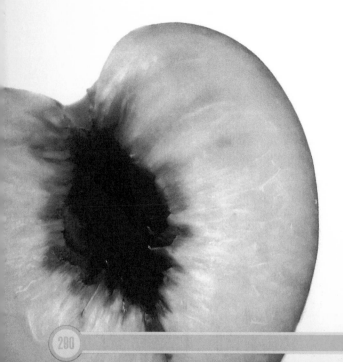

PEANUT BUTTER CLUSTERS

10 ounces peanut butter chips
½ cup dry roasted, unsalted peanuts
½ cup uncooked regular oats (not instant)
½ cup raisins
1 teaspoon ground cinnamon

Microwave chips in a bowl on high until melted, 1½–2 minutes. Stir until smooth. Add remaining ingredients; mix thoroughly. Using your hands, form into 1-inch balls. Cool in refrigerator until hardened.

MAKES ABOUT 3 DOZEN BALLS

PER PIECE: 63 calories, 3 g total fat (2 g saturated), 7 g carbohydrate, 3 g protein, 0 g fiber, 19 mg sodium.

Blood sugar sank nearly 30 percent in diabetics who ate ¼ teaspoon of cinnamon twice a day, in United States Department of Agriculture tests.

SCIENCE SAYS

PUMPKIN "BEAN" CAKE

1 (19-ounce) can chickpeas, rinsed, or 2 cups cooked
4 eggs, or 1 cup egg substitute
1 (15-ounce) can pumpkin
1 cup no-calorie sweetener such as Splenda, or sugar
2 tablespoons real maple syrup
½ teaspoon baking powder
2 teaspoons pumpkin pie spice
6 ounces whipped cream cheese
2 cups confectioners' sugar
1 (11-ounce) can mandarin oranges, drained
¼ cup walnut halves

Preheat oven to 350°F. In a blender or food processor, process chickpeas and eggs until smooth. Add pumpkin, sweetener, syrup, baking powder, and spice; process again until smooth. Spray a round cake pan with oil. Fill with batter. Bake for 60 minutes, until a knife inserted in the middle comes out clean. Cool. (Be sure the cake is completely cool before removing it from the pan, because it is very moist.)

Combine cream cheese and confectioners' sugar. Spread over top of cake. Decorate with mandarin orange slices and walnuts.

SERVES 8

PER SERVING: 340 calories, 13 g total fat (6 g saturated), 49 g carbohydrate, 8 g protein, 3 g fiber, 212 mg sodium

SCIENCE SAYS

High beta carotene foods, such as pumpkin, reduces your odds of developing macular degeneration, a leading cause of blindness, say Dutch scientists.

RICH, EASY OLD-FASHIONED CHOCOLATE PUDDING

2 cups fat-free half-and-half

¼ cup cornstarch

1 (11½-ounce) package Ghiradelli 60% cocoa bittersweet chocolate chips

3 ounces Amaretto liqueur, or rum

In a medium saucepan, stir together 1 cup half-and-half and the cornstarch until smooth. Add remaining half-and-half. Over low heat, bring to a simmer, stirring constantly to prevent sticking. Remove from heat. Put chocolate and Amaretto in a small bowl; microwave on high for 20 seconds. Stir until chips are mostly melted. Return milk to low heat. Add chocolate and stir continuously, scraping bottom and sides of pan, until pudding thickens. Cool. Serve chilled or at room temperature.

SERVES 12

PER ¼ CUP SERVING: 202 calories, 11 g total fat (6 g saturated fat), 23 g carbohydrate, 1.8 g protein, 1.8 g fiber, 40 mg sodium

Dark chocolate can help lower blood pressure, discourage blood clots, and keep arteries flexible, find several studies.

SCIENCE SAYS

SAUCY SUMMER FRUIT SALAD

3 large peaches, peeled and cut into chunks
1½ cups blueberries
1½ cups sliced strawberries
2 bananas, sliced
1 tablespoon fresh lemon juice

ORANGE-YOGURT SAUCE

1 cup fat-free or low-fat vanilla yogurt
2 tablespoons frozen orange juice concentrate
Mint sprigs, for garnish

Combine fruit and lemon juice. In a small bowl, mix yogurt and orange juice concentrate. Put fruit into a large glass bowl or 6 small bowls or parfait glasses. Drizzle sauce over fruit and top with mint.

SERVES 6

PER SERVING: 145 calories, 0.5 g total fat (0.1 g saturated), 34 g carbohydrate, 3.6 g protein, 4.5 g fiber, 30 mg sodium

SCIENCE SAYS

Fruits, including cranberry, apple, red grape, strawberry, peach, lemon, pear, banana, orange, grapefruit, and pineapple, retarded the spread of cancer cells, in test-tube studies at Cornell.

SPICY WALNUT COOKIES

2 cups walnut pieces
⅓ cup sugar
1 tablespoon ground cinnamon
2 egg whites, whisked until frothy

Preheat oven to 350°F. Grind nuts, sugar, and cinnamon in blender or food processor. Combine with egg whites. Drop by teaspoon onto an oiled cookie sheet.

Bake for 15 minutes. Cookies will be soft; do not overbake.

MAKES 15 COOKIES

PER COOKIE: 123 calories, 9.9 g total fat (1 g saturated), 3 g carbohydrate, 2.8 g protein, 1 g fiber, 9 mg sodium

Eating one and a half ounces of walnuts per day as part of a diet low in saturated fat and cholesterol may reduce the risk of heart disease, says the Food and Drug Administration.

SCIENCE SAYS

THREE-BERRY TRIFLE

1 (13⅔-ounce) Entenmann's fat-free loaf cake or other fat-free yellow cake
2 (8-ounce) containers fat-free vanilla yogurt
1 (15-ounce) carton part-skim ricotta cheese
½ cup confectioners' sugar
2 cups fresh blueberries
4 cups fresh strawberries, hulled and sliced
½ cup dry sherry or almond-flavored liqueur such as Amaretto
½ cup slivered almonds, toasted
1 (12-ounce) bag frozen raspberries or 2 cups fresh raspberries, pureed and sweetened to taste

Cut cake into 10 slices. Stir together yogurt, ricotta, and confectioners' sugar. Reserve a dozen each of blueberries and strawberry slices for garnish. Combine remaining blueberries and strawberries.

To assemble trifle, place 4 cake slices in bottom of a clear glass bowl. Drizzle on one-third of the sherry. Sprinkle one-third of the berry mixture over cake. Spoon one-third of the yogurt mixture over berries. Make two more layers with remaining cake slices, sherry, berries, and yogurt. Sprinkle almonds over top and decorate with reserved berries. Refrigerate for at least 3 hours.

To serve, spoon into dessert bowls and top with raspberry puree.

SERVES 12

PER SERVING: 279 calories, 6.3 g total fat (2 g saturated), 46 g carbohydrate, 9.2 g protein, 2 g fiber, 222 mg sodium

SCIENCE SAYS

Blueberries and strawberries are antioxidant-rich and prevent and reverse brain aging in animals, according to Tufts University researchers.

10-MINUTE BERRY BURRITOS À LA MODE

2 (12-ounce) bags frozen mixed berries (strawberries, blackberries, raspberries, blueberries)
2 tablespoons cornstarch (reserve 1 teaspoon)
¼ cup no-calorie sweetener such as Splenda, or sugar
¼ teaspoon ground cinnamon
2 (10-inch diameter) flour tortillas
Butter-flavor cooking spray
3 cups fat-free vanilla ice cream

Preheat oven to 425°F. Thaw and drain mixed berries: do not discard juice. Pour 1½ cups berry juice into a microwave-safe bowl. Add I cup of the berries. Set aside to use for the sauce.

Combine the remaining berries, 1 tablespoon plus 2 teaspoons cornstarch, sweetener, and cinnamon. Spray bottom of pizza pan or cookie sheet with butter-flavor spray. Spread tortillas open on pan. Place equal amounts of berry mixture down the middle of each tortilla. Roll up like a burrito; place burrito seam side down; spray top of burrito.

Bake for 10 minutes, or until slightly browned. Let cool for 10 minutes.

To make the sauce, stir 1 teaspoon cornstarch into berry mixture. Microwave on high for 40 seconds, or until thickened. Cut each tortilla in three pieces. Serve each piece on a dessert plate with ½ cup ice cream. Top with warm sauce.

SERVES 6

PER SERVING: 231 calories, 2 g total fat (0.2 g saturated), 49 g carbohydrate, 3.6 g protein, 2.2 g fiber, 138 mg sodium

Among all fresh fruits, blueberries, blackberries, cranberries, strawberries, and raspberries rank highest in antioxidant activity, in that order.

SCIENCE SAYS

TOTAL® CALCIUM COOKIES

4 cups whole-grain Total® cereal

¾ cup quick-cooking oats

2 teaspoons ground cinnamon

1 teaspoon ground ginger

1 teaspoon baking soda

2 beaten eggs, or ½ cup egg substitute

1 packed cup brown sugar

1 jar (2½ ounces) baby-food prunes

1 cup chopped walnuts

Preheat oven to 350°F. Crush Total cereal in a blender until it looks like coarse flour. Add oats, spices, and baking soda, and stir. In another bowl, combine eggs, sugar, prunes, and nuts. Add dry ingredients to wet ingredients and combine thoroughly. Spray a cookie sheet with canola or olive oil. Drop cookies by the teaspoon on the sheet about an inch apart. Bake for 10–12 minutes.

Makes about 40 cookies

PER COOKIE: 64 calories, 2.3 g total fat (0.3 g saturated), 10 g carbohydrate, 1.3 g protein, 0.6 g fiber, 63 mg sodium

SCIENCE SAYS

High amounts of calcium not only help maintain strong bones, but also can help prevent the recurrence of polyps leading to colon cancer.

Index